Red Iron
Over the Canyon

JOE IRVING

An autobiographical account of
growing up and working in the ironworker trade
in British Columbia during the early and mid 1900s

Coordinating editor
ROB D'EON

Note for Librarians: A cataloguing record for this book is available from Library and Archives
Canada at www.collectionscanada.ca/amicus/index-e.html
ISBN 1-4120-8185-8

*Printed in Victoria, BC, Canada. Printed on paper with minimum 30% recycled fibre. Trafford's print shop
runs on "green energy" from solar, wind and other environmentally-friendly power sources.*

TRAFFORD
PUBLISHING™

Offices in Canada, USA, Ireland and UK
This book was published *on-demand* in cooperation with Trafford Publishing. On-demand
publishing is a unique process and service of making a book available for retail sale to the
public taking advantage of on-demand manufacturing and Internet marketing. On-demand
publishing includes promotions, retail sales, manufacturing, order fulfilment, accounting and
collecting royalties on behalf of the author.

Book sales for North America and international:
Trafford Publishing, 6E–2333 Government St.,
Victoria, BC V8T 4P4 CANADA
phone 250 383 6864 (toll-free 1 888 232 4444)
fax 250 383 6804; email to orders@trafford.com
Book sales in Europe:
Trafford Publishing (UK) Limited, 9 Park End Street, 2nd Floor
Oxford, UK OX1 1HH UNITED KINGDOM
phone 44 (0)1865 722 113 (local rate 0845 230 9601)
facsimile 44 (0)1865 722 868; info.uk@trafford.com
Order online at:
trafford.com/05-3151

10 9 8 7 6 5 4 3

Red Iron Over the Canyon

JOE IRVING

An autobiographical account of
growing up and working in the ironworker trade
in British Columbia during the early and mid 1900s

Coordinating editor
ROB D'EON

Joe Irving

An Ironworker From the Kootenay

I was born by the banks of the Kootenay
On a bright October day
'Twas back in the year of eleven
Where my folks had come to stay

The fruit was ripe and the leaves were red
The trout they spawned in the stream
Maw smiled at paw, and paw smiled back
And they said we've created our dream

My hair was red, my eyes were blue
The neighbours came to see me too
The oohed and aahed
And said by gawd, here's one that will surely do

Time rolled by beneath the sky
Of the Kootenay's wonderful blue
I went to school to learn the rule
So I would know what to do

The place we lived, they called it Thrums
A beautiful place to grow some plums
The story of a window clear
You could open it wide to breath fresh air
The railway built a siding there

For the trains to pass with room to spare
The station was built beside the tracks
And the window in Thrums had a home at last

I learned to ride and rope a cow
And harness the big horse too
I could swing an axe and pull a saw
The make the under cut true
To drop the tree where it ought to be
To cut the logs right through
To be kind to your horse, and love your dog
And respect your parents too
I was young at the time, but I learned to climb
Where others feared to go
I connected the steel with the wonderful feel
Of a job well done today

And here at last, was the other side
That seemed so far away
An ironworker they call me now
And then be a foreman to show them how
To connect the steel, and tighten the bolts
To drive the rivets white hot from the forge
And try not to drop them into the gorge

Then to greater things I went
To build the dams and pour cement
To erect the steel for the bridges high
Where we worked seemed to be in the sky

With the derricks and cranes we hoisted the steel
To the men up high who had the feel
To walk a beam only inches wide
While the people below watched them with pride
And the ironworkers took it all in their stride

Some bridges we built to carry the rails
For the trains to run and haul the mails
The passenger trains had the right of way
While the freights they took to the hole

The Kettle Valley was the wonder of all
For over the mountains it did crawl
The bridges there both big and small
But they carried the trains to the coast as they went
Loaded with applies and power poles too
And ore from the mines and smelter's brew
And this all came for the Kootenay too

And cable ways to make the news
The crew the needed lots of booze
Two miles in length, they needed strength
To carry the power through

The contractors there were quite a few
Northern Construction and Dominion Bridge too
Commonwealth Construction along the way
With Canadian Bridge we thought it O.K.
But plans were changed most any day
Bickerton Steel was might tight
To get new tools you had almost to fight

The war was going mighty strong
When the call from Uncle Sam came along
To go to the States for Bethlehem Steel
To build the plants to make the guns
To go on the ships to kill the huns
And also the Japs who wanted to fight
We sure would show them we had the might
We got this done and the war was won
Then back to B.C we did come

We settled down and built more dams
To control the rivers for Uncle Sam

Now in Crescent Valley I settle down
In an old log house that is miles from town

This place we call it Rainbow Pines
And here you can rest with peace of mind
An ironworker can use his hands
For a lot of things concerned with the land
With horses that are the Dapple Greys
He gives sleigh rides on the winter days

In the summer time a garden grows
Of corn and squash and spuds in the rows
And then in the fall to cut the wood
To keep things warm when we watch the snows

By this time I am ninety-three
Nature has been kind to me
I have good health and a wonderful wife
To share this place for the rest of my life

Joseph A. Irving, 2005

Acknowledgements

IN THE PREPARATION OF THIS book I wish to give special thanks to my good friend, Rob D'Eon, for all of his help with the typing and computer work, without which I would never have been able to complete this book. Also, to my wife and partner, Sylvia, who looked after me in a thousand ways and always reminding me to keep busy and to finish the story. There was always a nice hot meal and a nice clean house and an encouraging word to keep me going. Also, thanks to my good friend, Ila Maber, for the sketches of the tools and a lot of encouragement.

Glossary

Tools and terms used in the iron trades

Anvil – for working iron

Axe and adz – for wood working

B&O – a punch

Banjo – a tool for holding rivets

Basket pole – a gin pole used on tower erection

Black wall hitch – a hitch used in rope work

Bucker up – man who holds rivets while they are being driven

Bull pin – a pin for lining holes ready for bolts

Bull stick – a hardwood handle for turning a derrick mast

Boars nest – bunkhouse

Bull wheel – a wheel to turn a derrick

Catty – man who gets around on steel quickly and easily

Cat's ass – a snarl in a cable

Cope – to cut iron to fit

Dead man – a buried anchor

Dogleg – a kink of twist in iron

Dog house – a shack for changing clothes or maybe a lunch room

Donkey – a hoist engine

Dolly – self-contained roller for moving pieces of iron

Dolly bar – a steel bar of shafting for holding rivets

Drag – a pay advance

Dog – a device to hold the load on a hoist

Drift pin – a pin, tapered on both ends, used to line holes in iron

Dunnage – temporary timber blocking

Ginnywink – a small A-frame derrick

Gooseneck – a dolly bar with an offset

Gut hammer – a triangle steel gong used at mealtime

Heater – the man who heats the rivets

Jib – the extension on a crane boom

Jumping shoe – temporary foot for a derrick boom when jumping a
        derrick

Mouse – string or twine used to secure ends of wire rope

Needle beam – a wooden beam used to support a hanging scaffold

Old man – a portable drill press

Pusher – an iron-working foreman

Reeving – threading rope or cable through multiple sheave blocks

Shore – shoring temporary timber supports

Snap – a rivet die

Snatch block – a gate block used as a fair lead

Spud wrench – a connectors wrench use to connect structural steel

Whirly – a revolving crane that can turn 360°

Forward

Joe Irving has written this book telling the story of his life. But really, he is telling the story of the development of British Columbia, and in particular, the story of the Kootenay area. That is where Joe was born, and grew up, and the part of B.C. that he truly loves.

Joe worked at Ironwork. He was a proud member of the International Association of Structural Ironworkers. Myself, as an executive of Dominion Bridge Company, I had many negotiations and dealings with the officers and members of that Union. Once an agreement was signed there was no deviation. The contract was good. Joe Irving is that kind of man. His word is good. One respects that kind of man. We did many projects together in the Kootenays. Once I got Joe started, I could leave him for a week. When I returned all would be proceeding in accordance with the plan.

At the age of 93 years, Joe completed his Grade 12 high school education – a remarkable achievement. Not many people that age care to continue their education. He has now written this book, which is also a desirable undertaking. Joe helped develop the Kootenays from the early days to the thriving area it now is. Joseph A. Irving is an outstanding citizen and deserves much recognition and credit. We wish him well.

John S. Prescott, Professional Engineer

Introduction

THE FOLLOWING PAGES WERE COPIED from handwritten notes that Aunt Mollie gave to Dorothy in 1988. (typed by Dick Greyson Feb. 20, 1996)

These recollections of Irving family history have been gathered for the family of Richard Irving Greyson, son of Violet Margaret Greyson, nee Irving, and are given to his wife Dorothy Greyson by Violet Greyson's sister, Mary Agnes Irving (Auntie Mollie) in Vancouver, B.C. ON MARCH 22, 1988.

OUR PARENTS

IRVING, Edward Bond
born Aug. 15, 1857
at Piety Hill, Dry Gulch (Red Bluff)
near Rhonerville, Shasta County, California
died at Nelson, B.C. Feb. 20, 1936
buried in Nelson in RC Cemetery

IRVING, Mary Bridget Theresa (nee McCormick)
born May 8, 1879
at New Albin, Kalamakee County, Iowa
died July 13, 1962 in Mt. St Francis, Nelson, B.C.
buried at Kinnaird (now part of Castelgar, B.C.)

Dad and Mother
were married in Rossland in B.C. in 1898,
where Dick's mother was born on May 4, 1900.

OUR PATERNAL GRANDPARENTS

IRVING, James
born Jan 28, 1808 at Carlisle, Cumberland, England
died 1883 or 1888 in Victoria, B.C.
buried in Ross Bay Cemetery, Victoria, B.C.

IRVING, Sara (nee Bond)
born Oct. 29, 1819 at Manchester, England
died Feb 20, 1902
buried in Everett, Wash.

OUR MATERNAL GRANDPARENTS

McCORMICK, John
born in the south of Ireland probably sometime in the late 1840s
died in Omaha, Neb. in 1906

McCORMICK, Mary Margaret (nee Nicol)
born in Ballymene, Ireland sometime in the 1850s
died in Omaha, Neb. sometime in the 1920s or early 30s

IRVING CHILDREN

Violet Margaret	Vi	Rossland	1900 – May 4
Mary Agnes Susanna	Mollie	Omaha	1902 – Aug. 7
John Latham		Spokane	1904 – Jan. 18
Eileen Estella		Spokane	1906 – Aug. 12
Bernard James	Ben	Portland	1909 – Oct. 28
Joseph Anthony Leslie	Joe	Thrums	1911 – Oct. 10
Robert Eden	Bob	Shoreacres	1915 – May 8
Marie de Lourdes	Dollie/		
Theresa	Dee Dee	Trail	1918 – Nov. 3
Josephine Marguerite	Dawn	Trail	1921 – Sept. 5

(Bob born the night the *Lusitania* sank)

OUR MATERNAL GRANDPARENTS

I'm sorry to say I can tell you very little about our maternal grandparents except that they both came from Ireland, that our grandmother was born in Ballymene, near Belfast, probably sometime in the 1850s and that she died in Omaha, Nebraska sometime in the 1920s, I think.

Mother's mother, Mary Nicol (there may be another 'l', but I'm not sure) came to America to keep house for her elder brother Henry, who had emigrated earlier. I remember hearing that she came on a "sailing vessel", "sat at the Captain's table", and that the voyage took six weeks. Another snippet – her mother (or aunt?) someone in the generation ahead of her, had been "a marvelous horsewoman who road to the hounds."

There was also an Aunt Catherine in Scotland, who may have been a sister of Mary and Henry Nicol. Uncle Henry was still ALIVE IN 1907 WHEN HE CAME TO VISIT MOTHER IN SPOKANE. I DON'T REMEMBER WHEN HE DIED BUT I DO REMEMBER BOOKS AT HOME THAT HAD BELONGED TO HIM WITH HIS NAME WRITTen in a beautiful flowing hand. Dawn remembers that he was a graduate of Nocohollit College (wherever that may be!) in Ireland – a fact I never knew. One thing I did know – Mother was very fond of him.

I don't know where Mother's father was born, apart from the fact that he came from the south of Ireland and that he had been too young to fight in the American Civil War. I also know he was a gentle soul, whom Mother greatly loved – and that it was from him that the three redheads in our family, Ben, Joe, and Bob, got their beautiful red hair. When our maternal grandparents met and married I don't know – only that at one time they lived in Iowa, where our Mother was born, and later in Omaha, Neb., where they owned quite a lot of land and had a transfer business. Uncle Henry kept the books. They also had a large blacksmith shop here and had horses for hire.

There were four children in the family, John, Susan, Bernard (after whom our brother Ben was named) and the youngest, Mary – our Mother.

Aunt Susan was the last to go. She died in the late 1960s, several years after Mother's death in 1962.

OUR PATERNAL GRANDPARENTS

Our paternal grandparents met on board ship crossing the Atlantic, and were married in New Orleans.

When our grandfather, James Irving, came to this continent – he was a widower with a twelve-year-old son, Robert Eden (after whom our brother Bob was named). Some time after his wife's death, his business had been ruined, when a partner in what must have been a prosperous merchant-tailoring business absconded with thousands of pounds, leaving James with five thousand to sink or swim (whether in this connection or not, I don't know, but we always knew there was family money, quite a lot of it, tied up in something or some place called "In Chancery", though where it came from or how it got there I have no idea. Anyway, it sat there, year after year, just sat there, and nobody could do anything about it. Uncles, or somebody, had battled to their sorrow and loss, and we knew you could not fight Chancery – whatever it was).

In any case, with a brother (or other relative) already in North America, emigration became the answer at this time of crisis in the life of our grandfather. I know neither the place nor the date of embarkation, but it must have been the days of steamships when James and his young son said good-bye to England.

Among other passengers aboard ship they met a Mrs. Gilmour, a young widow with two little girls (Anne and Margaret) who were on their way to join a sister living in New Orleans. The long crossing of those days provided ample time for friendships to develop. By journey's end James and Sara Gilmour were engaged, and while still on board they were married by the ship's captain when they reached the port of New Orleans.

Perhaps they stayed on for a while in New Orleans – I don't know – but some time after arrival they left (by boat, probably, up the Mississippi?) for Keokuk, in Iowa, where I think James' relatives were living (I have seen somewhere a contemporary reference to the Irving Brothers of Keokuk, so it would seem that members of the Irving family did settle in that city).

The newcomers lived some time in Keokuk, but somewhere around the date of the California Gold Rush in 1849, they joined others who were headed west and traveled out to the Pacific Coast.

The journey this time was made by covered wagon and many a time

we were regaled with tales of that long trek. One particularly stands
out as a disaster – when some Mormons stole their cattle (sorry, but it's
true!) though they were all recovered later because one member of the
party of travelers knew Brigham Young. We were intrigued, too, with the
story of grandmother's tea-set which went safely across those plains and
mountains with her. Blue Wedgewood, according to Dick's mother and
confirmed by Dawn. Crown Derby in Eileen's memory, probably faulty.

At the time our grandmother had a married sister living in California.
The husband, whose only name I know is his surname of Toft, had been
a British Army officer in India and was now retired. At a time when
England claimed all of what is now called northern California, the
British authorities had given him a grant of land near Rhonerville (in
Shasta County?) where the Tofts had become established, and there the
new Irving family joined them. It was there, too, in 1857, that our father,
Edward Bond Irving was born. (He added the name Joseph as a baptismal
name when he was baptized as a Catholic in Nelson, B.C. many years
later. Probably nicknamed in childhood, he was always called Ned. He
may have been brought up as an Anglican. His mother's brother was an
Anglican clergyman, so it is more than likely that she was one too).

James and his family remained in California until the time of the
American Civil War. England favoured the South, and the Irving's
sympathies were with England. Perhaps British claims about California
boundaries were still a matter of some dispute, too. In any case, the
Irvings wanted to live in secure British territory, "under the British flag."

So once again they moved on – by boat this time, up the coast of the
Pacific Northwest to the British Crown Colony of Victoria, on Vancouver
Island. (From Dick's mother's account, it seems likely that James' eldest
son, Robert Eden, had preceded them north at the time of the discovery
of gold on the Fraser River. She states that he died in Yale, in the Fraser
Canyon and was buried there).

Vancouver Island was still a wilderness but Victoria became home,
complete with "British flag" – and the Wedgewood. As the years passed
the city grew and became an English "enclave" where long established
habits and customs continued. Books and music were still cherished
greatly. Dad's family read aloud to one another by their fireside, and it
was there that his lifelong love for Shakespeare and other literature was
instilled. Dad's mother had a beautiful voice, which he inherited and
passed on to most of us – so that as music held an important place in

their lives, so too, it has in ours.

Not surprising, this love of music, as our grandmother came originally from Wales. Her father, we are told, was a "Welsh squire", so he must have been a landowner somewhere in Wales, but I have no idea where. I understand, though, that at one time the Bond family owned a great part of what later became Old Bond Street in London, and that the now-famous street was named after our grandmother's family.

After some years in Victoria Dad returned to California to his aunt and uncle. They had no children of their own, so, for whatever reasons (school, for one perhaps?) Dad's parents allowed him to live with the Tofts in California for several years. He often spoke with affection, I think, of his Aunt Maria (pronounced Maria) but the army officer uncle was a bit too strict and they clashed. One day, when Dad was about seventeen, they had a final disagreement and Dad walked out, took a boat to Victoria and rejoined his family.

As a young man Dad knew and loved the whole of California. During the early years, before the CPR was built, all the travel from Victoria was north and south. San Francisco and Seattle grew like mushrooms. Theatres and even an opera house flourished, where all the greats of the last half of the century came at one time or another, and Dad saw and heard them all – Sarah Bernhardt, Ellen Terry, Henry Irving (no relation!), Jenny Lind, Caruso, Melba – they were all household names to us as Dad told us of his own younger days. David Belasco was a friend for many years – and it was one of his one-act plays that Puccini used to create his opera Mme Butterfly! (I don't know that until I read it recently). We learned too about the California Missions, and Dad particularly loved Santa Barbara.

But back to Victoria. Dad's very early memories of his first years there held pictures of himself and a group of little boys being accompanied to school by priests with muskets on their shoulders. They still had timber wolves to fear. Among these school fellows were the Spencer children (later well known as the David Spencers of Vancouver); the Tolmies (I remember meeting Dr. Tolmie as an MLA when I was a child – when he was still one of Dad's friends); the Douglases, whose father became Governor of the Island and later the first premier of the new Province of British Columbia.

James Irving entered government service in Victoria, and there were some amusing tales of life in the so-called Birdcages of the old legislature buildings – too bad these stories are gone. One comes to mind about a goat and a window, but it's all lost in the mists of time. The old Birdcages are long gone, but pictures of today's Legislature Buildings in Victoria are always a reminder of our grandfather. The present buildings were designed by the English architect Francis Rattenbury (who, by the way, also designed the courthouse and the post office[1*] in Nelson, Dick may be interested to know. They are both designated heritage buildings).

One more interesting fact – our grandfather was for many years secretary to the famous "Hanging Judge" (B.C.'s first), Judge Mathew Bailey Begbie, whose own fascinating story is now British Columbia history.

I wish I had asked some of the many questions that now come to mind, questions that children simply don't know enough to ask. I have read much about the early days of Victoria, the Island and the Province always with the thought that some of our own were there living out their lives as part of that history.

James Irving died of a stroke in either 1883 or 88, and is buried in the old Ross Bay Cemetery in Victoria. A picture of his grave, taken by his great-grandson (my brother Ben's son, Douglas) shows the name and the date on the tombstone but the last figure is not clear. It could be a 3 or an 8. The picture also shows two of James Irving's great-great grandsons, Robert and Andrew, standing beside the headstone. It was taken one day when Ben, his own son and two grandsons made a special pilgrimage to Ross Bay to find our grandfather's grave.

After her husband's death, our grandmother went to live in Seattle with her son George and his family (children Myrtle and Henrietta). She could not be buried next to her husband as the Ross Bay Cemetery in Victoria was no longer in use. She must have been living in Everett, Wash. at the time of her death, as that is where she is buried.

[1*] since made into the Nelson City Hall

CHAPTER 1

The early years

THIS IS A BOOK ABOUT the history of my life and also a part of the history of structural ironwork in the Province of British Columbia and other places that I worked.

Structural ironwork was the occupation I followed for most of my working life. I also became a very efficient boilermaker. First of all though, I will go into my own history that starts with my parents coming to the Kootenay Valley in British Columbia.

This is the history of my parents as far as I have been able to trace it. My paternal grandfather, James Irving, was born on January 28th, 1808 in Carlisle, Cumberland, England. He died in either 1883 or 1888 in Victoria, BC and is buried in Ross Bay Cemetery in Victoria. My paternal grandmother, Sara Bond, was born on October 29th, 1819 in Manchester, England. She died on February 20th, 1902 and is buried in Everett, Washington. My maternal grandfather, John McCormick, was born in the south of Ireland sometime in the late 1840s. He died in 1906 in Omaha, Nebraska. My maternal grandmother, Mary Margaret Nicol, was born in Ballymene, Ireland sometime in the 1850s. She died in Omaha, Nebraska sometime in the 1920s or early 1930s.

My father, Edward Bond Irving, was born August 15th, 1857 in Piety Hill, Dry Gulch (Red Bluff) near Rhonerville, Shasta County, California. He died in Nelson, BC on February 20th, 1936 and is buried in the Nelson

Roman Catholic cemetery. My mother, Mary Bridget Theresa McCormick, was born May 8th, 1879 in New Albin, Kalamakee County, Iowa. She died on July 13th, 1962 in Mt. St. Francis hospital in Nelson, BC and is buried in Kinnaird (now part of Castlegar), BC.

Dad and mother were married in Rossland, BC in 1899 and had 9 children. Violet Margaret was born in Rossland on May 4th, 1900. Mary Agnes Susanna was born in Omaha, Nebraska on August 7th, 1902. John Latham was born in Spokane, Washington on January 18th, 1904. Eileen Estella was also born in Spokane on August 12th, 1906. Benard James was born in Portland, Oregon on October 28th, 1909. I, Joseph Anthony Leslie, was born in Thrums, BC on October 10th, 1911. Robert Eden was born in Glade, BC on May 8th, 1915. Marie de Lourdes Theresa was born in Trail, BC on November 3rd, 1918. And lastly, Josephine Marguerite was born in Trail, BC on September 5th, 1921.

Now we come to my parents settling in the Lower Kootenay Valley in the West Kootenays of British Columbia. The place where I was born on October 10th, 1911 is called Thrums. I was the first child ever born there. My mother was attended by Dr. McMillian who had come out from England with his family a short time before and settled a couple miles away in a place called Tarrys. It was fortunate for the people in this area to have a doctor living close by because in those days transportation was by train, on the days the train was running, or by horse and buggy which was a very limited mode of transportation due to the condition of the early day pioneer roads.

Mother and dad met each other in Spokane, Washington at the railway station. Of course all travel in those days was by railway. This was in 1898. When they met, Dad was on his way to Rossland, BC as he was very interested in the mining business, mostly the prospecting for ore, because he had made a study of geology for the sake of knowing all the different types of ore. The Kootenay country was in the news everywhere telling about all of the fortunes being made there. The country was booming. Railways were being built, paddle wheel steamers were on the lakes and rivers, towns were being built, new mines were opening almost daily, and smelters were built to smelt the ore at Trail, Nelson, North Port, Pilot Bay, Grand Forks, Greenwood, and Boundary Falls.

Mother had grown up in Omaha, Nebraska where her father had a blacksmith and livery business. It was evidently a very good business – the shop going steady and teams of horses being hired out all the time. She told her dad that she wanted to take a trip and see the western country. He said OK and gave her money for traveling. She met Dad in Spokane. He told her that he was on his way to the mining town of Rossland. She then told him that was where she was planning to go. She wanted to see what a mining town in the mountains was like, because she had been born and raised in the American prairie country. Most of what she had seen was corn and grain fields, so a mining town would really be something different.

The railway to Rossland was part of the Great Northern Rail complex. It was called the Spokane Falls and Northern, and from North Port to Rossland it was called the Red Mountain Railway. There was also another railway to Rossland from Trail. It was part of the Columbia and Western originally built by Augustus Heinz, the man responsible for building the smelter at Trail. Well, they traveled to Rossland together and the love bug must have bitten them because a short time later they got married.

Mother was a very attractive looking girl. She had dark brown eyes and a beautiful head of long black hair. She had a good education and dad was a very handsome well-built man, so it was no wonder that they fell for each other. I don't know too much of what dad worked on after they went to Rossland, but I know he knew how to prospect, stake a claim, record it, promote it, and then sell it. He was also a good tradesman. He was a good carpenter and also a good stonemason, and could turn his hand to almost any job. Dad and mother settled down in Rossland and dad worked there at various things. Violet, my oldest sister was born in Rossland on May 4th, 1900. This was a very historic day in the Kootenay country for it was the same day of the big fire in Sandon, BC when most of the town burned.

There is a book by Al King called Red Bait, which is a history of the Mine Mill Union in Trail and Rossland. In this book there is a chapter written by Rosa Jordan. The chapter written by Rosa gives a lot of the details of the strike of 1901 in Rossland and points out the meanness of the mine companies against the miners. In this chapter Rosa states that Ema Coombs was the first girl born in Rossland in 1902. By this time Violet was two years old and had a sister born in 1902. This makes my sister Vi the first girl born in Rossland.

By 1901 there was a lot of trouble in Rossland. The miners were fighting for the eight-hour day without a loss of wages and the mine owners were dead against the miners. Some of the mine owners were also in a big court battle over the ownership of the famous LeRoy mine. The Rossland trouble of 1901 is very well covered by Rosa Jordan's chapter in Al King's book. Al King became the president of the Mine Mill Union for Local 480 in Trail, BC.

With all the labour trouble going on with the miners strike, court battles by the mining companies, etc., dad and mother decided to go to Spokane, Washington where dad could work at carpenter work. Mother also wanted to take a trip home to Omaha to see her folks and show off her beautiful daughter. By this time she was also pregnant again so my sister Mollie was born in Omaha, Nebraska on August 7th, 1902. When she came back to Spokane, dad was working at carpenter work. One of the buildings he worked on was the big Paulson building. Dad worked in Spokane for several years and during this time they had two more children, John and Eileen.

About 1907 dad took a job with the O.R.&N., the Oregon Railway and Navigation Company. In doing this the family found it necessary to move to Portland, Oregon. Dad was now a skipper on a tugboat for the O.R.&N. My brother Bernard James, or Ben, was born in Portland on October 28th, 1909. The following year mother decided she would like to take a trip again to see her folks and to show off her now quite large family. One day, dad came home from work with the tickets for all of them to have a trip to Omaha. So mother and her now large brood took a nice trip on the train to Omaha. They had sleeper tickets for the Pullman car. The rail service in those days was very good. This was about a three-day trip each way.

When mother and the family got back to Portland, dad said he would once again like to see the Kootenay country. Mother said OK but this time she thought they would stay there. Dad must have made good money in those days to be able to have the family do so much traveling. This time they all came to Nelson, BC and after meeting with the Powers family decided to settle in the Lower Kootenay Valley at Thrums, BC. I guess by this time I was in the mixer, so I was born in Thrums on October 10th, 1911. Where the house stood that I was born in, you could throw a rock that would just about land in the Kootenay River.

CHAPTER 2

Thrums and Tarrys

THE COLUMBIA AND KOOTENAY RAILWAY, which had been taken over by the Canadian Pacific Railway, had been built through the Kootenay Valley from Nelson, BC, going by way of Castlegar to the smelter town of Trail and the mines at Rossland. The railway crossed the Columbia River at Castlegar on a new steel bridge that was comprised of two through-truss spans and a swing-girder span centered on a circular stone pier on the east end with two more short girder spans.

The Columbia was a navigable river with boats running from Arrowhead on the Upper Arrow Lake to North Port, Washington on the Columbia River. It was federal law that all railways or highways build bridges that could accommodate marine traffic. Hence the swing span in the Castlegar bridge. It is still in place today although locked into position for the railway track. The boats on the lakes and rivers were called stern wheelers. The railway was also being extended westward from Castlegar by way of Grand Forks and Midway to eventually reach the west coast at Vancouver. There will be more on this railway later on in the story.

From Castlegar the railway was known as the Columbia & Western. It so happened that a lot of little flag stations had not yet been named, although in some cases the sidings were in place for the trains to pass each other. Well, in this case, the train had stopped when someone asked what the name of the place was. It had not been given a name yet. Now there was a lady on the train reading a book called "The Window in Thrums" by J.M. Barrie (publisher Charles Sasrlenen, New York). When she heard this she said why not call this place Thrums. She eventually got the approval of the railway people and the place became known as Thrums. The family that settled on the west side of the railway track opposite the station and siding was a family that had recently came from Scotland, Mr. and Mrs. Robert Chalmers. Years later they built a small store and had a tea room there that they called "The Window". After that people talked about going to the window for tea.

The people who settled on the lower or east side of the railway were the Powers family. A short time previously the Powers had moved west from Manitoba. They took over a piece of land that had been already cleared and cultivated by the Rebalkan family. The Powers moved into a new house on this place, so now they offered to rent the older house to my parents.

Along with the other goods and items that the Powers brought with them was a thoroughbred horse. This horse had won the Manitoba derby of 1910. Just before they moved west, his name was Twig, the name of an early-day Manitoba politician. People might wonder about a family bringing a horse all that distance, but if you were going to farm, it was very important to have a horse. You could ride the horse or hook it up to a buggy to drive where you had to go. You could plow and harrow your land, cultivate your crops, skid your fire wood out of the forest, and move anything that had to be moved – a very useful animal. You could also grow the horse's feed on your own land, which you can't do with your car today. It would be quite a few years before they had successful small farm tractors.

As mentioned before, my mother had been raised on the American prairie country so she was well acquainted with the use of horses. One day, about this time, she walked up to the Chalmers' place to see them. There were two families living at this place. The Chalmers and the Wykes. The Chalmers family had acquired a horse so they ordered a set of harnesses from the T. Eaton Catalogue. They received the parcel of harness in the mail, which came all disassembled. When mother arrived at the Chalmer's place they had the horse standing there and the parcel of harness on the ground. They had the catalogue open showing a picture of a horse in harness, but they didn't seem to know anything about what to do. Mother explained the harness to them and showed them what to do. Before long they had it all figured out and the harness placed on the horse. For greenhorns, as new people to the country were called, there was a lot to learn about these things.

If you didn't have your horse harnessed properly you wouldn't get any work done. There were a lot of different parts to the harness for a horse. First of all was a collar that fitted around the horse's neck and came against the shoulders to take the thrust when the horse pulled forward. Next came the hames that fitted over the collar. They were connected at the top and bottom of the collar with straps called hame straps. Then there were the tugs or traces. These were what pulled the load. These fastened to the hanes with a bolt. Then there was a back pad which held up the traces and also a belly band to keep these all in place. Then there was a set of breeching to go over the horse's hips. The breeching had straps that ran forward and fastened to the hames and straps that kept the traces in place – quite a complicated affair for a person who has never put it all together. Then there was the bridle that held the bit to go into the horse's mouth and lines to drive the horse with. I guess you would call this pioneer technology.

The house where I was born, as mentioned before, was only a short distance from the Kootenay River. An orchard had been planted there, and also some beautiful Hawthorne trees. If a person can pick a place to be born, this was a real nice choice. I was the sixth child born in the Irving family. I had red hair and so did my brother Ben and also Bob when he was born a few years later.

Another reason that my folks settled in Thrums was the fact that a one-room school had just been built there. It was within walking distance of where we were going to live so Violet, Mollie, and John would be able to go to school there. The distance to the school was a little over a mile. Today they would be able to ride a school bus. This is a type of bus that I never got to ride in.

This school was located halfway between the two flag stations of Thrums and Tarrys. That way it would serve all of the people for about four miles or more. The first teacher at this school was Mrs. Mansfield. The early-day families sending kids to school there besides the Irvings were, the Collins family, the Dodds, the Pratts, the Richards famly, the McMillians, and the Montgomery family. Other families that settled in the Thrums and Tarrys area were Chalmers, Wykes, Morrisons, Rebalkins, Couts, Mansfields, and the Wallace family, and of course the Tarrys.

At this time, the provincial government was in the process of building a road through the valley. Mr. Powers became the road foreman. He wanted dad to work for him on his this project. Dad was good at almost any job, so he took the job. It didn't bring in much money but I guess every bit helped. They liked having dad on the job. He did the blacksmith work for them sharpening and tempering the tools and building culverts. This type of work in these days could only be carried on when there was no frost in the ground. All power for this work was manpower and horsepower. It was during this time that dad and mother acquired a piece of land in Glade, which was about four miles to the north in the valley. There was a flag station on the railway there but you had to use the Shoreacres post office another mile or so to the north. This post office and store was run by the Oliver family.

The station two miles from Thrums was named Tarrys after the Tarrys family that settled there and acquired a lot of land and timber there. The senior Tarrys family was the first family to settle in the area. The Tarrys family built a sawmill there and had a siding installed on the railway for the loading of cars with lumber ties and poles. Their sawmill and planner were run with steam power.

Frank Tarry was the son of Mr. and Mrs. James Tarry. He married Florence Dodd the daughter of Mr. and Mrs. Thomas Dodd. Mr. Dodd became the first postmaster at Thrums. There was also a post office established at Tarrys. This was run by Mr. Richards. These families had recently come out from England.

As the timber was cut and sold, the Tarrys family sold blocks of land to the settlers and the valley gradually became a small farming valley. There were quite a few sources of water from small creeks that came down off Sentinel Mountain. Some people had springs on their land and some people dug wells. The first child born to Frank and Florence Tarry was a girl they named Hazel. She was six months younger than me, and the first girl born in the Thrums and Tarrys area.

The Tarrys family lived and farmed in this place for a good many years. Frank Tarry built a very big modern-type dairy barn and silos for his cows. The dairy barn could hold up to 40 cows. He also raised a lot of corn for silage. They also had a nice big orchard, some good sized hay fields, and raised a lot of ground crops besides their house garden. They also raised a big quantity of fruit – apples, cherries, and pears. They built a nice big packing shed for preparing the fruit for market. Then it was taken to the railway station for shipment.

Frank Tarry was a very industrious man and had a very good knowledge of machinery. Besides the sawmill he also built a wood pipe mill to manufacture wood pipe for water lines and irrigation pipes. He ran this mill for a good many years. The power for the mill was a Pelton waterwheel run with a water line, with water diverted from Tarrys creek. The timber used for this was second growth larch. The pipes were 8-foot sections. These were drilled with a wood auger and the ends were milled with a type of wood lathe tool so that they were milled to a male and female joint. The pipes for pressure lines were barked and turned with a lathe tool and then wrapped with a No. 9 wire and creosoted. The ones for irrigation were only done on the ends for joints.

The larch timber, being second growth, could be skidded to the mill with one horse – mostly in tree lengths to be cut at the mill. There was a cut-off saw about 30 inches, also run by the Pelton wheel which was used to cut the tree into 8-foot lengths. The ends that were too small for pipe were cut up for firewood. The 8-foot logs were rolled into the mill on a deck ready for milling. After the timber was made into the pipes, the pipes were loaded on a wagon and hauled to the railway for shipping. Frank Tarry had previously advertised this pipe material in various papers around the B.C. interior. He manufactured these pipes until he sold out his farm in 1928. He then moved with his family to the north Okanagon.

The British Columbia Encyclopedia published in 2000 gives a very small amount of space to its description of both Thrums and Tarrys. It is a very poor description of both places. It states that Thrums was a Doukabor settlement and also Tarrys. The only thing I can see that is the proper information about these places is the naming of them. All the places at both Thrums and Tarrys were settled by English and Scotch Canadians and Americans. Starting in the early 1920s and running through to the early 1930s the M.L. Bruce Timber Co. of Sand Point Idaho had a very big timber operation going on up Ten Mile Creek across the river from Tarrys. They had a sawmill, a ferry for crossing the river, and also a big high line to bring the lumber and poles across the river. They had four or five miles of water flume to bring the timber down out of the mountains. This flume was about one foot wide at the bottom, close to five feet wide at the top and about four feet high, and carried a real big flow of water. It could handle any amount of saw logs and cedar poles up to 100 feet in length. The flume ended at the mill pond.

There was a big millpond at the sawmill level created by a bay on the side of the river. The logs and poles were sorted at the pond. The saw logs went to the jack ladder at the mill. The poles were pulled out of the water and skidded under the high line where they were bundled and had cable chokers placed around the bundles and hoisted up and taken across the river on the high line. At this place there was a railway siding that came under the high line so that the poles could be directly loaded onto the railcars. The high line consisted of a timber tower on each side of the river carrying a 2-inch high line cable. The carriage ran on this line. It was powered by a big 3-drum steam donkey engine. The sawmill also had steam power. All of the skidder power in the woods was done with horses. The company had a boarding camp at the mill site and two more camps up in the woods for all the men, and also barns for the horses and feed.

In 1929 Mr. M. L. Bruce was killed in a car accident on the long wooden bridge over Pend d'Oerille Lake at Sand Point, Idaho. After this, the company was taken over by the Shafter and Hitchcock Company of Sand Point. The operation at Tarrys continued until 1930 when a very large forest fire put the company out of business at Tarrys.

Here is a list of most of the early day settlers in the Thrums and Tarrys area: The Powers, Chalmers, Wykes, Collins, Morrisons, Couts, Pratts, Mansfields, Irvings, Tarrys, Richards, McMillans, Montgonerys, Wallaces, and Dodds. Early settlers in the Glade, and Shoreacres area: Holmes, Markins, Schiavons, Passmores, Balaneys, Allens, Olivers, Shepleys, and Rotchfords. I think there were more, but I don't remember any more names.

CHAPTER 3

A childhood in Thrums and Glade

WE HAD NOT LIVED IN Thrums for very long before dad and mother acquired a piece of land at Glade about five miles north in the valley. It was on this place that dad built a log house from timber found on the land. The first thing he did was build a good stone foundation. There was one part of the land that was covered with rock. Dad decided to build the house on top of this rock. He put the foundation together with a good mortar of cement, sand and lime. He bought the lumber for the flooring, the cement and lime for the foundation, and the glass for the windows. He made the window sash and the door frames. He had very good tools and was a good carpenter. He split the shakes for the roof from cedar logs and also the laths for the walls, which he plastered. To split the shakes and the laths, he used a froe and a mallet. Cedar is a very suitable wood for these products. He also had to buy the doors and hardware for the doors and windows. The windows were all casement style. The timber for the house walls, shakes and laths etc. all came from the property. Mother kept track of the money spent for the materials used to build the house. One time, many years later, I was talking to her about the building of the house at Glade. She told me about keeping track of the cost. She had marked everything down and when it was all finished, the total cost for the doors, window glass, hardware, flooring, cement, lime and nails had come to a total of seventy-nine dollars. Today it costs that much to hang one door with its hardware.

The West Kootenay was a great country for cedar. Cedar timber, being a great source for power line poles, was shipped all over North America. Also, millions of bundles of laths and shingles were shipped from West Kootenay sawmills. Another big timber item from the West Kootenay was white pine. Millions of feet of this timber was milled in the West Kootenay as a match supply. White pine lumber was processed in Nelson at the match block factory of the W.W. Powell Co. and then shipped east to become manufactured to matches.

Dad built our house on a bench that sat about 15 feet above a creek that ran behind the house. The land below the house had good soil and a good water supply. The land along the creek was good garden soil and therefore my parents cultivated their garden on this land. My dad also dug out and constructed a root cellar between the garden and the house. This made access to the food supply very handy.

The one big problem with living in the country was the fact that there were very little work opportunities for men. This was the time just before the First World War and the country was in a depression. Money was almost non-existent. As soon as the house was built, my parents promptly moved from Thrums to the new house in 1913.

About the same time that the school had been built at Thrums, there was a one-room log school being built at Shoreacres about six miles from Thrums. This is where my brothers and sisters went to school. Their walk to school was a little further than before. Their new walk to school was a mile and a half. In years later, I also went to this school. The teacher there was a young lady by the name of Miss Donaldson. I don't remember anything about living at Thrums so my first memories are from Glade. I remember the nice, big garden and also that the folks had chickens and pigs. I also remember we had a dog that had pups. The dog was called Rags and the pups were Ceaser and Ghost. They were Airdales.

My dad was quite musical and he played the banjo. My sisters were also musical and became very good singers. Violet was a soprano and Mollie a contralto and when they sang together, it was really beautiful to listen to. There were also other families up and down the valley that had sons and daughters that were musical. At times we would have visits from them and there would be some great singsongs.

One of my first memories was when a lot of the young men from the valley were going away to war. Arthur and Fred Pratt were two of these men. Arthur Pratt played the violin and Fred Pratt played the banjo.

Arthur was not old enough to go to war, so Fred advanced his age a year so that if Arthur did the same, he would be old enough to go. Then there was Jack Ballaney, Jack Powers and Titch Montgomery. Titch was killed overseas in France. There was also Edgar McMillan, who was the son of the Doctor that attended my birth. He died in England. The only son of the Wallace family was killed in France. Art and Will Oliver also went to war. Art Oliver married the first teacher at the Shoreacres and Glade school. Before they went to war, quite a few of the men came over to our house for a musical evening. Some of them played the violin, some played the banjo while others played the accordion. Some of the songs that were very popular at the time were from the U.S. civil war such as Marching Through Georgia, Tenting on the Old Camp Ground and the songs of Steven Foster. A few of the old time songs were My Old Kentucky Home, Carry Me Back to Old Virginia, Darling Nellie Gray, Oh Susannah, Swanee River, Old Black Joe, I Dream of Jeanie with the Light Brown Hair and When You Wore a Tulip and I Wore a Big Red Rose. There were also many Irish and English songs such as Annie Laurie, My Wild Irish Rose, Killarney, Mountains of Morin and Doy Kin John Peel etc. I remember all the singing and playing and the talk of them going away. Some of them never came back.

In later years my two oldest sisters, Violet and Mollie, played the leading parts in some famous Gilbert and Sullivan operas. These operas were produced and played in Nelson and Trail by the Nelson and Trail Amateur societies. A few of these plays were, the Country Girl, The Pirates of Penzance, Pinafore etc. It was also at about this time that my brother Bob was born on May 8th, 1915. He was born on my mother's birthday.

When we moved to the log house at Glade I was about two years old. Therefore my first memories are naturally connected with the log house at Glade. One of my first memories is the time I pulled a bunch of carrots from the garden and I went around giving everyone a nice raw carrot. I remember another time when my mother came out in the yard and I was sitting down and eating with chickens all around me. I also remember when our dog Rags had her pups. They were Airdales, a breed who commonly had their tails chopped off short. My dad did not want to perform this operation, so a friend, Mr. Bill Ridge who was the line foreman for West Kootenay Power Co., told dad he would carry out this task. When I found out about this, I told my mother that dad's friend was the meanest man in the world. However, the pups survived and they were named Ceaser and Ceaser's Ghost. One day when dad was carrying a big block of wood over his shoulder with an axe, he dropped the block where he intended to drop it. Unfortunately he dropped the wood on top of the pups and killed them. I felt real bad for quite a while, as I was quite the animal lover.

Another time dad had a big pig on a rope. He tied the rope to a log or something and went back to the house. I untied the rope and the pig started to go. I hung onto the rope and the pig pulled me down and I cut my chin on a sharp rock. I still carry the scar. We were too far from a doctor to have it stitched up.

I also remember a community picnic. It was held by all the people from around the valley in the vicinity of the Slocan River Bridge. This bridge was about a mile from our place. The picnic was at the site of a nice meadow. I was about four years old at the time and I suppose I was interested in the bridge and the river. Anyway, I wandered off from the crowd and when they found me, I was sitting on the bridge railing which was about 50 feet above the river. Someone came along and lifted me off the railing and took me back to the picnic where mother, or someone else, minded me to make sure that I would not wander off again. Then there was my first ride in a motor vehicle. We had some friends come from Nelson and they had a motorcycle with a side car. They put me in the sidecar and away we went. It was quite a thrill. These friends were the McHardy's, the real estate family from Nelson.

There was very little work in the valley for my dad. About this time the Consolidated Mining and Smelting Company at Trail had acquired a grant from the federal government to build a zinc plant at the smelter in Trail. They were hiring carpenters and other tradesmen. Dad decided to go there and work. The trouble was that he could not get home very often because a lot of the time they had to work seven days a week. This was not very satisfactory for mother and since the older girls now had to go to high school, it was decided that we should move to Trail. Dad bought some property in East Trail and started to build right away. It was the summer of 1917 when we went to Trail. My older brother John had already gone there and was living with dad and giving him a hand to build. This was the summer of a terrible forest fire in the Columbia valley. The fire burned all the way from Blueberry south towards Trail. It swept around the mountains behind the smelter at Tadanac and down the valley below Trail as far as Waneta. There it jumped the river with flying sparks and started up on the other side of the valley. Then the wind changed and forced the fire back up the valley to trail and beyond. The fire had probably started by a hot spark from a steam railway locomotive as all the power on the railways at that time was steam. The fire was still burning in some places when we moved to Trail. Men were still working on putting it out when we arrived.

CHAPTER 4

The Doukabors

A FEW YEARS BEFORE I was born the Doukabors came to the West Kootenays from Saskatchewan, and from Russia before that. They were able to purchase all the land at the lower end of the Kootenay River where it empties into the Columbia River. This was the land on the east side of the river from Castlegar where the railway had been built. They called this place Brilliant. They also landed across the Kootenay River where the Castlegar airport is today. All the land around there they called Ootichennia, "Valley of Contentment". They purchased all this land at the same time. Brilliant is a place that comprises several hundred acres of land. Ootichennia is a bench land above the Columbia and Kootenay Rivers and is about a mile wide and approximately four miles long.

All of this land was cleared and cultivated by the Doukabors and they planted a lot of orchards, and also raised a large quantity of fruits and vegetables. On the Brilliant side of the Kootenay River they built their jam factory beside the railway and had a siding installed for the loading of the boxcars for the jam. Then they needed to bring the produce from Ootichenia to Brilliant. So with help from the government they constructed a suspension bridge over the Kootenay River about a mile above the mouth of the river. They used a ferry across the Kootenay until the bridge was built.

At this point there was solid rock on both sides of the river, so this is where they built the concrete towers that would support the cables from which the bridge span would be hung. The cables were anchored in the solid rock and the span was a steel truss with a wooden deck. The span and deck were hung with cable suspenders from the main cables which were strung over the concrete towers.

With the new bridge, all the produce from Ootichenia could be transported by wagons to the jam factory. The people living in the Doukabor community also had much easier access to the trains and other parts of the area. This bridge is no longer in use, but can be seen from highway 3 as you go across the new steel arch span over the Kootenay River on the way to Castlegar airport.

The Doukabors, under the leadership of Peter Verigin were a very hard working industrious group of people. They lived a communal style of life in villages about half a mile apart. Each village contained two large houses and sheds and workshops and barns at the back. Approximately 40 or 50 people lived in each village. The houses were all about 30 feet square and all two stories with hip roofs. Some of these houses had brick veneer on the outside. There are still a few of these community houses in the area.

The Doukabor community built their own factory to manufacture the bricks for their houses. They also had their own flour mill. There were many good carpenters and tradesmen among the Doukabors. Besides carpenters, there were blacksmiths, shoemakers, harness makers and millwrights. The Doukabor women were also great at needlework, knitting, quilting, and great gardeners.

The Doukabors also acquired a lot of other land in the West Kootenays. They established a community on the east side of the Columbia River at Champion Creek about 8 miles south of Castlegar, also on the east side of the Kootenay River at Glade, another settlement at Shoreacres and one at Krestova, Pass Creek, and Grand Forks.

The land of Ootichenia and also at Brilliant was a very sandy loam type of soil so it naturally required a lot of water. To acquire enough water to irrigate all this land, the Doukabor community built two big wood stave pip lines to supply the water. They built a small dam on Pass Creek above the lower falls about a mile upstream. From this dam they ran a two-foot diameter wood stave pipe. They ran this down along the flat at Brilliant and then across the suspension bridge to Ootichenia. The second line was tapped into McPhee Creek on the mountainside a mile or so above the site of the Brilliant powerhouse on the opposite side of the river from the railway and highway. The pipeline was constructed through the area that is now the Castlegar golf course and it ran at that level above the Kootenay River to where it tapped the Creek. This pipeline was about 16 inches diameter.

It was mainly because of these two water lines that the community was able to produce all their produce and crops that they needed for their own consumption and supply all the fruit necessary for the jam factory. The jam they made at Brilliant was sold under the trade name of K.C. Jam (Kootenay Columbia). It was very good jam and was sold and shipped by rail all across the country. The Doukabor colony was known as the Universal Brotherhood of Doukabors in Canada.

The Doukabor community carried on very successfully under the leadership of Peter Verigin, but fell apart after he was killed in a blast on the railway at Farron, BC. There were several other people killed in this blast which still remains a mystery to this day. There was another segment of the community known as the Sons of Freedom that had previously caused trouble in Saskatchewan. The community eventually broke up, the jam factory was ruined in a blast and various other buildings were burned and destroyed.

It is a terrible disgraceful shame when you think of all the work the Doukabor people did to get their family community together and productive. The water lines they built, the jam factory, the bridge, and a lot of the thousands of hours of work that went into all of it. Then to have it all wrecked by a group of selfish religious fanatics

The story of the Doukabors is very well covered in several different historical books written about them: *Terror in the name of god* by Simma Holt, *Doukabors – The spirit wrestlers* by Pierre Burton, and *Doukabor daze* by Hazel O'Neil. Hazel O'Neil (her maiden name was Hulls) taught school in the Ootichenia Doukabour community for several years.

CHAPTER 5

Living in Trail, 1917

WE MOVED FROM GLADE TO the town of Trail in August 1917. Dad had not yet started to build the main part of the house. We therefore had to temporarily move into a large shack, probably comparable to a single- wide trailer according to today's standards. This was rather small quarters for a family. However, it wasn't very long until he got going with the remainder of the house. The lumber and building materials all arrived, delivered by teams of horses and wagons. Dad had some carpenter friends he had been working with at the smelter job who came to help with the building work. It was also at this time that all of the men working at the smelter went on strike. This then freed up time for them to give dad this help. They didn't think the strike would last very long, but it lasted about three months until the men were forced back to work for less wages. Winter was coming on so they could not keep the strike going.

Dad laid out all the lines etc. and everything seemed to go like magic. The house was built two stories high about 24 feet square. It had a hip roof. He incorporated the shack part into the back of the house, being enough room for a kitchen, bathroom and one small bedroom. The big front part became the living room and all of the upstairs was bedrooms. Dad framed all the rafters on the ground and the other men put it all together and it seemed as we had a house built all at once. It is a wonderful thing what good carpenters could do with lumber and other building materials without the help of power tools.

All the time the men were busy on the house, mother was busy cooking and serving meals to them. After the building was all up and everything in place, there was still a lot of finishing work to take care of. This was done over a period of time with my older brother John doing a lot of the work. He also became a first class carpenter and took up the trade of molding. He went to work at the smelter foundry with these skills. At the foundry, castings were made as it had a pattern shop and molding facility. Many castings were made for all of the machines on site.

In later years, my brother Ben served his time in the smelter pattern shop to become a pattern maker and subsequently he became a first class carpenter. I should add here that when Ben was in school and taking manual training (woodwork), he took the first prize for all the kids in Trail and his work was displayed at the Fall Fair. He was presented with a drafting set from Blaylock, the Consolidated Mining and Smelting Company manager.

During this time, there was a two-room school being built in east trail, although it would not be ready for the September opening. However it opened a little later on and this is when I started school. So I guess you could say that I am a charter member of the east Trail school as I began school on the day the school opened. The first teachers were Mrs. McDowel, our principal, and Miss Black, the primary teacher. This school was later named the Laura J. Morish school in honour of one of the teachers.

Miss Black was very strict and rather of the mean type. I remember if a child did something wrong, she would make them put their hands face down on the desk or some other hard object and proceed to hit their knuckles with a ruler or a pointer. Well, she only stayed at the East trail school for one term. The next teacher, Miss Wilkinson, was a real nice person. She and the kids got along real well together.

For heat in the school they had wood burning stoves – heaters they were called. The wood was delivered in 4-foot or cord wood size. They would come with wagons and teams of horses and unload the wood in front of the woodshed. The woodshed was built close to the primary room at the school. Then, in the next day or so, they would come with another wagon on which was mounted a gasoline powered buzz saw. Then they would cut all of this wood on the buzz saw to stove-wood lengths. The boys from the senior room would all work together, piling the wood in the shed. There would be a nice pile of sawdust, left from the cuttings, right in front of the shed. Some of us kids got the idea that it would be great to jump into the sawdust pile from the shed roof, so one day during the lunch hour we moved a lot of blocks of wood to the back of the shed and piled them up like a pyramid so we could climb up on the shed roof.

When the weather was nice, the teachers would line all the children up in two lines outside of the school. Senior students were in one line and primary students were in the other. The students would then march into school when the bell rang. On one day the bell rang and the kids were all lined up and ready to go into the school. About half a dozen of us were now up on the roof. The last one to climb up on the roof of the shed had knocked the blocks down. The teacher came over in front of the shed and was telling us to come down and get in the line. We said we couldn't get down because the blocks had fallen down. She then instructed some of the boys to start piling the blocks back in place and then she was going to come and help us down. When she came up on the back of the roof, we all jumped down into the sawdust pile and ran over to the line. Now we were in line and the teacher was on the roof. The senior room teacher then had to get some of the bigger boys to re-pile the blocks and they all helped to get the teacher down from the roof. When we all finally went into school, we got a lecture about the mischief we had created. Some teachers would most likely have strapped us for this but Miss Wilkinson knew how to handle kids and she was well liked. I have often thought about this incident and wondered what would have taken place if the inspector or other school board authority had showed up at this time.

We had a good time at school in those days. We were always getting into mischief but never any real serious trouble. We were always playing cowboys and Indians and imagining ourselves to be great cowboys heroes or Indian chiefs. Another memory of those days was Armistice Day at the end of the World War 1. The teachers lined us all up from both rooms and we marched downtown to where they were holding the Armistice day celebration. It was a distance of about two miles and being November, it was cold. It was a great thing for the war to be over, although a lot of us younger kids didn't realize what it was all about. There were bands playing and a lot of speeches but we were glad when it was all over.

Yet another great pastime at school was playing in the winter time. We would pick sides and build snow forts from big snowballs. We would roll up and make a wall, then we would make a lot of snowballs and start the war. It might be Wolfe against Montcalm, the English against the Americans, the allies against the Kaiser, Napolean against Wellington or other famous battles we read about in the history books. Other winter sports were sleigh riding and skating but we didn't always have the best of sleighs or skates.

In the spring we would all be down in the mud playing marbles. When the weather was nice we would all be playing baseball, although we didn't have the fancy equipment like the kids have today. In those days the school did not supply sports equipment for the kids.

CHAPTER 6

Blueberry, 1918

ON THE THIRD OF NOVEMBER 1918 my sister Dolly was born. Mother named her Lourdes Marie but my younger brother Bob thought she was a doll so she was always called Dolly. This was the year that my oldest sister Violet was in Vancouver going to the Normal School studying to be a teacher. She got her certificate in June 1919. When she came home that summer she applied for a teaching job at the little community of Blueberry. It is situated about 13 miles from Trail and about 6 miles from Castlegar. The people who were in charge of the school there had advertised for a war widow or someone who had a child of school age as there were not enough children to keep the school open. The ruling was a minimum of six children. My sister told them that naturally she did not have any children of her own but that she could bring her young brother. This was agreed between them. So, when it became time for school to start we went to Blueberry.

At this time there was very good train service in the area. The train would leave Rossland about 6 AM and it would come down the mountain road to Tadanac where the smelter was located. Then there was a switch back road down the hill to Trail. It would back down the hill to the top end at the gulch. Then, after the switch was thrown into place for the lower track, it would go forward down to the station in Trail. The order was reversed when the train went back out. This train ran through to

Nelson and was a 7-day-a-week service. It also made this trip in the evening but only as far as Castlegar and West Robson to meet the boat on the Arrow Lakes, and the west bound train to the coast from Nelson. I should mention here that this train would stop at all the flag stations along the line to pick up passengers or express items. Although it made about a dozen stops between Trail and Nelson, it would make the trip in 2 hours. Steam was a wonderful source of power.

We went to Blueberry and got started in school there. The people that we boarded with were the Beresford family. At the school, which had been built in a coulee below the Beresford house and the railway track, is where I met the rest of the school children. There were three children from the Judkins family: Geraldine, Harold, and Woodrow. This family was homesteading almost three miles back in the hills. They were all nice kids to know. The other kids were from the Harrison family. There was Irene and May and they also had another girl but she was not old enough to go to school yet; this was Ellen. May was my age and Irene was two years older. Their mother ran the store and post office and this was about half a mile from the school. Their father was not home from the war yet.

Mrs. Beresford was the secretary of the school board. Something that my sister Vi did not know about at the time is that Mrs. Beresford was from England and that she hated anybody or anything from Germany. If it had not been for her attitude in this regard I would never have been able to go to Blueberry. There was a family living at Blueberry by the name of Gopp. The Gopps were of German decent so Mrs. Beresford, being the secretary of the school board, would not have any of the Gopps children at the school. Today she would have been brought to court for this kind of action. I wonder how she felt about the Royal Family of England being related to the rulers of Germany?

The war was still going on in Europe at this time. In later years one of the Gopp boys became a very good friend of mine and he was one of the best people you could meet. His dad was also a very fine fellow. He was already a widower at this time. Should we say three cheers for British justice? There was even a big wall clock in the school that had been manufactured in Germany. Mrs. Beresford had that taken out and replaced with a different make.

We settled down in school and we enjoyed it. My sister, we had to call her Miss Irving was a good teacher. She was conscientious but also strict. She seemed to understand teaching very well. She did not have trouble with any subjects. She even taught us music and singing, of course, because she was very musical and a good singer. In later years she specialized as a writing teacher. Quite often the Judkins' girl, Geraldine, was not at school. Miss Irving inquired of her brothers about this and she found out that Mrs. Judkins was very sickly, and also that the family was very poor. Miss Irving was worried about this, so one day after school she arranged with Mrs. Harrison to go and visit the Judkins home. They made a pot of soup and put it in a good container with a lid to take it to Mrs. Judkins. They took a lantern with them and hiked to the Judkins place about three miles away. They found Mrs. Judkins in bed and not very strong. They fed her the soup and instructed Geraldine about how to look after her mother. Mrs. Harrison and Miss Irving did not get home until about 10 PM that evening, aided by having the lantern with them. Eventually things did improve at the Judkins place and the kids attended school more regularly. Although, in the winter when the snow was deep, they missed a lot of days.

Miss Irving put on a school Christmas concert and had a Christmas tree and presents for all the kids. She had canvassed the area for small donations. Everything was very successful and everyone was happy. Mr. Harrison had returned from overseas so the Harrison family was quite happy.

After school one day I had gone to the Harrison's place with May. We were playing and she said that we would go see my grandmother. I looked at her and told her that couldn't be done because our grandmothers and grandfathers all lived a long way off. My dad's relations were all scattered up and down the west coast and mother's relations lived in Omaha, Nebraska. Therefore, I had never known a grandparent or an aunt or uncle or cousin. But May said that I was living at her grandmother's place. We went there and what a surprise I had. The Beresford's had a small farm and kept some chickens and cows. Everyday after school May and I would go look for the cows and bring them home for milking. Sometimes the cows wandered a long way off. They had bells on them so we would listen for the bells in order to find them. We would do this before supper on the shorter days, but in the spring and summer, when the days were longer, we would all spend time playing before supper and bring the cows home afterwards.

On the weekends I often went home to Trail on the train so I got to know a lot of the men that worked on the trains. Some of these early day trainmen were Charlie Brett, Tom Peck, Matt Bradshaw, and a Mr. Shaw. These men were conductors, brakemen, and baggage care men. Others were Mickey Erskine, Charlie Kellerman, Harry Mansfield and a lot more names I don't remember. The engineers and firemen we didn't get to know as well as the trainmen. From riding the train on the weekends I got to know Mr. Brett very well. His wife and daughter became good friends of my sisters. I had a big thrill for an 8-year-old kid one evening when my sister and I boarded the train at Blueberry. Mrs. Brett was on the train. We went to Castlegar and then to West Robson where the train met the boats. On this occasion the boat was the Bonnington, the largest boat on the lake. Mrs. Brett took me all through the boat so I could see everything. It was a wonderful experience that I never forgot. Up to that time it was the greatest thing I had ever seen.

I remember other weekends when they took me to their home in Rossland. That was another thrill to watch the train climb the mountain from Trail to Rossland. The grades were steep and there were several places the train climbed by way of switchbacks. When it got to Rossland it was in the upper part of the town. Quite often when I was on the train I would ride in the baggage car with all of the trainmen. They would get me to sing for them and we all became great friends. I learned all of the train-whistle signals and how to pull the chord to signal the engineer to stop the train for the stations along the line. From the ticket book that the conductor carried I learned the names of all the stations in the West Kootenay districts. I thought the railway was a wonderful organization and decided that when I grew up I would be a railroader. But, by the time I grew up everything had started to change in that line of work so I didn't go to work on the railway. That is until much later in a different capacity.

The Harrison family wanted me to stay on with them in Blueberry so that the school would have enough children to keep it open. I did this for about another three years. I enjoyed living with the Harrisons and had a lot of fun there. When Mr. Harrison came back from the war he got a grant to a piece of land at Blueberry and decided they would homestead there. This place was on the hills to the west of the railway and government road. At the end of the school term my sister decided she would teach at a different school as she wanted more teaching experience. So, she applied for a different school.

CHAPTER 7

Growing up in Trail

WHEN WE WERE JUST YOUNG kids living in Trail, I had something happen to me that almost changed everything for life. I think this was when dad was working as a night watchman at the smelter. He used to go to work late in the afternoon around 4 o'clock and finish early in the morning. This incident happened in the late fall when the days were getting shorter. Mother had gone shopping and the only ones home were my younger brother Bob and myself. Bob suggested that we play a game of "The Hunter and The Lion". I said OK, so we made sure all the lights were turned off. I would be the lion and he would be the hunter. Without me knowing what he did, he went to the kitchen and got a really sharply pointed knife. I was crawling around the living room and hiding behind some of the furniture. He being the hunter came up behind me and grabbed me by the hair and of course I had a big mop of hair, so it was very easy for him to get a good hold of my hair. He pulled my head back and stabbed me with the knife. He made two of these stabs. I don't think the knife came right out after entering until I let out a yell. The knife had gone in right over the top of my right eye. There was a lot of blood and when we got a light turned on, it really scared the hell out of Bob. He started to cry and did not know what to do. I took the knife from him and got a towel to stop the bleeding. The wound didn't seem to hurt though. The knife had gone in right over the top of my eyeball, but it didn't seem to do any damage. The sight of blood really upset Bob. I told him to stop crying and not to say anything to anyone. I got the blood stopped and got it all cleaned up, washed the knife, and put it away. Mother came home a short time later and she never did get to know about this until long after we were grown up. I still have a fine scar over my eye. I guess all is well that ends well. While on this subject, I might as well tell of a few other incidents while growing up.

In the town of Trail, it seemed they always had something going on for the kids. Quite often at the theatre on Saturday afternoon when the matinee was on, they would have a contest for the fattest kid in town, or the one with the most freckles, or the kid with the reddest hair. At one of these contests, my brother Ben took the prize for the one with the most freckles, while I came first for the reddest hair of all the kids in Trail.

There was a forest fire that swept through the valley around Trail in 1917 and had cleaned out all the young coniferous trees. So it was almost impossible to find a Christmas tree anywhere near Trail. My brother Ben, who was two years older than me, decided that this would be a good way to make some Christmas money. He had a friend who he worked for on weekends and holidays. This was Mr. B. Williams. Mr. Williams had come to the area from Alberta where he had a cattle ranch. He brought some livestock (cattle and horses) with him. Ben talked the Christmas idea over with him and he said he would do it with him. They took Mr. Williams' team and wagon and some axes and left early one morning – this was about the beginning of December. They went out towards Fruitvale by way of the old Sand Hill short cut. Mr. Williams knew where there was a good stand of Christmas trees. They came back with a big load of them. Then Ben got busy taking orders for them and he sold all of them. To deliver the trees, Mr. Williams loaned him a horse and a smaller wagon and he delivered all of them. After paying for Mr. Williams for his horses, he had made himself 75 dollars – this was a lot of money for a teenager in those days.

I had a friend, Pat Ewings, from my grade-one days in the East Trail School. We thought we could make ourselves some Christmas money too. So on a Saturday morning we took a couple of axes – small ones (the axe I had was Dad's carpenter hatchet) – with us and we headed up the mountain. After a couple of hours of hiking we got to where there were some nice fir trees. The trouble was that they were all really big ones, but the tops looked like good Christmas trees. We started chopping at one of these big trees. These fir trees were about two feet in diameter at the stump and about 80 feet tall. Finally it started to fall, but it got hung up on another tree. We chopped at that one until it was ready to fall and then we ran out of the way. Well, the two trees came down and we cut the tops off of them and then we headed for home with the two trees. It was long past dark by the time we got home. We were tired and hungry. Our folks were wondering where in the world we had been. We told them and after having some supper, we went out to sell the Christmas trees. We must have been very poor salesmen, because all we got for them was 15 cents each. That was the end of our Christmas tree business. My brother Ben and everyone had a big laugh over it, but we said: "Well, we tried anyway".

We didn't have very many toys or play things from the store, so we made things of our own. We would go where there were some bushes growing and cut some of these to make bows and arrows. For the bows, we used the hazelnut bush and cut pieces about four feet long and about one inch thick. For the arrows, we cut the small pieces of willow and sometimes split a block of cedar into equal pieces and whittle all these into shape. On one occasion, I was shooting some arrows and one arrow hit Bob in the cheek. Another time we made some golf clubs. We took a piece of willow about three feet long and fitted it into an iron pipe elbow. This made a pretty good club. One time Bob had his club and was behind me. I didn't know he was ready to swing and as I turned around he swung his club. The pipe elbow hit me right under the jaw. It didn't knock me out but it did break the flesh and hurt like hell. Another time we had been given a peashooter each. These were just a piece of metal tubing ½-inch in diameter and 12 inches long. Plastic had not yet been invented. We got some dry peas from the house and had quite a time shooting peas at every one that came around.

One time we had a piece of 2-inch by 12-inch plank over the top of a big block of wood for a teeter-totter. I was on one end and Bob on the other. We had been using our peashooters. All of a sudden, Bob jumped off when his end was at the ground. Of course, my end slammed down to the ground with a bang. I still had the peashooter in my mouth and when the plank hit the ground, the peashooter, being a metal tube, hit the roof of my mouth and stuck there. I let out a yell and I had to pull the peashooter out of my mouth. I had a sore mouth for some time after that.

Another time when the weather was hot and I came back from school,

I asked if I could go swimming. My mother said no. Well, it seemed there weren't any kids around to play with and I got another idea. Mother told me I couldn't go swimming, but she didn't say I couldn't go to the river where all the kids were swimming, so I hiked down to a place we called Dry Creek. This creek only ran when the snow was melting. It made a nice bay on the river and it was all good clear sand. This bay was quite narrow in the upper part of it and the water was actually in two levels. Many years ago, a cottonwood tree had fallen across the creek and it was now buried in the sand. This made the little bay into a good place for young kids to learn to swim, as the place above the log was only about three feet deep, but on the river side it was at least eight feet deep or more. When I arrived at the swimming place, the smaller kids were all playing in the shallow water above the log. These kids were all just learning to swim. Some of the older kids were just getting undressed for swimming. I must have looked like Huckleberry Fin as I had on a pair of bib overalls and I was wearing a straw hat. Bob was there in the water just above the log. He had gone there direct from school without asking permission. He was right at the edge of the log and all of a sudden, he was in the deep water – and of course, he could not swim. One of the bigger kids, Casey Bishop, was a good swimmer. I called to him to hurry up and get in the water to get Bob, but he was taking off his clothes very leisurely. Meantime, I was wondering what I could do because I couldn't swim either. The banks going down to the water were quite steep – about a 30-degree incline. I got an idea like a flash. If I ran down the bank and dove in the water right in line with Bob, I could grab him and the momentum would take us to the other bank. I did this – straw hat, overalls, and all. I was bare-footed at the time because I went around that way a lot at the time. Well, that is exactly what happened and as we reach the far bank, some kids helped get us out of the water. Casey had not even got in the water yet. I dried out and then went home to supper. Mother never knew about it.

One other thing that mother never got to know about, was how a lot of us kids would go across the bridge. The city had built sidewalks on both upstream and downstream sides of the bridge for the pedestrians. Then, some of the kids thought it would be a good idea to walk the hand railing. The railing was a 2x6 at about four feet off the ground. Many times we walked the rail right across the bridge – it was close to 800 feet long. I don't think that anyone ever fell off the bridge, but it scared the hell out of a lot of people because the Columbia River is an awfully big powerful river – but kids don't bother thinking about danger.

One other memory from those days concerns my brother Ben. He and I were playing hooky from Sunday school. We would just go for a long walk somewhere and then come home about the time it would be over. We hated the idea of going to Sunday school when other kids could be playing. A few months later, Bob was big enough to go, so mother told us he had to go with us. The old priest said to us "Are you boys new around here, I don't remember seeing you." Well, when we got home Bob told all of this to mother and she gave us hell for it. What it really amounted to though, was turning us more away from the church. For me, I got to hate the idea of going to church. First of all, on Sunday morning you had to get all dressed up with your shoes shined. We lived two miles from the church, so we had to walk this distance, have the communion and whatnot, and then walk back two miles home again – all before breakfast. After, we could finally get into some play clothes and get into a game of some kind, then first thing we knew we had to get cleaned up for Sunday school and go down town again two miles and two miles home again. On Saturday afternoon when we were in the middle of a game, we would be called to go downtown to the church to go to confession.

I am very sure I would never have made a priest. I am glad I became an ironworker so I could do some good for the country and build bridges, dams, and powerhouses. I could most likely write a whole book about the escapades that we got into when we were growing up. One incident comes to mind. This was after we moved out to Tarrys. There was a nice big flat area near the Tarrys barnyard. The kids used this area for ball games and things like that. Somebody had planted a big round cedar post there – I think for tying up horses. It was flat on top and about five feet or more above the ground. John Tarry, Bob, and I got hold of a big 2 x 12 plank about 20 feet long. We drilled a hole in the middle of the plank and we got a bolt from the Tarrys blacksmith shop and then drilled a hole in the post. With some grease on the top of the post we had a merry go round. I took a piece of rope and fastened it to one end of the plank. Bob and John Tarry each got onto the plank, one at each end. I got onto one of Tarry's horses and started riding around in a circle. John and Bob thought this was great so I got the horse running in a circle, going faster all the time. They were getting dizzy so when I had it going quite fast, I let go of the rope. They were hanging on for dear life and both of them yelling. By the time it slowed down they were both sick and throwing-up.

They didn't want any more merry-go-rounds. It's really great being a kid.

Another time, Bob and I were at the Pratt farm and we were helping with the hay. The hay had been cut and raked and put into haycocks for curing. Now we were loading the hay onto the wagon. Bob and I were on the wagon to build the load. Mr. and Mrs. Pratt were both forking the hay onto the wagon. It was a good crop so we soon had a good load. The wagon was pulled by one horse. We started to leave the hay field and on the way out there was a small side hill to go up. The old horse decided that there was some good grass on his left side and he started to turn to the left. I should have jerked the line on him, but I didn't, so the turning cramped the wheels against the wagon frame, and being on a hill, we tipped the whole thing over. It scared Mr. and Mrs. Pratt but we crawled out from under the hay. Then the wagon had to be straightened up and all of the hay reloaded again. We finally got it all done and the hay taken into the barn. No one was injured and no damage was done to the wagon, and the nerves of Mr. and Mrs. Pratt calmed down.

I have recently noticed a lot in the news about bullying in schools. We had lots of it too. I got into some real bad fights on account of it. For some reason, it seemed quite a few kids liked to pick on me. But I had a temper and though I was smaller than a lot of kids, I fought back. I remember one kid that came from Scotland and he evidently had taken some boxing lessons. One day after school, he picked a fight with me. I didn't back up and he gave me a bloody nose, but that didn't stop me. He kept ducking his head but I hit him several times on the side of his head. I didn't realize how hard I hit him but on about the third or fourth blow he collapsed in the snow. There was blood all over the place. Now with him lying in the snow a lot of other kids were scared. We put snow on his head and he came out of it. I washed my face in the snow and went home. After this Scotty and I became good friends.

There were a couple more kids that were always wanting to fight me: Dan Skinner and Willie Mcouch. I could handle either one by myself, but the two together was a little too much. One day after school, they said they were going to get me. I said you will have to catch me first and I took off. It was several blocks to our place but I was a fast runner. Just before our place there was a short steep hill. There were a lot of rocks on this hill. I got to the top of the hill just when they reached the bottom. I grabbed some rocks and started throwing. They started throwing rocks too but I had the advantage of throwing downhill. I hit each of them and they gave up. Another day they caught me as I was coming home from the store with a dozen eggs in a paper bag. My mother had sent me to get the eggs. Dan and Willie said "Well, we've got you now". I smashed the eggs right on both their faces with on quick swing. They both took off for home and then mother sent me back to the store for more eggs.

One time in the summer when we were staying out at Thrums during the summer holidays, Bob and I had gone up to the Tarry's farm to play with John and Hazel. On the way home, as we walked along the dusty road, a gopher ran across the road to his hole beside a fence post. It was a double hole – one going in at an angle on each side of the post and entering from the road. When the gopher reached his hole he stopped there and sat up to watch us. I said to Bob you just stay still and I will catch the gopher. I moved along where the gopher could not see me. Then I headed back to the post in the dust and didn't make a sound. I reached the post – it was a good size. I put my right had behind the post while the gopher was still watching Bob. I put my left hand to the other side. The gopher immediately jumped back towards the hole and I grabbed him by the back of his neck. He wasn't able to bite me because of the way I was holding him. Bob said he could hardly believe it. Now we had a squealing gopher that we didn't really want. I carried him up the road for a little way, then let him go. He beat all gopher running records getting back to his hole. Now we had an adventure story to tell mother at suppertime.

With the help of some of the older men in town we formed the junior football (soccer) league and drew up a game schedule for the four teams that had been formed. I was named captain of the East Trail team (AKA The Outlaws). We, the kids that lived in East Trail, were quite lucky because we had more access to the ball grounds than some of the others, since the ball grounds were located in East Trail. We used to have other school games on weekdays and afternoon games on Saturdays. At the end of the season, we had play-off games and also games with Rossland and Nelson. We also had baseball games with these same teams.

At this time, I should mention some of the men that helped us form the junior football league. There was Jack Kitchen, Dick Styles, Mr. Balfour, and Mr. Forrest. There were others, but I don't remember any more names. These men had all been great soccer players in their day and they were very good coaches. In fact, they still played on the men's teams in Trail. They had all come out from England and Scotland where soccer was their national game.

We had another game that I have never seen since those times. We called it knobbies. We would go out in the woods and cut a piece of willow or hazelnut bush for a knobbie stick. The stick would be cut between three and four feet long with the end having a fork on it projecting about three to four inches from the main part. We would then take two pieces of garden hose two inches long and tie them together with a leather lace 12 inches long. With this, we had our equipment ready for playing. The only equipment you had to pay for was a pair of running shoes. The rules of the game were the same as lacrosse, but we could not afford to play lacrosse because real lacrosse sticks with leather nets were expensive.

When we were kids, Halloween was just Halloween tricks. Trick or treat came much later. We never got treats so we tried to play a lot of tricks. East trail was a great place for this. Most of the houses did not have bathrooms yet, but they all had outhouses at the back of the lot. Most all the kids thought that it was great sport to push over and upset the outhouses. There were quite a few houses that were near the riverbank with the back end of the lot at the edge of the bank. This was usually where the outhouses were situated. When you pushed these over, they naturally fell down the riverbank and sometimes right into the river. I guess Halloween helped with the advancement of indoor plumbing.

I remember one incident that happened out in the valley at Thrums. There was a place where the school teachers boarded. It was the home of a widow woman. I wasn't in on this deal, it was done by kids younger than me, but I got the story first hand. My younger brother Bob was with them when it happened quite late at night. They boosted one of the kids up on the roof of the back porch of this house, and he stuffed a gunny sac into the top of the chimney. Then they all got together and moved the outhouse to the rear entrance to the house at the back porch. In those days, everyone used a wood-burning stove for heating and cooking. The first job in the morning was to light the fire to get breakfast going. The fire was started in the kitchen stove and immediately the house started to fill up with smoke. The lady of the house and the school teachers went to the back door to open it and were greeted by the site of the out house right at the back porch. This was an awful Halloween trick but it really happened.

Another time we got someone's cow and we put some horse harness on the cow. We then put a horse wagon on one side of a wire fence, and the cow on the other side, with the shafts of the wagon through the fence and the cow hitched to the wagon. I guess the cow did a lot of bawling and that was the way the farmer found her. It's amazing where kids get ideas from.

CHAPTER 8

Blueberry

WHEN MR. HARRISON CAME BACK from the war in France, he was able to get a big piece of land for a homestead as part of a soldier settlement deal. This piece of land was just above the town of Blueberry. It ran from the Government Road back into the hills. The lower part of the property had been logged but there was still valuable timber near the back. There were also good springs for supplying water. This valuable part of the land was on a bench several hundred feet higher than the rest of the land and was therefore the area where Mr. Harrison chose to build the house and the barns, etc.

Mr. Harrison had a friend who had been a logger and was out of work. He offered to help to cut the trees for the log supply and to raise the log frames for the house and barn. To raise the logs on the buildings, they erected a gin-pole for a rig to hoist the logs. Once the logs were raised onto the building, they would be marked and notched on the lower side of the log on both ends with an axe. This would allow for the logs to interlock with one another. This job was done for all the walls of the buildings. If two rounds of logs were placed in one day, this would be considered a real good days work. To hoist the logs there was a pulley block near the tope of the gin-pole. This block had a line running through it. The line was rigged through a fair lead block pulley at the bottom. This in turn was hitched to the single tree that was hooked to the harness of the horse.

This is considered real horsepower. It was simple and very effective. The horse could skid the logs out of the woods and then raise the logs on the building. The fuel supply was simple and consisted of hay, grain, water, a barn to eat in, and of course some grooming and care.

Before the house could be lived in, it required doors, windows, flooring, etc. Mr. Harrison decided to obtain the lumber for the inside of the house from the mill at Birchbank. This was six miles away on a very poor road. He borrowed another horse to add to his own horse, in order to have a strong enough team for a wagon. The horses were not in the best of shape. He placed a plank on the bolsters of the running gear of the wagon to make a seat.

One day he got the horses ready early in the morning. His daughter, May, and I were going to join him for the ride. We left Blueberry at about 7:30 in the morning. It was November and the days were cold and short. We arrived at the mill around lunch time. Mr. Harrison took May and I to the cook house at the mill to have lunch. He told us that he would join us as soon as the lumber was loaded. The cook gave us a nice hot lunch, which we enjoyed. We also warmed up after our trip on the wagon. Mr. Harrison came in to eat and informed us that we would be heading back as soon as the team was ready and had eaten their grain. The mill where we picked up the lumber was a planer mill. It was located beside the railway on a bench above the Columbia River at a town called Birchbanck. The lumber that supplied this planer mill was rough lumber from a sawmill up in the mountains approximately five miles away. The lumber traveled from the sawmill to Birchbank in a water flume. After it arrived it was put through the planer mill and was ready for shipping. The mill was owned and operated by Mr. Joe DeChamps. He was a big lumber operator in those days. There will be more about this mill and owner in another chapter.

It was a long and slow trip back. We were all sitting on top of the lumber. Mr. Harrison was up front driving the team and May was sitting behind me. About two miles from home it started snowing and was getting progressively colder. The snow was acting like sand on the wagon wheels, which made it more difficult for the horses to pull. Pretty soon there was two or three inches of snow covering everything. When Mr. Harrison looked around to see how we were doing, he suddenly grabbed a handful of snow and put it on my face. I asked him what that was for and he said my nose was freezing and the snow would take the frost off.

Well, it was dark by the time we got home where the store was and where they were also living at the time. He unhitched the horses and put them away to feed them. May and I were real glad to get into the house to get warmed up and eat our supper. Later on Mr. Harrison had to move the lumber to the homestead with a horse team and sleigh. People really worked hard for what they got and to get work done in those days.

Mr. Harrison and his friend, Al Osmsby, worked on the house and barn at the homestead. By the end of the year, they had both ready. The family moved up to the homestead after Christmas. Of course I was with them. When the Harrison's left the store for the homestead, they made a trade with Mrs. Harrison's mother, Mrs. Benesford. They turned the store and post office over to Mrs. Benesford in exchange for her livestock. The livestock consisted of only cows and chickens, as they already owned a horse. The name of the horse was Prince. He was a big gentle horse, possibly a Percheron breed. All of us kids liked him.

With the cows and everything in the new log barn it looked more like a homestead or farm. Some of us kids had already learned how to milk cows while the cows were still at the Benesford's place, so when the arrivals were moved to the new place, we kept up with the job. It didn't seem to be a big problem to perform such a task. Irene was a couple of years older than May and I. Between the three of us we did all of the chores at the place and I seem to remember enjoying these tasks. Anyway there was always something to do after school.

When they moved to the homestead it was winter time. There was a big hill going down from the place so Mr. Harrison helped us build a nice big bobsled. This was done by building a bunk on each of two small sleighs with the front one made so it would turn. On top of the bunks, a 10-foot plank was placed and fastened solidly to the rear sleigh. With a hole drilled in the front bunk and through the plank, the sleigh could turn on a pivot bolt. Turning was controlled by a rope. There was a piece of wood fastened to the front at the plank. This piece was there for the person steering the sleigh. They were to brace themself with the rope as it ran up along the sled, beside their feet. We had lots of fun with this sleigh as we could all ride on it together. It was all downhill to Blueberry, which was a mile and a half although it was sure a long haul back.

One time we were all on the bobsleigh together. I was sitting in the front to steer the sleigh. We were on the steep part of the hill and going quite fast. The steering rope broke and we had a bad upset. We were all thrown off of the sleigh and bruised up. The girls were mad at me and told me I didn't know how to steer a sleigh, but after they realized the rope had broken I was forgiven. It was a wonder that we were not badly injured as the snow on the sides of the road was all frozen. Winter clothes save a lot of bruises.

When we lived at the homestead in the log house there was not much entertainment. There was no radio or TV, but we did have an old hand wind-up phonograph. In the evenings we would listen to a record or two after we finished our homework or maybe we would sing songs before bedtime.

In the spring after the snow was gone we would pick a lot of wildflowers. We learned the names of all the wild plants and flowers as they came into season. The first flowers to appear were the dogtooth violets, or Easter lilies as some people would call them. Then the little yellow and purple violets would bloom, followed by the tiger lilies and wild roses. Finally the Indian paint brushes, trilliums and blue bells would appear. We always had bouquets of wildflowers in the house for Mrs. Harrison. In about the beginning of June the wild strawberries were ripe and we would pick a lot of them. Then there were thimbleberries and wild blackberries, and later in the summer there were huckleberries. In any case we would always find a lot of things to do. We also liked to ride the horse and we learned how to harness the horse and hook it up and drive it. I find it difficult to understand today when I hear people, especially young people, say that farm and ranch life is boring.

Before we moved to the homestead we had a lot of things happen both at school and outside of school hours. The railway passed approximately 250 feet south of the school. It ran over a big fill and culvert over Blueberry creek. Here it made a big turn to the south and ran along the side of a hill which was a clay bank and was therefore subject to sliding. One time a slide came down at night and collided with an ore filled freight that was headed to the Trail smelter. The engine, a big 2-8-0 job was derailed and went down the bank, along with several ore cars. I don't remember hearing of any serious injuries.

When I say a big 2-8-0 job, I'm referring to a steam locomotive. Steam locomotives were designated by their wheel alignment. The first number indicates the leading, or pony, truck. The second number indicates the number of driving wheels and. the third number indicates the number of wheels under the fire box, or the engineers cab. To remove the train wreck, they built a track down the hillside and then with the aid of the Big Hook, they pulled the cars out, put the engine back on its feet (or rather wheels) and then pulled it up onto the main track. Then they took all of the wreck to Nelson where it was all repaired and returned to service. In those days the railway company maintained a complete car and machine shop service in Nelson. This was all very exciting for all of us kids to see something that weighed well over a hundred tons to be pulled back into place.

Another time a slide came down in the early evening. We ran in and told Mrs. Harrison. She said we had to stop the night train on its way to Trail and Rossland as it would soon be coming. We needed a red lantern to signal the train to stop to alert them of the danger. We didn't have any red cloth to place over a lantern, so we cut an old tobacco bag and fastened it around the lantern. This served the purpose for a red lantern and we stopped the train. This is about the only time I know of when tobacco helped mankind. The railway people were very grateful and Mrs. Harrison was given a railway pass for a year.

Another time, a lot of us and Mrs. Harrison had a real bad scare. About 100 feet from the store building where we were all living at the time, there was a big Ponderosa Pine tree growing beside the road. It was in the evening after supper and we were all playing outside. We saw a squirrel run along the ground and then up this pine tree. We ran over to the tree thinking we might catch the squirrel. I thought I could climb the tree and get the squirrel. There were no heavy limbs for about 12 feet up the tree and then for quite a few feet there were only stubs of limbs. We found an old ladder and with the aid of this I managed to get hold of some of the limb stubs. I kept pulling myself up until I reached some branches. Pretty soon I was a long way up in the tree. The squirrel was a little excited and all of a sudden he ran down the tree on the opposite side from me. I started back down and the kids near the bottom of the tree were all yelling. They were yelling because the squirrel went up again. I went up again. Now he went down again. The kids were all still yelling. I then went down again. I was down at the bottom of the branches. I was holding onto a dead limb above my head. The limb broke and I was falling through the air. I could see the kids running on the road and I could hear Mrs. Harrison scream. I landed on my back on the ground. Just a few feet from where I landed there was a big pile of rocks. The wind was knocked out of me and I had an awful time to get my breath back. However, I didn't have any broken bones but I had one broken tooth. It was truly a wonder that I wasn't killed. Mr. Harrison looked at the tree later and told us the distance I had fallen was 45 feet. Any way we all had a bad scare out of the incident.

One time when the afternoon train had stopped on its way to Trail, I was riding a saddle horse that they (the Harrison's) had. It was a nice warm day and the train men in the baggage car had the side door open. When they saw me on the horse they all shouted. The horse was scared and he started to buck. I was thrown off and I landed face down on the gravel road. The men on the train all laughed and as the train pulled away the engineer or fireman blew the whistle. My face was all bruised and scratched and I looked like I had tangled with a wild cat.

When we lived at the store we had to bring the water all the way from Blueberry Creek, which was a good half-mile away. Two of us would go together and take a big wooden bucket to the creek. We would fill the bucket and, with one of us on either side, we would carry it back. About half way back we would reach the railway. When we got there we would set the bucket on the rail and then we would just skid it the rest of the way on the rail. There was also a man with a horse who used to bring the water in barrels, but he was not always available.

We liked it better when we moved to the homestead because the spring where we got the water from was quite close to the house. The first spring that we lived on the homestead we started to cultivate some of the land and plant a garden and some hay crops. It was at this time when Mr. Harrison got a job with the BC Forestry department. They wanted him to move to Rossland as that was where the Forestry office was located for all of that portion of the West Kootenays. The head Kootenay office of course was located in Nelson. They got a house in Rossland and at the end of the school season they all moved to Rossland. They sold all of the livestock and left the homestead vacant. When this happened I went back to Trail and the next season I continued school there. This was a disappointment for me as I had really enjoyed living at Blueberry.

However I would at different times go to Rossland to visit with them. I would go up there on the local train. Mr. Harrison had a little Model-T Ford pick-up truck that belonged to BC Forestry. We would go to high places around the area with a pair of field glasses and look for signs of forest fires. I liked this very much. Of course another reason that I liked to go to their place was the fact that from the first day I was at school at Blueberry I met May and fell in love with her. I don't think I ever got over it. To me she was the most wonderful person in the world, but I was always too bashful to tell her that I loved her. Then later on as we grew up I didn't get to go to Rossland very much and of course she met other people. Then later on after high school she worked for the BC Telephone Company. Later on she married and moved away so I never got to see her anymore. Although, one time years later after I had been married I met her in Penticton. She was living in Penticton. We had a nice long talk about the old days when we were kids together. I guess the moral of this part of the story is that if you have missed the boat you are not liable to catch it again. Also, it's better to have loved and lost then never to have loved at all.

CHAPTER 9

School in Glade and Shore Acres

IT WAS SEPTEMBER 1924. My mother came up with the idea to move out in the country again to Glade. The house in Trail was to be rented, and the one in Glade would be a lot cheaper. So, she thought she would be making some money. But moving costs money, so unless the move is for a long time, there isn't much gained.

We moved into a vacant log house on the Jack Balleney place. It was a good place, not a modern house, but warm and comfortable. For myself, I was happy to be living in the country. We had about a mile to walk to school. It was a one-room school built out of logs. All grades from one to eight were taught there. The teacher, Miss Wadds, was a nice person but she had a big job to teach that many grades. October was the month of my 14th birthday and I was full of energy and always ready for mischief.

I like riding a horse and Jack Balleney had a nice horse that I cold use a lot of the time. I repaid Jack by doing a lot of work for him. Jack was a veteran of World War One. He was a very nice person, but he was lazy and very low on ambition. He used to loan us his horse to bring in wood, and then I would help him with his wood. The weather had been very good all during October. But, towards the end of the month a snow storm came. At this time, Jack had not dug his potatoes. My mother got all excited about the snow and told us kids, Bob and I, that we would not be going to school one day, and instead we would be helping Jack with the potatoes. We went to Jack's house to tell him, he had to borrow a plow from his neighbour Mr. Passmore. We got started with the job, but what a horrible mess to pick the potatoes out of the wet sloppy ground. Well, we did the job and by the time we finished we were a soaking wet muddy mess. Jack loaded the sacks of potatoes onto the stone boat and hauled them to his root cellar. He left the plow in the field.

My dad had been teaching Bob and I a lot of woodcraft. For example, he taught us how to make the under cut in a tree to be able to fell it where you wanted it to land. He also taught us how to skid and deck logs and how to handle a rope to rope a cow, and how to tie all of the different knots in a rope. When the weather was nice, the teacher had all of the kids line up outside the school just before starting time. It seemed that I always had my rope with me. One day when the kids were all in line, I tied my rope to the doorknob and then took a turn around a porch post with the rope. The teacher rang the bell. When she tried to open the door, it would not open until I let the rope go. When the door opened suddenly, she fell back into the room. After she picked herself up, she came out with her hair flying and her face all red. "Who did that?" she asked. A little girl in the line said "Please Miss Wadds, Joe Irving did that." She asked me why I did it. I told her I was showing the kids how to hold something with a rope. I don't know what she thought, but she didn't say anything more about it. She could have given me hell, but she never did.

Well, time went on and we got through the winter. One nice day in spring, Miss Wadds asked the boys to bring some alder catkins to school for a drawing lesson. I said I would do that. I had a nice boys axe that my dad had given me. Near the bridge over the Slocan River, which was on the way to the school, there was a group of alder trees. My brother Bob was with me and with my axe I cut down one of these alders. Then I cut about 12 feet off the top of the tree. We took this to the school. We were a little late on purpose. I told Bob to open the door and then I came in with the tree with the butt first, so that the branches wouldn't spread. Miss Wadds jumped up and shouted "What are you doing?" I said that I had brought enough catkins for the whole class. She said that we didn't need that many, only a few, and to take that out of the schoolroom. The kids were all laughing.

To get the tree out I had to chop all the branches off and the kids were all still laughing. Miss Wadds placed some of the catkins in a jar for the drawing lesson and I took the remainder of the tree outside. She never said anything more about the prank. She probably thought that someday I would forget about playing pranks and be sensible.

At this time it was spring and time to plant gardens. Jack Ballaney asked me to go and get the plow. He would plow the garden. I didn't know that he had left the plow in the field all winter, so I went to the Passmore place to get it. What a blast I got from Mr. Passmore. I was to tell Jack Ballaney what he thought of him for leaving borrowed equipment in the weather. Then I went to the field where we had dug the potatoes the previous fall and got the plow. Then I gave Jack Mr. Passmore's message. It didn't bother Jack very much, but I thought about it quite a bit.

Time rolled along and the school season was ending. I had to go to Nelson to write my high school exams. Mother made arrangements for me to stay at the Strathcona Hotel. Both Dad and Mother knew the people that ran the hotel and it was only a block from the school. We had two exams each day and one in the morning, and another in the afternoon. When the afternoon exam was over, I walked down to the wharf at the lake to watch the big lake boat come in. The train would meet the boat to pick up the passengers and express. This was called the Crowe boat that had met the train from Crowsnest at Kootenay Landing. This was the transportation life line of the Kootenay Country. The train ran from Nelson to Vancouver by way of the Coquihalla Pass.

I did very well with my exams and passed with the highest marks among the valley students. I was awarded a prize from the Women's Institute. Miss Wadds was now on a holiday at Banff and she noticed the write up in the Nelson News. She sent me a card of congratulations, which I still have to this day.

September came and we once again moved back to Trail.

CHAPTER 10

Trail, 1925-28

AFTER I HAD PASSED MY exams to get into high school we moved back to Trail in 1925. I went to the high school downtown on the corner of Cedar Avenue and Portland Street. I liked school and I did quite well in my studies. There were also a lot of sports for the kids. I played soccer again and baseball, and I also did some track running.

We had a big deal that fall. There was an indoor track meet between the towns of Nelson and Trail, in the Trail arena. The arena was one of the old wooden structure arenas. The one in Nelson was up the hill by the old streetcar barns. The one in Trail was at the south end of Bay Avenue where it starts to follow the river towards the old bridge. When the track meet was held in Nelson, we went to Nelson on a special train, which was paid for by the amateur athletic association. And when the track meet was over they had a banquet for all the kids and all the track meet officials. This was all a big thrill for all the kids, since there were not very many affairs like this taking place that kids had a chance to attend. Also, it was a real treat to be able to go on the train for free. We did not get back to Trail until about 2 AM – a tired but happy bunch of kids.

One other thing I enjoyed doing was climbing the mountains behind east Trail. There is a lot of big rugged rock bluffs at this part of the valley and a lot of us kids hiked up these bluffs. Actually there were some very dangerous places for kids to climb. Sometimes we had a rope with us and with the rope we managed to climb a lot of dangerous rock bluffs on the mountain. Today a lot of young people have mountain bikes, but we were always on foot. In fact, I never owned a bicycle of any kind. I rode my brother's bike though from time to time. He used to work after school and on Saturdays for the Trail Merchantile Company so he was able to buy a bike at wholesale prices.

Well, I was not able to stay in high school for very long. The following spring my folks made a deal on the Trail property. They traded the house and lot in Trail for the old Tarrys house and a piece of land of about three acres. In the month of May the deal was complete so we moved all the furniture and household goods to Tarrys and this would be our home from then on. But there were no high schools anywhere other than in either Nelson or Trail. I started doing odd jobs for different farmers around the valley, but of course there was hardly any money involved in these jobs. I realized a long time later that I should have taken my high school by correspondence, but didn't know about it at the time. I realized in later years after I was working in construction that I needed more education, so I took several night school courses and an awful lot of study at home.

So for the next couple of years, I worked for various farmers around the area for little money. For instance one time I looked after four dairy cows for one of these farmers, while he and his wife and kids took a holiday with their touring car. They were actually looking for a different place. I got my younger brother Bob to help me. We had to milk the cows twice a day. We had to put the milk through a cooler, put it into 10-gallon containers, and then take these containers to the railway station where they were shipped on the morning train. We then brought back empty containers, cleaned the milk house, and looked after the cows. This job lasted about 10 days. For this we were given the large sum of $1.50 each, which came to about 5 cents an hour for our labour. Today no one works for less than $8 per hour.

Well, in the following spring of 1928 I saw an ad in the paper for a farm and ranch hand. I applied for the job. The place was in Fruitvale and the farmer was Mr. Williams, the fellow I spoke about before on the Christmas tree deal with my brother Ben. I took the job and I went to Fruitvale where I spent the next five months. At this place, Mr. Williams had a lot of land and some of it had to be cleared of brush, broken with a plow and a team of horses, and brought under cultivation. Then there were also ground crops to cultivate and harvest. We always worked about 12 hours a day, 6 days a week. I stayed with this until October and then went back home to Tarrys. For this work, I received the large sum of $15 per month.

CHAPTER 11

Bonnington, 1928-29

JUST AFTER I HAD FINISHED working on the ranch at Fruitvale for M.B. Williams, I was in Trail and I happened to meet Fred Pratt. He was an old time friend of our family from Thrums. After the First World War was over, he went to farm in the Peace River area on the soldier settlement scheme. This turned out to be a very tough deal so came to Trail and was working at the smelter. This was a very unhealthy place to work so he had just quit. We had both heard that there was a construction job starting in Bonnington on the Kootenay River. The City of Nelson was going to build another unit on their hydro plant. Fred and I talked about this. He said to come along with him in his car, a new Model-T Roadster. We did this and we were both hired. For me, this was the start of my life of construction work. I had just turned 17 on the 10th of October so I was all eyes and ears for this kind of work. Also, the pay would be much better than what I was used to.

The superintendent was a man by the name of Bill Faust. He had worked his way up from a bridge carpenter and pile driver to superintendent. On this job they were going to build a big-timber stiff leg derrick to handle the lifting and placing of the material for the job. The place picked out for the derrick setting was at the front end of the existing fore bay that served the power plant. This was about 40 feet higher than the generating floor of the existing powerhouse.

They constructed a timber bridge across the fore bay for access to the derrick site. The foot block of the derrick mast was placed there and then the mast placed by rigging a pole with power from the steam donkey engine from the opposite side of the fore bay. The gin pole was also used to place the top end of the stiff legs over the gudgeon pin at the top of the mast. The stiff legs had special iron fittings for this. The gudgeon pin was about 4½ inches diameter. The mast was an 18-inch square timber 40 feet high. The stiff legs were 14-inches square by 60 feet. All of this was held in place by a special bolt. One stiff leg had its base on the fore bay, the other on the rock bluff, which was actually the mountain. A big timber crib was around each base and filled with rock to stabilize the derrick. The boom of the derrick was 14 inches by 16 inches by 70 feet long after being spliced.

The timbers for the stiff leg derrick were all No. 1 coast fir and these all arrived at the job site in forty-foot lengths. The ones for the stiff legs and the boom all had to be spliced together with 4-inch timbers on both sides of the splice and held together with ¾-inch diameter bolts, nuts, and O.G. washers. This was quite a job in itself, because we did not have any power equipment on the job such as front-end loaders or boom trucks or mobile cranes. Everything was done the hard way: by hand — even the drilling of the bolt holes for all of the big splices.

If the operator could not see the work from his position at the hoist when a crane or derrick is set up ready for work, a man had to be designated as the signal man to give the signal for all the work and hoisting to the operating engineer. The signal man had to be in a place where he could see all of the work, and where he could be seen with ease by the operator.

I had been working with the carpenters that were doing the timber framing for the derrick. One day when we had it all together, Bill Faust called me. I went to see what he wanted. He said: "Hey kiddo, you think you could give signals for this rig?" I said I couldn't see why not. He said: "OK, go over there and talk to Dave Hodges, the hoisting engineer, and learn all of the derrick signals". And then he said: "And don't you ever hurt anybody". I had a good talk with Dave and from then on I was the signalman for the derrick. I kept my mind on the job and everything went OK. This was the first derrick or crane I had ever worked with. But, in the following years I worked with every kind of rig that was ever invented.

I sometimes wondered why I had been picked for this particular job, and then I thought about an incident that had happened. One Saturday night we were all in the bunkhouse when a truck driver came in. He said he had left Nelson that afternoon with a big load on his truck to be delivered to the construction job at the city power plant. The truck was now bogged down about 5 miles back on the road. The labor foreman told him to take an empty bunk and he would tell the superintendent in the morning. The next morning Bill Faust took charge of things himself. He had the company truck driver take the truck to the tool shed and they loaded up tools and rigging and men. They took all of this up the road to where the bogged-down truck was. This truck driver was a fellow by the name of Pat Deferro who drove for the Nelson Transfer Company. As far as I know, he spent most of his life driving for the Nelson Transfer Company.

We got the truck jacked up and out of the mud and with the aid of some planks, back onto solid ground. The road was only a dirt road and also very narrow. The truck was a GMC 5-ton truck with a single rear axle as all trucks were at the time. The load consisted of a big penstock section, a 9-foot diameter elbow, and a lot of steel for the trash racks – about 10 tons all together. We got down the 49 Creek Hill and were headed up the hill on the south side of the creek. All of a sudden the outside of the road gave way and the truck was in the ditch. The load was well tied down with chains and cinchers so it stayed on the truck. Now they had to widen the road all the way up the hill, pull the truck back onto the road, place timbers under the truck, and finally get it back onto firm ground. In those days there were no tractors or equipment around so Bill Faust sent the company truck and some men back to the job. They brought back more blocking, jacks, and rope rigging. Then they started jacking up the truck with the load and placing timber under it. To hold the truck up to the higher side of the road, they placed several sets of rope falls anchored to trees above the road and hooked onto the truck. The men from the job were mostly laborers, good men, but not with much knowledge of rigging. It was while we were hooking up this rigging to the trees that I believe I got myself the job as the signal man for the derrick.

I was working beside the labor foreman, Nels Teri. Bill Faust was on the road below us, and he called up to Nels to put rope lashings around the trees to hook the rope falls on. He told him to take several turns of rope around the tree and then tie a square knot in the lashing and use two or more parts for the hook of the rope block. Nels didn't know how to tie a square knot so I took the rope, made the turns around the tree, tied the square knot in the lashing, and then hooked the hook of the block into a couple of parts of the rope with the hook going in from the underside of the rope. We did this with all of the sets of rope and when they were pulling on the ropes all stayed in place properly.

We finally got the truck jacked up, pulled up on the road, the road widened, and the truck up the hill. It was only a few days later when Bill gave me the signalman job. Dave Hodges and I became good friends and I learned a lot from him. Many years later when I was running jobs for some of the bridge companies, I had Dave for an engineer as we were still using steam power until the 1960s. Some times we talked about Bonnington and how I had started out as a green kid and we would have a laugh as we thought about those days.

When we first started using the derrick, the main job at the time was the excavation of the power site. All the rock was lifted out of the hole with the derrick and dumped to the side. Most of the rock work was done in the winter, then the concrete work took place. By spring, they were ready to start placing the steel and machinery. The first piece of equipment was the big draft tube. This goes down into place before the turbine. In a hydro power plant, the water comes from the dam to the fore bay, then down through the penstocks to the scroll casing and through the speed ring where the governor blades are that control the flow of water to the turbine. After doing the work of turning the turbine, which in turn, through the shaft, turns the generator up above on the generator floor, the water goes out again to the river through the draft tube.

After the draft tube was positioned, it was concreted in place. The next things were the speed ring and the scroll casing, which fastened to the speed ring and looked like a large snail. It was built from boilerplate steel, the same as the penstock. All of these parts of the scroll casing and penstock were pre-drilled and then bolted together and fitted. Then they were all riveted in place. Nowadays this is all a welded job. When the turbine finally went into place, it was fastened to the speed ring and the governor blades. This was all handled by the derrick from its location on top of the fore bay.

On this job all of these parts of the job were supplied and done by the Canadian Allis Chalmers Company. The man that came to look after all of this part of the work was Jim Shore. He came out from Montreal. During the time of the riveting of the scroll casing, for example, the derrick was tied up. Jim Shore came to me and wanted me to work on their crew. I said OK but I didn't want to give up the signal job. He said that was OK and that whenever the derrick has to work, I would still be the signal man. This deal worked out OK because during this time there was no work for the derrick. By doing this I learned about the fitting and riveting of steel, of which I had no previous knowledge.

Whenever a lift had to be made, I went back up to look after the derrick and signals. For instance, some times a heavy lift had to be made and then the rigging at the load line changed from single to multiple parts and I would take care of a lot of this. The power for operating the derrick was a 2-drum steam engine, which also had two swing drums. The donkey engine was placed on the land side of the fore bay with the cables running out to the derrick. The top drum was used for the cable that raised or lowered the boom. The boom was rigged with four parts of ¾-inch diameter cable with the becket or dead end of the lines going around the boom at two-thirds the distances from the base of the boom and held there with cable clamps. When the boom was raised to the working position on the boom drum, it was then held in that position with a steel fitting that was called the dog. The load line was on the lower or front drum and then went to the derrick and run through a sheave or pulley at the front end of the boom and then to the load block. The load line could be changed at any time from single to multiple lines. The derrick was capable of handling 15 tons at a radius of 60 feet. For handling loads of this size, the boom was rigged with four parts of load line. The heavy loads included the draft tube, the speed ring, the turbine shafts and penstock sections, and generator parts.

The mast of the derrick, which held the boom in place, was turned by means of a bull-wheel at the base of the mast. This was done by two cables that come from the swing drums on the donkey engine and then in turn went around the bull wheel. When the line on one drum was taken in, the other line went out so the bull wheel turned and consequently the boom with the load could be placed wherever necessary.

The construction company doing the main part of the work was the Stewart Cameron Company of Vancouver. This company was associated with the Cassidy Engineering Company of Seattle, Washington. In the spring of 1929, Bill Faust, the superintendent, left Bonnington to take over the project at Ruskin, B.C. on the Stave River, another hydro job for the B.C. Electric Company. He was followed at Bonnington by Mr.

Cassidy, who came up from Seattle. Mr. Cassidy, being an engineer, was also a very capable construction supervisor.

I stayed with this job through the summer of 1929 until we shipped out the equipment and loaded it out in Nelson. I was the last man on the job. Then for some time I only had odd jobs around the area. Work and jobs were slowing down and becoming non-existent after the stock market crash of 1929. During the first half of 1930 there was very little work. But that year the Consolidated Mining and Smelting Company (Cominco) in Trail B.C. decided to build the fertilizer plant at Warfield, which is on the bench above the Smelter at Tadonac, which is on the bench above the City of Trail, B.C. I went there in July 1930 and applied for a job. Being young and having a lot of construction experience, I was hired right away.

City of Nelson power plant extension project
1929

CHAPTER 12

Trail/Cominco, 1930-32

IN 1930 COMINCO WAS HIRING quite a lot of men. If you had construction experience, so much the better. They made you go on the labour gang first and you then graduated from there. I was placed on the crew that was unloading material from the rail cars. I worked at this for a few weeks and then I was transferred to work with the ironworkers. They called us the steel gang.

The first building I worked on was the big phosphate plant. There was a lot of steel in this building – about 2000 tons. I went with the crew that was constructing the top part of the building. The name of the foreman was Alex Smith. I could get around up high very well, so I got along with the crew very well. My experience from Bonnington came in very handy here. When we finished the work at the phosphate plant we went down to the smelter at Tadenac. There was a lot more work there that was part of the fertilizer plant job. We worked on a job at the Wedge Roaster plant and at the new acid plant there.

In the acid plant, in each building, there were three heat exchangers. These heat exchangers were built just like a vertical boiler. They stood about 30 feet high and were six feet or more in diameter. Each one contained 1,344 2-inch diameter tubes that had to be rolled at both top and bottom. There were three of these to each plant for a total of nine heat exchangers. The job of rolling tubes is done with a set of tube rolls or tube expander. This is a tool that fits inside the tube. It is smaller in diameter on one end and it contains three rollers. Inside this you place a mandrel, which has a morse taper. You power this tool with an air motor run by compressed air. As the mandrel turns to the right, or clockwise, the rollers turn to the left. The set of rolls or expander are forced into the tube and the tube is expanded against the boiler plate which is known as the sheet. At one time, this job was done by turning the rolls by hand – a very slow tedious job. I ran into this kind of tube rolling some years later while we were on a job in Port Alice on Vancouver Island.

In Port Alice, we installed a boiler at the Rayonier Pulp Plant and worked for the C.C. Moore Company of San Francisco. On this job we installed a second-hand boiler that came from the Granby Mining and Smelting Company in Anyox, on the north west coast of B.C. This was a B&W boiler – named after Babcox and Wilcox. It was an odd type of boiler that consisted of two steam drums and a system of tube headers that hung with the tubes horizontally under the steam drums and were connected to the steam drums with 4½-inch nipples. It so happened that these were an odd size and had never had power tools made for them, so these had to be done by hand. This was a new experience for me, but everything worked out OK.

I should mention here how I came to have so much experience at the tube work on boilers. When I was working for Cominco in Trail, at the time they were placing the heat exchangers in the acid plants, I was able to get in on this kind of work. The heat exchangers for the acid plants were designed and fabricated by the Thomas Piggot Company from Newcastle on Tyne, England. There was a boilermaker working for Cominco in Trail who was sent out to the acid plant to roll the tubes in these heat exchangers. The heat exchangers were erected in place and they were in the process of installing the tubes. This boilermaker's name was Fred Clary. He started rolling tubes and he told Hughie Palmer, the boiler shop superintendent, that we could not roll these tubes properly into the boiler sheet. Palmer took Clary's word and the company wired the Thomas Piggot Company to cancel the rest of the order as the tubes could not be rolled properly. The Thomas Piggot Company wired back and said they would send a couple of their men to do the job.

We continued to place the tubes in the heat exchangers to be ready for rolling. In a couple of weeks the men arrived from the Piggot Company. They came out to the job with Hughie Palmer and looked it all over. They told Hughie everything would be OK, and that all they needed would be a good helper. I was on the crew that was placing the tubes, so Hughie called me over and I met the English boilermakers. Hughie laughed and said to them that here is the best damned helper you can get. He then turned to me and said: "Joe, you stay with these men until the job is finished and make sure they have everything they need." I replied that I would stick with them. We started the job the next day.

Cominco always started work at 7 AM. But, these fellows didn't get on the job until after 8 AM. I waited for them. They went to work once they got there, and of course I was with them every minute. They had brought their own tools with them. Helping them was an easy job. These tubes were a heavy gauge tube known as heavy wall. The secret of making them tight against the sheet was to roll them and then reset the rolls and then roll them again. These men would go down town for their lunch and also have a beer. I would stay at the job and wait for them after eating my lunch. Cominco crews quit at 3:30 PM but these fellows worked through to 5 or even 6 PM. I would stay with them and my time went on until they quit. So I got in a lot of overtime at time and a half.

Well, I was their helper all the way through the job and learned a lot about the job of rolling tubes. When we gave the heat exchangers the cold-water test, similar to that done for a boiler test, everything was OK. Cominco renewed the order for the other heat exchangers and the boilermakers went back to England. I now had a lot more knowledge about boilers. At a later date when they built the other acid plants Hughie got me to go on the tube-rolling job again. A funny thing about this was that they had apprentice boilermakers who never got the tube rolling experience that I got. In later years I made good use of it.

I worked at this kind of work at the steam power plant in Princeton. This was a combustion-engineering boiler. I also worked on the big Tomlinson type boiler for the pulp and paper plant at Ocean Falls, which at that time became the highest pressure boiler in Western Canada – then another B&W boiler at Fraser Mills in New West Minister, then Port Alice, and several years later another B&W boiler for the B.C. Electric Company at Brentwood Bay on Vancouver Island. In between these boiler jobs I was always working in structural ironwork.

Now back to the Cominco and Trail Smelter. By the time the fertilizer plant at Warfield, and the first acid plant at Tadanac, were finished, the depression was setting in and it could be felt everywhere. It seemed that as every week went by there were more and more men laid off until soon all of the crews that had been erecting structural steel for all of the different plants, were all gone. Somehow I managed to hang onto my job and I was sent to the boiler shop to work. It seemed that I was able to work with any of the boilermakers or shop men and I kept learning more about the trade all the time. The automobile at this time was one item that everyone thought was the ideal thing to have – at least the younger people. A lot of young fellows had bought older model cars and cut them down to look like racing cars and called them bugs. One of the fellows that had been working with us, Bill Wilson, and was now laid off and said he would sell me his bug. I asked him how much and he said I could take it for 40 dollars. I said OK, but first I had to get a drivers license.

I went to the provincial police office to get the license. The policeman there was a big fellow who I knew from my school days in Trail. His name was Mr. Johnson. He told me to save my money and not to buy any car since there was a big depression coming. I told him that I had already told the fellow that I would buy the car as soon as I got my drivers license. He said OK, but that I should remember what he told me.

Well, I didn't know much about car mechanics but I soon started to learn. Of course the roads in those days were not like the paved highways that we have today. People didn't travel very far by car back then, but I made good use of the bug. I used the bug on weekends to go home to Tarrys. I even took my mother for a ride.

It was late August when I bought the bug. The work in the boiler shop hung on through the fall and the winter. But the next spring, in April, I was laid off along with a lot of other men. I went to the place where I had been staying, paid my board bill, and went home to Tarrys in my bug.

At this time, there wasn't any work of any kind going on anywhere in the country. I stayed around home for a while and then one day when I was in Trail, I met Hank Unger. He wasn't working either, so he suggested we take a trip to the prairies and work in the grain harvest. I said that might be OK. He had a sister living in Saskatchewan on a grain farm. If we went there we would be able to get a job on their farm.

We made arrangements to go and another young fellow from Trail wanted to come with us. His name was Alfonso Vendremie – a nice young person. We arranged to meet in Nelson where we could all catch a ride on a freight train together. So we met in Nelson and caught our ride. The weather was real nice and we all had seats on the observation cars (box cars). The price was right for our pocket books. That evening we stopped in Yahk where we jungled up (camped), as it was called. For us it was a holiday. The next stop was Cranbrook, where we camped again, then on to Fernie where we stopped over for a day, then on to Crow's nest. This was the division point on the railway where the railway crews changed and the engines were serviced.

From here we travelled out onto the prairie. This was something new for me as it was the first time that I had seen the prairie. It was so much different than the mountains. It was hard to believe that there was so much flat land. Although, before we got to the town of Lethbridge, we crossed over one of the highest and longest bridges in Canada. We stopped in Lethbridge for the day, then on to Medicine Hat, then Swift Current, then Moose Jaw.

Seven miles east of Moose Jaw the SOO Line branches off to the southeast for Wayburn and the North Portal. This was the route we took. At Wayburn we had to wait around for a day to catch a ride on the branch line freight to Talmadge where we went to the Jones farmland to meet Hank's sister and her husband.

When we got to Talmadge, we found out that the Jones farm was three miles east of town so we hiked out there. We arrived in the late afternoon and they were sure a surprised couple. After we met them, Dave Jones asked us what we were doing out there on the prairie. We told them that we wanted to work in the harvest. He laughed and said that there wasn't any harvest. But he said he had about 30 acres of hay to harvest and if we wanted to give him a hand he would appreciate the help. He couldn't pay any wages, but he would give us room and board. We said OK and he said we could start the next day.

We all had a good supper and they had lots of room for us to sleep upstairs. The next morning after breakfast we all went out to the barn. Dave was still using horses. Although he still had a tractor, he said he couldn't afford the fuel to run it. Dave had a nice big horse barn. He didn't have any cattle. He had eight big draft horses in the barn with all the harness for each horse hanging on a post beside each horse. Dave said that he had to go back to the house to see his wife because he had to take her to town. When Dave went back to the house I started to harness the horses. When he got back to the barn I had four horses all harnessed and standing outside the barn. Dave could hardly believe it. He asked Hank who did all of this. Hank said "Joe is the horseman, we don't know anything about horses." Dave was real happy to know that one of us knew horses.

Dave had the mowing machines ready to go. We hitched a team to each mower and went to the hayfield with Dave driving one team, and I driving the other. We started to mow and after a couple of hours we stopped to give the horses a rest. Dave said that was the first time he had met anyone from B.C. that knew anything about horses. I told him that they use hundreds of horses in B.C., but that a lot of it was for logging. Then he said he was sure glad that we had come out there.

The mowers were each equipped with 6-foot blades. By changing teams after lunch we were cutting about nine or ten acres each day. When the cutting was finished we raked it all into windrows. Then, with a big timber sweep, we brought it all to a stack. Hank and Alfonso worked on building up the stacks. Because the prairie harvest was so poor that year, when the hay was finished, we decided that we would go back to B.C. as there wasn't too much hope of finding work there.

We said goodbye to Dave and his wife, and then worked our way back to B.C. When I arrived home, I found everything pretty much the same. My brother Ben was home and he found out that if you had wood for sale, you could sell it in Nelson. There was an old man at Tarrys who had a lot of timber on the back of his property. We arranged a price with him, and also with the freight trucks to haul the wood into Nelson on their return trip from Trail. We could get a horse for the care and feed. We had axes, crosscut saws, hammers, and wedges. Now we had jobs and went to work. I didn't realize it at the time, but this work would carry on for the next year and a half. This was the fall of 1932, and it was the only thing I worked at until I received a letter from Cominco in February 1934.

The letter from Cominco said that I had a job again in Trail if I wanted it. I went to Trail to find out when to start, then went home to pack my bags and go back to Trail to work. First thing I had to do was find a place to stay. I went to see the Wilsons, who were friends of the family when my folks had lived in Trail. They were glad to see me and I moved in. This would be my home for more than 2 years.

Lead furnace flues for
Cominco plant extension project, Trail
1934
(Author is on far right hanging from wire)

Trail, Boiler shop, 1934-36

IT WAS LATE FEBRUARY 1934. When I went to Trail I had to find a place to stay so I went to see the Wilsons. We knew the Wilsons, Omar and Edith, from when we had lived in Trail. They were glad to see me and said they would like to have me stay with them. This was good for me as there would not be any transportation needed to go to work. I had only to walk a block then climb the smelter steps.

By this time they had a little boy, Kenneth, who now thought he had a big brother in the house. Both Mr. and Mrs. Wilson were wonderful skaters, and Mrs. Wilson was a very good pianist. In the silent movie days she played in the theatre.

I worked at various jobs in the boiler shop as a helper to different boilermakers. The work took us to almost every building in the smelter. Later on, there were some more buildings to erect such as the acid plants. It was at this time that the lead furnaces would be rebuilt and a lot of other work that was associated with them – actually a lot of dirty work. Also, there was an extension to the zinc leaching plant, and extension to the general office, and more buildings in connection with the fertilizer plant at Warfield.

At this time, one of the main sports in the town of Trail was baseball. This was the sport that I enjoyed most. There were several senior teams in Trail, so I joined up with one of them: The Saskatchewan Life Team.

We played against the other Trail teams, and also against teams of the surrounding area such as Salmo, Rossland, Ymir, and Castlegar. It was all good sport.

At work, I was getting experience at every branch of the trade and getting to be a key man on the crew. I could connect the steel, work in any part of the rivet gang including the rivet heating, splice cable, and reeve blocks. At that time, I could also read the blue prints for a multi-story building without any problem. I was thinking that I could go anywhere and hopefully get a job as an ironworker. I also knew how to roll boiler tubes.

I think at this point, I should explain a little about the work that was done by a rivet gang. First of all, the gang needed a scaffold in order to work. Most of the time it had to be hanging scaffold. The hanging beams that supported the scaffold were known as needle beams. These were made from clear 4"×6" coastal Douglas fir timber. The scaffold planks also had to be clear edge-grain material. This type of scaffold was hung with 1-inch Manila rope. The ironworkers using the scaffold had to know how to tie proper knots in the ropes such as the scaffold hitch, the bowline, the square knot, the stopper or rolling hitch.

When the scaffold was hung ready for work, the point or connection was measured and counted by the rivet heater (the person who heated the rivets prior to driving them in). There were usually several different lengths of rivets. The heater had to be able to deliver all of the different rivets when they were called for by the men on the scaffold, and keep track of the count. It was little wonder that a lot of the men never learned the art of heating rivets.

The riveting was done with an air powered hammer known as a rivet gun. This was a precision tool, made to very fine specifications, and also a heavy one at about 40 pounds. The end of the gun carried a die known as a snap. These snaps come in various shapes and sizes to form different types of rivet heads. The inside of the gun had a smooth bore and carried a plunger that travelled back and forth in the bore at a very high speed. The bore of the gun was generally $1^{1}/_{16}{}^{th}$"× 9". This was known as a ninety gun, and was preferred by most men for driving rivets. The plunger in this size of a rivet gun was $1^{1}/_{16}{}^{th}$"× 3".

Now, the tools for holding the rivet while it was being driven, these were called the bucking-up tools, and were held in place by one of the men who was known as the bucker-up. The rivet had to be held tight in

the rivet hole while it was being driven. A loose rivet would be rejected by the inspector.

There is a long list of tools for this part of the job. On open work, the common tool was the dolly bar, which was a piece of shafting with a curve in it to fit the work place, with a rivet die forged into the end of the tool. There were a lot more tools to fit various places on the iron connections. Some of these tools have some strange names, such as the banjo, a shackle dolly and a no.9. There were times when special tools had to be made for a specific job. On bridge work, the air jam was used a lot of the time because the work was in the bridge chords which are double sections. The air jam was built similar to a hydraulic jack but ran with air power and was much more versatile. It held a rivet die in the front end and had what was known as a spud to hold the back end against the iron – a very efficient tool.

Nowadays, most of this type of work is history. That's because the high tensile bolt has taken over the place of the rivet. Some people still debate the issue though. The labour costs are a lot less with bolts, but the bolt costs a lot more than a rivet, and doesn't fill the rivet hole like a hot driven rivet. But, you can't stop progress.

Erection of structural steel is still done in more or less the same manner, bolted and pinned the same way, with enough bolts and pins to stabilize the structure. When the holes are punched or drilled in the iron in the bridge shops they are nominally $1/16$" larger than the bolt or rivet that they will receive. But, the drift pins are made, the full size of the hole. Therefore, when the pins are driven they bring the iron into proper alignment. Also, the drift pins are tapered on each end so that they can be driven either way. When the points or connections are fitted up either with bolts or rivets, all of the loose bolts, pins, or any loose material has to be placed in pails or buckets for safety.

Besides the names that the rivet tools have, there are a lot of queer names for the tools used in the erection of structural steel, such as spud wrench, comealong, molly Hogan, beater, cat's paw, oldman, push, drag, and a dozen more.

One evening while I was still staying at the Wilson's, there was a knock on the front door and I answered it. Here was a fellow from Castlegar, who I had known for a long time, by the name of Jack Killough. You could tell that he was distressed. He asked if I could do him a favour? I said "sure". He told me that his wife Lilly was in the Trail hospital and that she needed a blood transfusion as soon as possible. So far they had not been able to find any one that could match her blood. He wanted me to go to the clinic to see if my blood would match. I said I would and went there immediately. They did the test and Doctor Daly phoned me a little later to tell me that my blood was the proper match, and if I could go to the hospital right away where they would take my blood for the transfusion. As it happened, I only lived one block from the hospital. They took the blood and then gave me a shot of brandy. When I came back to the house, Mrs. Wilson gave me an eggnog before I went to bed. The next morning I felt fine. A week later Lilly was out of the hospital and returned home. I never heard of any more problems with her.

I heard a story about this several years later. I never saw Lilly again, but the story was that the next children she and Jack had were born with red hair, but I never saw either one of them again. I suppose that it is possible.

It was shortly after this that I quit Cominco and left Trail.

CHAPTER 14

Leaving Trail to go to Vancouver and Kimberley, June 1936

THERE WAS A YOUNG FELLOW by the name of Jack Marcus who quit Cominco about this same time. He had some friends by the name of Rodgers and it happened that they were all going to Vancouver in a car that the older Rodger had. His name was Chic. Anyway, we all decided to go together. I went home to Tarrys first to tell my mother of our plans. This made here rather sad but she realized that young people want to get out and see the world.

They came the next day to pick me up and the four of us travelled together in Chic's car. It was a 1926 Chevy sedan equipped with luggage racks on the running boards. We decided that we would do some touring before going to Vancouver, so we went by way of the Slocan Valley to the north Okanagan, then to Revelstoke, then back to Kamloops, then Cache Creek, and finally the Fraser Canyon to Hope and onto Vancouver.

The Rodger boys both played the guitar and did some singing. I also had my guitar and I did quite a lot of singing too. When we reached Cache Creek we stopped at the tourist camp. The lady who booked us in noticed the guitars and asked us to come to the office in the evening and to please bring our guitars. We went there after supper and very soon a man came in carrying a violin in a Hereford calfskin. The lady from the tourist camp introduced us to him. His name was Ernie Madden, and what a wonderful violin player. We were all very interested in his playing. After talking to him we found out that he had been a violinist in the Seattle Symphony Orchestra.

He was making saddles and horse harness, and doing repairs. Then on the weekends, he would join in with a local band and play for dances throughout the Cariboo ranch country. After we had all played and done some singing, he wanted us to join him. He said he would teach us the art of working with leather. Then on the weekends we could all play and sing at the local dances. I was all for going with him, but Chic owned the car and he wanted to go to Vancouver, so that is what we did. There are times though that I wished we had gone with Ernie Madden.

When we got to Vancouver, we all got rooms and got settled. One of the first things that I did was to go to the ironworkers hall to find out about work. That was a big disappointment. Work was very scarce and a lot of ironworkers were looking for jobs. However, there was work of a kind in the evenings if you cared for it. This was singing and entertaining in the night spots (actually bootleg joints). But you could make a few dollars a night if you wanted to do this. Chic thought that it was O.K., but I didn't care for it.

I kept in touch with the union hall, but had no luck there. I had a notion about going to Kimberley, so one evening Jack Marcus and I took a ride on the east-bound freight. We went as far as Golden and then started to hitch hike to Cranbrook. A short ways out of Golden a fellow picked us up and gave us a ride. He asked us if we were looking for work. We said "yes"!! He said to come with him because he had work for us. He drove us to his place, which was near a little place called Parson, which was a flag stop on the Kootenay Central Railway. He said his name was Jake and he and his brother were living together. They were in the process of building a new log house, and needed some help.

When we arrived at his place, his brother was in the process of making a stew for supper. They invited us to have supper, which we did. Jake noticed the guitar and asked if we would come with him to his neighbour's place and give them a little entertainment. Well, this was something to see. It was real hillbilly for sure. The woman was getting the kids ready for bed. She was slicing a loaf of homemade bread and smearing the slices with jam for each kid before they went to bed. There were six or seven kids and each one waiting in line for his or her slice like a set of stairs – and all bashful. I don't think these kids saw many strangers. The little ones were peeking out from behind their mother's skirt. However, after I sang a few songs, the kids were all smiling and seemed to be happy. Jack also played the mouth organ for them. They made you think of shy little animals. But I think they all enjoyed the music.

We said goodnight to them and went back to Jake's place where Jack and I slept on a bunk in a small bedroom. The next morning Jake made some breakfast and then asked if we could skid some logs out of the woods for their new house. He showed me where all the rigging was for the horse and I got the horse ready for work. Jake was rather surprised that I knew how to handle a horse. I took the horse to the woods behind the house where they had a number of logs cut ready for skidding. The horse handled easily and was familiar with the work. I skidded logs all morning. Jack was decking them into a pile and was pleased with the work. After lunch we asked Jake when the train ran. He said that there would be one that day. I told him I would skid some more logs and then we would head for the station. He said O.K., thanked us for the work, and said he would drive us to the station when it was time. We thanked him and worked a while longer with the horse. Afterwards, we put the horse in the barn, washed up, and Jake drove us to the station.

This was a mixed train service of only a couple times a week. A bunch of fellows came over from the sawmill to see the train come in – one of the busy days for the little town of Parson. When these fellows came from the mill, they noticed my guitar and asked if I would play for them. I took the guitar and started playing and singing. Jake took off his hat and went around the crowd. He told them "look, these guys need a treat too". He came back with several dollars in change and gave it to me. I played a song or two and then the train came in.

When the train came in, the CPR welding track crew was on the train. They were in the process of moving to the Crows Nest area for another job. I had known this gang when they worked in the Thrums and Castlegar area. When they saw me, they called out: "Hey Red, what the hell are you doing here?" I told them that we wanted a ride to Cranbrook. "Well climb aboard and have a beer", they said. We said goodbye to Jake and thanked the mill crew, then climbed onto the train and joined the crew. They gave us beer and the train started out of the station.

This crew was actually having a travelling party between jobs. We were welcomed by the rest of the crew and we all had another beer. It wasn't long before the train stopped and the cook rang the supper bell. The fellows invited us for supper. We went with them to the cook car and had a good meal. Then it was back to the bunk car where we all had some more beer, and I played the guitar and the crew all joined in for a musical evening. Jack also joined in with the mouth organ. When it was time to sleep the fellows on the crew showed us some empty bunks, which we made good use of. At Windermere the train stopped for the night. The train crew had sleeping quarters here and this was a regular stopover for them. The next morning we had breakfast in the cook car with the crew. Some of them had a swim in Windermere Lake.

Then the train went on to Canal Flats where some cars were switched into the sawmill siding and some others were picked up to go into the train. Then we went to Bull River where the train stopped again. While we were stopped there, most everyone had a swim in the river – very refreshing. A little further south at the Coal Valley junction, all of the camp cars and the track welding crew were left there to be picked up by an east-bound train. Jack and I said good-bye to the gang and we went onto Cranbrook with the train.

We stayed overnight in Cranbrook to catch the train for Kimberley the next day. The next morning we were having breakfast in a café that was across the street from the railway. A rancher and a cowboy came in. They noticed the guitar and it was easy to see that they had been drinking. They wanted me to give them a western song. I said I would as soon as I finished eating. The rancher took some money from his pocket and said it was something to pay for my meal. I played a couple of western songs and he was quite happy. I told him we had to catch our train to Kimberley. They said good-bye and wished us luck. We left and went to the railway yard where we caught the train to Kimberley.

The railway line to Kimberley from Cranbrook has some heavy grades. While we were on this train, an incident took place that I have never seen again. Where the railway grade crosses the St. Mary's River, there is a downgrade on the Cranbrook side and then a heavy upgrade on the Kimberley side, then a passing track at the top of the grade. When the train was on the level on the bridge crossing, the trainmen broke the train into two sections. This was to lighten the load for the hill on the north side. The train was being pulled by two big 3600 2-8-0- engines.

Now, the train headed on up the hill, but before it reached the top of the hill, it ran out of power. They backed the train down to the bridge again and then unhooked from the train. Now the two engines proceeded on up the hill to the siding at the top of the hill where they switched the front engine to the rear. After that they hooked onto the train again, and this time they pulled the train up the hill without any trouble. They also took the other half up the hill without any further trouble. After the engines were hooked on again, we proceeded to Kimberley.

In Kimberley, we made enquires to locate my brother Ben and were directed further up the street. We didn't only find my brother Ben, but also my brother John. They were just in the act of hanging up a sign: "IRVING BROTHERS CONTRACTORS & BUILDERS". I didn't even know that John was in Kimberley. They were also surprised to see us. After the greetings and handshakes, Ben asked if we were looking for work. We told him we were. He then said that they were starting a job the next day to build a house and we could start tomorrow. There was also a room in the back of the shop that we could have and that we could have our meals at his place. That sounded good to us.

By this time it was late afternoon. We walked over to Ben's place where we met his wife Edna. Ben had met Edna in Nelson where she had been nursing at the Kootenay Lake Hospital. They had gotten married while I was away and that was why I didn't know about it. After a nice supper we walked around the town to look it all over and then went to our rooms. The next morning we had a good breakfast and then Ben took us to the job site. The first thing to do was excavate a basement. Ben had arranged to rent a team of horses and a slip scraper without a teamster. That would be my job because Ben knew that I could handle horses and that Jack could handle the scraper.

CHAPTER 15

Kimberley, Summer 1936

WE STARTED ON THE JOB of excavating. It was a tough job as all the ground in Kimberley was. It was all heavy gravel and boulders but the team worked O.K. and Jack soon got the knack of holding the scraper. At this time there was not any equipment such as backhoes anywhere in the country.

We made fairly good time with the job and John and Ben were busy getting the basement forms all cut. We had to do some work by hand in the corners, but most of the muck came out with the scraper. When this was done we helped with the forms and when the forms were ready, they placed all of the floor joists and sub-floor which became the deck for the pouring of the basement walls. Then we helped with the pouring of the concrete. We had a concrete mixer that they rented and we mixed all of the concrete and poured it all using wheelbarrows.

By this time, summer was coming to an end and we thought maybe that things would have improved in Vancouver. So, Jack and I decided to return to Vancouver. We again rode the freights as this was the cheapest way to travel. This was now September, but when we arrived in Vancouver we were again disappointed to find out that things were much the same as when we had left.

We looked for work in a lot of places but did not have any luck. Once in a while I would try the night spots again but this was not satisfactory.

The rainy season was now here so the theatre was a cheap place to spend your time. So, I saw quite a few shows during this time. By the time winter was coming on, I was getting low on money so I went back to Tarrys. But this time I bought a ticket and rode home on the cushions.

As it turned out, I was not long at home when I had job offer with a survey crew that was doing a job on the highway. I liked the work and I got along real well with the crew and the engineer who was in charge of the work. The work lasted through the winter and shortly after Easter I returned to Vancouver. This was when I found out about the boiler job at the Grandby Consolidated Mining Company in Princeton.

I found out where their Vancouver office was, so one morning I went there. I had put on a clean shirt and was wearing a suit so that I was presentable. The Granby office was on the 18th floor of the Royal Bank building. I went up the elevator and went into the office. A receptionist asked me what I would like? I told her that I was looking for a job on the Princeton project. She said that all the labour would be hired in Princeton. I told her I wasn't looking for a labour job, but that I was a boilermaker. She told me to wait a minute and she went into the back office. She returned in a very short time and asked me to come in to the other office.

I did this where I found a man sitting at a desk. He asked me what kind of boiler work I could do. I told him I could do almost anything connected to a boiler, but especially the tube work. He then asked me if I could leave for Princeton that day. I said I could. He then told me to come back at 2 PM to pick up my train ticket. Then he asked me if I knew of another boilermaker that could go, but I had to say no.

After going back to the Granby office and then packing my bags, I went to the CPR station at train time. There I met a fellow who I had worked with in Trail. This man was Chuck Burns. I asked where he was going and he said Princeton. So, that meant we would be working together, which would be good. We boarded the train and arrived in Princeton at 4 AM. We each got a room at the Tullameen Hotel and had a sleep. Later that day we walked out to the power plant. We were signed up at the office and looked the job over and walked back to the hotel.

The next morning we went to work. The job was a combustion-engineering boiler. The drums were already in place. The man who would supervise the job was Bill Deadman. He showed us where the tools were and the sequence for the tube installation. Then, we went to work. The first job was to place the tubes, then to roll them. Later, there would be the headers for the furnace walls and then to install the tubes for them.

About a week later two more boilermakers arrived on the job. We didn't know them. They worked for the Vancouver Iron Works and were on loan to Granby for this job. Their name was Laidlaw and one of them was quite old. At this time we were ready to start tube rolling, so we suggested that they could roll the tubes in the steam drum and we would take the mud drum. That way it would be easier and not so crowded up there. They thought this was a good idea so that was the way we worked the job.

All went well and the job was progressing very well until a few weeks later when Jimmy fell from a scaffold and injured his back and had to return to Vancouver. That left Chuck and myself to finish the job. When the tube part of the job was done, Chuck decided that he would also go back to Vancouver. There was still a lot of other work to be done in connection with the boiler, so I stayed on to finish it. Also, I met a girl who lived in Princeton, and we decided to get married. How foolish can young people be? My work held out until some time in September. Then I left my wife with her folks and I went to Vancouver to see about work. I met Chuck shortly after arriving there. He was working for the C.C. Moore Company on a job at the Fraser Mills in New Westminster to erect a B&W boiler job. He wanted me to work with him so I said O.K. and asked him when we would start. He said he would pick me up the next morning. I would be ready.

This job was inside an old building so we had to erect the drums with a gin pole, then place the tubes and roll them. While we were on this job, the C.C. Moore Company got another job to erect a second-hand boiler at Port Alice on Quatsino Sound on Vancouver Island. We would do that job as soon as the Fraser Mills job was finished.

We finished Fraser Mills in the first part of November and left for Port Alice. We travelled on the union steam ship "Cardena". We landed at Port Hardy where we had to take a small bus to Coal Harbour to catch the boat called the Granby. It was late at night when we arrived at Port Alice. The place where we would stay was the Jones Hotel.

The job there was to erect a second hand boiler that came from Anyox, an old copper mining town on the northwest coast of B.C. This was an old type of B&W boiler. These were an odd type of boiler – a turn of the century model. There were two steam drums and a system of large headers that hung below the steam drums and connected with large nipples of 4½" diameter. These nipples had to be rolled into place with hand tools, as they had never made power tools for this type of boiler.

The C.C. Moore Company, being an old boiler erecting company, had the hand tools. At Port Alice it rained almost every day so we were glad that our work was inside. We had a good crew and all of the work progressed at a good pace. Jack Murray and I did all of the tube rolling. When the water test was done and everything was O.K., it made us feel good about our work. We wanted to finish the job before Christmas so we were working a lot of overtime. The pulp mill company also wanted the job done as soon as possible. We managed to finish the work by the 17th of December and then headed back to Vancouver.

The trip back was the reverse of the trip to Port Alice except the ship this time was the S.S. Catala. After arriving in Vancouver I did some Christmas shopping. I bought some real nice clothes to take home to my wife before catching the train. I told my wife when I would arrive in Princeton, so she was at the station to meet me when the train pulled in at 4 AM. We took a room in the Princeton Hotel and went to see to her folks the next day. We didn't need a lot of room so we rented a cabin that would do us for a few weeks, since I didn't plan to stay long in Princeton. I stayed in touch with the news of work in Vancouver and about the middle of that month we left for Vancouver.

We got a housekeeping room in the west end and I kept in touch with the Union Hall. The Lions Gate Bridge was starting but it would be some time before the crew would be enlarged. However, there was a smaller job starting at Wood Fibre at the pulp mill. So, that is where I went first.

This job was being done by old Ed Bickerton. This was the first time that I met him. On the boat going to Wood Fibre he asked me if I was an apprentice or a journeyman? I said I was a journeyman. He said that I looked too young, to which I replied that I had a lot of experience. He shook his head in disbelief, but when we went to work he soon saw that I could handle any of the work.

A short time later I got a call to leave Wood Fibre and come out to Ocean Falls where the big Tomlinson boiler was going to be installed. I came out on the weekend and then we left for Ocean Falls. This was to be another C.C. Moore Company job and Chuck Burns would be the foreman again. This was already a big boiler job. It would be the highest pressure boiler in western Canada. It was all fabricated by the

B&W Company. The steam drum was three inches thick where the tubes entered the drum. The steam drum weighed 18 tons. When erected, it would be 70 feet above the floor.

The operating pressure was rated at 600 pounds per square inch. After all assembly and erection, the boiler was tested to over 900 pounds test. Boiler testing is done with cold water and a pump. The steam drum was supported on false work until after the boiler tubes were placed and rolled. There was also a super heater installed with this boiler. After the tubes had been placed and rolled, the false work was removed. Then on the side of the boiler a huge furnace was built. This was also built from tubes. These tubes were also water tubes that made up the walls, floors, and roof of the furnace. These furnace tubes weighed up to 1800 pounds each. These furnace tubes all carried a system of studs that held the compound for the walls. To place the boiler drums we used a steam donkey engine. For the furnace tubes we used an air tugger for hoisting.

The work at Ocean Falls lasted until June. When we came out, we all went to work on the Lions Gate Bridge which carried through to the early fall. At this time I took a trip home to Tarrys with my wife.

CHAPTER 16

Bonnington 1938 – 1939

I WAS ONLY HOME AT Tarrys for a few days when I got word of a job that was starting in Bonnington on the Kootenay River. The No.2 power plant was going to have a major extension. I went there to find out about the project and was hired immediately. The first part of the job was to erect a small railway bridge over the tail race of the existing power house. This was a second-hand C.P.R. Bridge from the Kicking Horse Canyon – a 160-ft truss.

This bridge would give rail access to the generator floor in the new powerhouse when it was complete. There had been a small beam span placed over the tail race, with a double purpose, before erecting the railway bridge. This would be used for false work for the railway bridge, and later be used for a narrow gauge rail bridge for the removal of the excavated rock from the powerhouse.

To erect the bridge, we placed rails on the beam span. As the bridge steel was placed, a double-flanged wheel was placed at every second panel point. As the erection proceeded, the span was pulled ahead so that the crane could erect all of the bridge steel from one position. After erection, the bridge span was moved sideways to its permanent position. This was done with hand winches, and by placing timbers and rollers under the ends of the span.

On the beam span a double narrow-gauge track system was placed so that the Dinky locomotive and rock cars would have a place to pass. It had spring switches at each end. The main track was for the loaded train. The empty train used the passing track to wait while the other train was being loaded.

I had taken a job as an operator on one of the Dinky locomotives. After drilling and blasting the rack at the powerhouse, the excavated rock was loaded onto the rock cars with a power shovel, then hauled away with the Dinky locomotive to the rock dump where a man with a jill-poke timber dumped the cars. This was done by holding a piece of timber at the corner of the rock car while the locomotive operator slowly moved the train ahead. This performance only took a matter of a few seconds for each car. Each train load consisted of four car loads.

We had been on the job for a few weeks. We were on the night shift and everything was going very well. My train was being loaded. After the train was loaded, I looked to see if the other train was on the bridge. It was. I started across the bridge, opened up the throttle and looked again. The other train had not moved. I knocked the throttle down and pulled on the big hand brake. My locomotive missed the other one but the corner of the first rock car caught the other locomotive and de-railed it just as I came to a stop. I looked for the other operator but he was not there. He had gone to the toilet and left his locomotive foul of the main line – a very serious offence in any kind of railway work.

We got the other locomotive jacked up and back on the rails and not much time was lost. We still hauled 110 loads that shift. But, the next day, I found out that I was fired. The other guy who had walked away and left his machine, kept his job. Such is justice.

It was only a few days later that a government engineer came to my place to tell me that I was wanted by the V.H. Macintire Company to work on a Department of Transport tower. This was to be a radio beam tower for the newly inaugurated Trans-Canada Air Service. I took this job. It was a timber tower 40 feet square at the base and 150 feet high. We did this job using hand winches and a basket pole. When the tower was finished they wanted me to do a lot of rigging work on a set of poles that were to be used in conjunction with the tower. I did a lot of this work for them, and finished about Christmas time. The Department of Transport wanted me to go east with them to another job of a similar kind, but I had to say no to the engineer because my wife was pregnant.

However, the first thing I knew, there was another job for me again in

Bonnington. They were ready to start work on the powerhouse and very soon they were hiring more ironworkers. Several men on the crew that I had been working with at Ocean Falls came to work on this job: Chuck Burns, Jack Murray, Archie Downy, Johnny Wallach, and several more. There was a lot of interesting ironwork to be done: the scroll casings, the control gates, the super structure above the gates, the powerhouse steel, etc.

We worked at all of this through the summer of 1939. Shortly afterwards, the union called us back to Vancouver because we could not make any headway with West Kootenay Power to come around to the union way. It was also at this time that war was declared in Europe. We all went back to Vancouver, but there was no work going on yet. My son, Joe Jr. was now six months old, so my wife and Joe Jr. and I got a house-keeping room and settled down to wait for work to develop.

Well, it turned out to be quite a long wait. It was not until March of 1940 that I received a call to work on the Nanaimo arena structure. This was for old Ed Bickerton. This job only lasted a few weeks, but Ed acquired more work shortly thereafter. The next job was the marine store building at Jericho Beach. That didn't last long either, so we were out of work again. Then there was a call from the C.P.R. for men to paint railway bridges, so several of us took this job and it lasted until the end of June. At this time, old Ed had a small bridge job to erect at Duncan on Vancouver Island. When this was finished there was a job on James Island to erect some tanks. After that there was a hammerhead crane to be constructed at Patricia Bay. So, I was busy most of the summer.

When we went to Patricia Bay for the crane job, I took my wife and young Joe with me to live in Victoria. There were two of these cranes to build – one at Patricia Bay and another at Prince Rupert. These were for the Department of National Defence.

These cranes were designed and fabricated by the Star Crane Company of Tacoma, Washington. The cranes were to be mounted on a 30-ft tower with rail trucks at the bottom in each corner, with the rails embedded in concrete. The crane cab and the superstructure would be another 20 feet above the tower. At the top of the tower there was a large centre bearing and a rail roller path on which the crane would revolve. The boom would project out 120 feet, and the counter weight would be suspended at the rear.

While constructing the boom, we had another problem. There were a number of blind holes and old Ed did not have an oxy-acetylene cutting torch. Northern Construction Company had a dredge working in the bay, so he arranged to borrow a cutting outfit from them. Hughie Bickerton, one of Ed's sons, went with me to the barge in a rowboat to get the outfit. We placed the outfit with the bottles in a concrete buggy and then with me in the buggy also, the crane hoisted me up so that I could cut all of the holes.

We got all of this done and Hughie and I took the outfit back to the barge. We handed the torch and gauges to the deck hand and then the oxygen bottle, which he took, then the heavy acetylene bottle. All this time the boat was rocking. We picked up the acetylene bottle and started to hand it to the deck hand. The end of the bottle was on the deck, but the boat was rocking. The deck hand stood there with his mouth open and the boat was moving away from the barge. I knew we were going to lose the bottle. I was on the low side. As the bottle fell on me, I grabbed it with both arms and went in the water with the bottle, then let go of it. When I came up it was only a few strokes and I had hold of the boat and climbed back in.

Hughie and I returned to the job at the crane. I thought that old Ed might offer to drive me somewhere so I could get dried up, but all I got from him was "there's a 35 dollar deposit on those bottles". The cheap old bastard. Well, a little while later they turned the barge and with the clamshell bucket they recovered the acetylene bottle. So, after all, Ed did not have to pay for it.

While constructing the counter weight a question came up. The specifications on the crane drawings called for 25 cubic yards of concrete. Old Ed questioned this figure. Was it 25 cubic yards, or 25 tons. He was told "you have your drawings". The structure was built accordingly. We finished the iron work on the crane and the job was turned over to the Department of Transportation. I returned to Vancouver with my wife and young Joe.

Old Ed had another job starting in Vancouver but it would be done at different times to coincide with the rest of the construction on the project. This was the Vogue Theatre on Granville Street. The first part of this was the steel at the front where the ticket office and the front entrance would be. This was a very small job and we finished it on a Friday.

That evening I received a phone call from old Ed. "My God" he said, "there's hell to pay". I asked him what the trouble was. He told me that the crane at Patricia Bay was lying in the water upside down, and that Sid Hogson, the machinist who was operating the crane, was dead. When the initial trial was being made, the crane was turned so that the counter weight was over the water. But, being too heavy, it fell into the water and in the process it turned the whole structure upside down and Sid was killed. He said that we would all have to return to Patricia Bay and salvage the crane and use the one that was fabricated for Prince Rupert.

I reminded him that he had questioned them about the counter weight. He said yes, but that now poor Sid was dead. He asked me if I could be back in Victoria for Monday morning. I said yes but that I would have to stay at a hotel. He said we had rooms reserved at the Westholme Hotel.

To salvage the crane we used a big floating barge and derrick from the Northern Construction Company. This rig had a one-piece coast-fir boom five feet in diameter and was 120 feet long. It was capable of handling 40 tons at a 50-foot radius. We went to work on the crane with cutting torches and lifted the pieces out with the floating crane. The tower had remained in place and it was all O.K. When the salvage was finished, we erected the one that had been made for Prince Rupert – this time with a much smaller counter weight. To my knowledge there was never any more problems with the crane.

When all this work was completed, we all returned to Vancouver. Old Ed had several more jobs ahead for us.

CHAPTER 17

Boeing plant, 1940

BACK IN VANCOUVER, OLD ED had picked up several jobs: Vogue Theatre Steel, Rodgers Sugar refinery storage building, and the erection of the timber trusses for the Boeing plant at the Sea Island airport. The ironwork (timber trusses, etc.) for these jobs would all be erected with derricks using steam power. The sugar refinery job was a storage building. It consisted of high columns of about 70 feet – roof beams, purlins braces, etc. Then this was riveted together. The Vogue theatre was a different structure. There was the small steel framework at the street level mentioned before. Then there was the large girder that would support the balcony along with two wing girders from the balcony girders at an angle connecting it to the concrete wall. Then came the sound effect steel above the stage and then the roof structure. These balcony girders were set in place with the boom of a guy derrick used as a gin pole. When they were in place, we placed this gin pole "guy derrick boom" on a foot block at the centre of the balcony girder on the floor of the building. Then we brought in the big derrick mast from the rear of the building. With the rigging on the boom, which was the gin pole, we hoisted the mast to its foot block on top of the balcony girder. This spot was the approximate centre of the building. All of the guys were put in place and then the boom, which had been the gin pole, was now hoisted to its position at the bottom of the mast. Now we had the guy derrick ready to work. From this position, all of the roof structure could be placed.

A guy derrick could work a full 360° circle. The mast was at least 10 feet longer or higher than the boom, so when the boom was raised to its full height, the mast and boom could be revolved to any position in the circle. Sometimes this was done with power; sometimes done with the aid of a bull stick. The base of the guy derrick being anchored down with the kicker cables and sitting on the greased bearing and the top revolving in a fitting known as the spider, one or two men could turn the boom and mast fairly easily.

Here is a little story about a bull stick. In another part of this story, I spoke about Hi Carpenter, an ironworker superintendent. This incident happened on the New Vancouver Hotel. There was an ironworker by the name of Red Jack MacDonald working on this project. The foreman was called a pusher. Old Hi always had a sense of humour and he enjoyed pulling a verbal joke on any of the men. He only had a rough whisper of a voice, but it never held him back. One morning as the men were getting ready to go up on the building to work, he came along and spoke to Red Jack. He said, "Red, I have a pusher job for you." Red Jack says, "Oh no, I don't want any pusher's job. I can't handle that." Hi says, "Oh yes you can handle this one. You go on up to Number 4 derrick on the sixth floor and you will be the pusher on the bull stick." A big laugh went all around the crew.

I should mention here how a guy derrick works on a multi-story building or what is also known as a skyscraper. On these kinds of jobs, the hoist engine stayed down on ground level with the drums holding a full capacity of cable. When the ironwork was erected to the height of what can be reached from ground level, we had to raise the derrick up a number of floors to be able to erect more steel. The guy derrick was a device that can pull itself up by its own bootstraps. When it came time to go up higher on the structure, it was done by what is known as "jumping the derrick". The boom was raised to maximum height by the boom falls on the mast. Then the boom pin was removed and a temporary foot block was fastened to the bottom of the boom. Now this mast assembly could be hoisted several floors higher. The boom would then land in position on its foot block and a set of guy lines run out to make a mast out of the boom. When this was done, the load line—which is running through the top of the boom for the load falls—was used to raise the mast. The foot block for the mast went up with the mast to the floor level that the boom was now sitting on. The foot block guys were placed, then the main mast guy lines all run out and anchored, then the boom line tightened up, then the boom pin again placed in position at the bottom of the mast, and then you had a derrick again at a position on the building several stories (usually four floors) higher and ready to erect another four floors of steel. On some of the big buildings, there were usually several derricks used to erect steel.

Just before the end of the year, about December 1940, we went to the job at Sea Island to build the Boeing plant. This was quite a large building and covered about 14 acres of land. The housing for this building was to be a large timber structure built of big timber posts and roof trusses. Each of these trusses and posts would weigh up to 20 tons. The plan was to set up two stiff leg derricks of 10-ton capacity each and work them together. The power for these would be steam donkey engines each with 3 drums and nigger-head drums. These rigs would be mounted on a big sled assembly that could be skidded ahead after each truss had been erected.

We put these rigs all together. The mast and stiff legs were mounted on the sled with counter weights at the bottom of the stiff legs. The derricks were both timber rigs. The stiff legs were 12 inches × 12 inches × 60 feet long. The masts were 16 inches × 16 inches × 30 feet high. The booms were 14 inches × 14 inches × 70 feet long. All timber was coastal Douglas-fir. There was a working deck built on the sleds. Also, the steam donkeys, the coal, water, and extra rigging lines, etc., were all on these decks. While we were assembling the derricks the carpenter crews were busy assembling the trusses. They did this by starting at the west end of the building. When one truss was assembled and laying flat on the ground, the next one would be assembled with the truss laying on top of the first one then another and so on. The second side was done the same way except it was laying the other way around. This was done so that when one side was all erected we could turn the derricks and erect the second side. As soon as a truss was erected, the derrick booms would be swung around so that the booms could be lowered below the level of the bottom chord of the truss. Then the line for the moving of the derricks was tightened up, the skids greased, and the rigs moved ahead to the next position. Then the booms were raised and hooked onto another truss and it was raised. These trusses weighed about 20 tons each and we generally raised 5 or 6 trusses a day.

When we had the rigs all assembled and ready to start erecting the trusses, we raised the derrick booms to what looked like the working height. Jimmy Fitzpatrick was the general foreman on the job and he also pushed the crew on the No. 1 rig. Eddie Bickerton, the son of old Ed, pushed the No. 2 rig. I was working in Jimmy's crew. One time, he called me over and handed me a long tape measure about 75 feet long. He said to go up the boom and when I reached the top, to send down the end of the tape and tell him what the reading was. That way we would know if we were high enough with the boom. We already had the chokers on the load as a set of spreaders. This was so that we were lifting the trusses from four points with the two rigs. I dropped the end of the tape to Jimmy and he called out that it wasn't high enough. He signaled to the hoisting engineer to boom up. I have a really big voice so I called out to the engineer – his name was Percy Chapman. I hollered to let the load run. He did this and when I read the right height on the tape, I called out to stop it. Then, the No. 2 rig could be boomed up by eye-balling it with No. 1. I came down off the boom and Jimmy called over to Ed and asked him if he was ready? He answered yes. "O.K." he said, "let's see what these rigs will do." The engineers put the boom drum dogs in place and the lines were marked for future reference.

Then they went ahead on the load lines. Well, the lines were tightened but the truss barely started to lift when the big chain at the top of the mast that holds the boom falls on No. 1 rig (the one I had just come down) broke and down came the boom. Imagine the feeling I had to think that just a few minutes before I had been on the top of that boom. We looked at the other one and the chain on it was parting. We lashed it off with several parts of good rope and lowered the boom. Now a new set of rigging had to be placed on both derricks. Old Ed ordered two special chokers for this made from new 1¼-inch cable. These were ready for us the next day. We placed these on the rigs and we went ahead with the erection. We had a small truck crane for filling in the brace sections and struts between the trusses, after moving the derricks ahead ready for the next move.

You can just imagine what these skid pieces were like as they were pressed into the mud as the heavy derrick sled passed over them – a load of about 50 tons. These skid pieces were almost out of site in the mud. Old Ed did not have any timber tongs for the men to pick these up with. He expected the men to get them out of the muck and carry them ahead to the next position. You could not even get a grip on them. I said this was no good. Jimmy Fitz replied that we just didn't have any timber tongs. These hand tongs are also known as Swede hooks. They are a pair of tongs attached to the middle of a five-foot handle for two men to lift. I went over to the general contractors tool shed to see if I could get some. The general contractor on this job was a firm by the name "Carter Hall & Aldinger. The man at the tool house asked me what I would like. I said I wanted two pairs of Swede hooks. He brought them out and asked what my number was. Of course, we didn't have numbers, so I just told him "Number 27". He marked it down and handed me the Swede hooks. I took them back to the rig and everyone wondered where I got them. I don't know what happened to them when the job was finished. I guess old Ed ended up with a little more equipment.

I should mention here about the pieces of timber used under the derrick sleds for moving the rigs. These were 4"× 12" timbers 6 feet long with a smooth piece of 2"× 6" nailed on top, which was greased. This made it easier for the derrick sled to move. After moving ahead, all of these pieces had to be picked up and moved ahead to the next position.

So, once we reached the west end of the building, we turned the derricks and came back on the next section. Then it was just a matter of repeating everything we had done on the first section. When we got back to the east end again, we erected the rest of the building, but it was a different set-up. The next section was mostly structural steel. It was made of six main trusses supported at each end by steel columns. It was an area of 240 feet by 240 feet, with only one column in the centre of this area. Between the steel trusses the roof was carried by 20 timber trusses, which was carried by the steel trusses. These steel trusses were erected by using some timber falsework to support them while erecting. When these trusses were erected, we riveted them all into place and then raised the remainder of the timber trusses. This completed all the work for us at the Boeing plant.

From there, we went to the hydro project at Stillwater near Powell River. This is the hydro project that supplies Powell River with power. This was a penstock job. The general work was being done by Northern Construction Company. We used their rigs for handling the penstock sections as they already had a couple of stiff-leg derricks built at this location. This was a short job, which we finished in a few weeks.

Back in Vancouver, there wasn't much work so I took a job with the Dominion Bridge plant where they were starting to make structural members for the first ships that would be built in the West Coast Shipyards. I stayed with this until the end of June 1941.

Changing a girder span on the Kettle Valley Railway
1941

CHAPTER 18

Canadian Bridge Company, July 1941

AT THE END OF JUNE 1941, I got a call from the Union Hall saying they wanted me to go to work for the Canadian Bridge Company. The job was on the Merrit subdivision of the Kettle Valley Railway. I went to the Union Hall to check things out. Here I was given a slip of paper addressed to the Canadian Pacific Railway Company that stated the following:

> Please supply transportation for Red Irving and ten men.
> Signed Frank Soucie
> Canadian Bridge Co. Ltd.

Frank didn't know my first name and most people knew me as "Red". I met the rest of the crew at the C.P.R. station where I presented the draft from Frank Soucie. This was immediately honoured by the ticket agent and we all boarded the Kettle Valley train. We went to a place called Brodie. This is where the Kettle Valley line divides to go either to the Coquihalla Pass, or down the valley to Merritt and Spences Bridge, where the Kettle Valley line joins the main line of the C.P.R. The Coquihalla line joins the main line west of Hope at Ruby Creek.

We caught the train in Vancouver at about 7:30 PM on July 1st, 1941. We arrived in Brodie at about 1:00 AM the next morning. They had already opened the camp there as the camp was all on rail cars. We were met at the train station by a fellow by the name of Bill Hesson. He was a blacksmith but had been in the employ of the Canadian Bridge Company as a watchman to overlook their camp railcars parked on a sidetrack. He showed us where to bunk and said breakfast would be on at 6:30 AM. We all went to bed and then up on time since there was a wake-up gong. In the morning we all got started to work. The derrick car had to be assembled and the hoisting engineer had to get the steam donkey on the derrick car steamed up and ready for work.

The job ahead was to reinforce and repair every bridge from Brodie to Spences Bridge and in some cases, replace the bridge spans. The bridge spans were all on the Cold Water River as far as Merrit and then over the Nicola River to Spences Bridge. We started at Brodie, on the first bridge, to reinforce the floor system. The rail system at Brodie forms a big "Y" in the little valley where the trains can go either way. One leg of the track comes down the hill from Brookmere where the C.P.R. had facilities to service the steam engines and accommodation for the rail crews. The west leg of the rails headed for the Coquihalla pass. The outside leg of the rails was close to the hillside and this is where our camp cars were located.

While camped at Brodie we worked on three bridges. These all had to be reinforced in the floor system. The reason for this was so they could use engines of a heavier class. The next bridge was about a mile down from our camp. The crew travelled from camp to these jobs on a railroad section pump car. Small tools and equipment were moved on a small rail push car.

At the first bridge, the one that was downstream from camp, there was a nice swimming hole in the Cold Water River. At this time of year the days were long and hot. In camp, after supper, several of us – mostly the younger fellows – would put one of the pump cars on the track and go down to the swimming hole. We would set the car off the track where it was safe and out of the way. On these jobs, all railroad rules had to be observed. One evening, while we were swimming, a thunderstorm came up. We left the swimming hole and headed up the trail to the track. About 50 feet from the track, the trail went right beside a big Douglas-fir tree that was about two feet in diameter. The lightening had been flashing all around. When we reached the pump car, we took hold of the handles to place the car on the track. Then: BOOM!. We were all laying on the ground and wondering what had happened. The lightening had struck the tree, just where a few seconds before we had passed. The tree was split wide open and the grass around it for about 30 feet was all burnt. The split in the tree was big enough for a man to put his arm through. Well, we all felt pretty shaky after that. We put the car back on the rails and went back to camp. Boy, what an experience, and we all walked away from it.

While camped at Brodie, we worked on three bridges. Then our camp, derrick car, and all the equipment were moved to Kingsvale. At this place we dismantled a deck girder span and replaced it with heavier girders. On this kind of a job, everything had to be made ready so that the girder span could be changed in between train times. We moved in and cut all the rivets loose in the bridge, and then replaced them with bolts and pins as the work proceeded. On this rail line, the train to Spences Bridge from Brookmere came down about 8:30 AM and then returned about 6:00 PM. As soon as the train was past, the dismantling took place. Pins and bolts were removed and all floor beams, stringers, bracing, and struts were lifted out with the derrick car. Then the girders, one at a time, were pulled out and a new one put in. Then all the lower bracing was placed, the stringers and floor beams were placed, the top bracing was placed, then everything was pinned and bolted ready for riveting again. When replacing the rails on a hot day, it was sometimes necessary to cool the rails in the river since they had expanded in the heat during the day. Everyone worked like hell to get everything done so the rail traffic could proceed. In the following few days, all the riveting was done and everything was cleaned up. Then, we moved to the next bridge.

The next camp was at a place called Glen Walker, where we reinforced the deck systems on two through-truss bridges. While we were on these jobs, there was no evening entertainment, no T.V.s or radios. On Saturday evenings though, a fellow who worked for the C.P.R. would come by in a gasoline speeder and a push car hooked to it with a couple of benches and he would take us to Merritt. In Merritt the stores were open on Saturday evening and of course, the beer parlours. The beer parlours closed at 11:00 PM. So afterwards, everyone would go to the café to have something to eat, and then back to the rail yard to catch the speeder back to camp.

The next place we moved the camp to was right in Merritt. Some of the men had their wives come up to Merritt from Vancouver, so I also did this. We rented a small cabin for a while and then managed to rent a nice furnished house in town. This was quite a nice house – kitchen, living room, three bedrooms, and nice porches. This was much better than Vancouver and we still had six months work ahead. This meant we could get ahead a little bit and save some money for a home.

Back on the job, we reinforced the small girder span in Merritt and then moved the camp and equipment to Canford, which is about 10 miles closer to Spences Bridge. We were camped at Canford for some time as we were able to work on several of the bridges from this location. The reason there are so many bridges in this valley is because the river winds back and forth while the railway tries to run in a straight line. We worked on these bridges up and down the line throughout the rest of the summer and fall.

Our next move of camp was further down the line to a place called Dot. At this place we dismantled a bridge that was exactly the same as the one at Canford. Both of these bridges were identical through truss spans of the pin and link model. At Dot, the bridge was dismantled and a new one erected in its place. The bridge from Dot was moved back to Canford and rebuilt outside the existing span. The reason for all of this was the wartime rationing of steel. The government let the company have only enough steel for one new bridge, since these bridge spans were identical.

The new span to be erected at Dot was being fabricated in the Canadian Bridge shops at Walkerville, Ontario. By using the derrick car with a short set of pile driver leads, we could carry the leads through the truss on a low boom and place all of the false work to carry the bridge before any dismantling took place. After finishing the false work, we dismantled the bridge trusses but left all of the floor system in place as a trestle to carry the rail traffic. Just at the time that we had finished dismantling the trusses, and while we were preparing to move, we were hit with a spell of rainy weather. The rain started in the afternoon and continued through the night. By the next morning, the river was rising. As the river rose, a lot of trees, stumps, and other debris were coming down the river. This debris started to pile up against the bridge false work. We started to remove it with the derrick car, but there was more of it coming all the time, and the river kept rising and running faster. By the late afternoon it was getting quite serious and piling up against the bridge faster than we could remove it.

When the false work had been placed we had left one panel open without bracing to let any drift wood go through. This worked for a while, but it was not nearly enough. All of this debris had to be cleared or else the bridge would be lost. Frank Soucie was getting worried, so at the normal quitting time he said we had better eat and bring the derrick car out again and keep pulling the drift wood out. We all worked like hell to get this done and it was one hell of a fight against nature. The days at this time of the year were getting very short. When it got dark all we had for light were two or three coal-oil lanterns. There was no power available.

We kept pulling out the tree stumps and everything else, but still the debris kept coming. There were a lot of big trees 2 to 3 feet in diameter and 50 or so feet long. This kind of stuff is hard to get a hold of when the light is poor and the water running like hell. If a man ever was to fall in the water, he would be gone. The river had risen about 8 feet in about 12 hours. It was running so fast, it looked like we might lose the bridge. The ends of the trees and logs in a lot of cases were going under the bridge, so when the derrick car was hoisting them out, it was pulling them against the bracing of the falsework, which did not help the situation.

Upstream from the bridge on the left bank, there was a big rock that looked like it was quite solid. I got an idea all of a sudden. I got a couple of men to help me and we put a chocker around the rock and hooked a snatch block to it. Then we took a piece of cable and ran it through, and then another snatch block on the bridge with this cable through it and then hooked it to the derrick car. We used the other end to hook to trees with a pair of tongs. Then we could pull all of this debris upstream out of the bridge and guide it to the open panel. The rain stopped and the amount of debris coming down the river was slowing down. By about midnight we were winning the battle. An hour or so after that, some of the men went back to camp to get some rest. Some of us stayed up all night to keep an eye on the river. By daylight there was no more debris coming down the river. We put the derrick car in the siding and checked that the switch was locked in line with the main track. Then we had some breakfast and flopped on our beds. Just some of joys of being an ironworker.

Before we moved back to Canford to erect the trusses from Dot to double up the Canford trusses, we moved the outfit north to a bridge closer to Spences Bridge. This was a place called Clapperton where we had to reinforce a deck truss and a deck girder span. This was only about a two-week job. When it was finished we moved all the way back to Canford. It was just when we were getting ready to move back to Canford when the bombing of Pearl Harbour took place. Now there would be a lot more war.

The train that moved our outfit was on the return trip from Spences Bridge. This happened on a nice mild sunny day. It seemed like the train was late. Now, on railway work, there were different items used for warning of approaching trains. One of these devices was known as a torpedo or track bomb. Some of the guys got hold of some of them and thought they would play a trick on old Frank Soucie. Our camp cars were about 400 feet from the south end of the bridge. Some of us were at the bridge where we could see down the line for quite a ways, so we knew when the train was coming. These track bombs were generally placed on the track so when the engine runs over them, they explode with a loud bang. Frank Soucie was getting anxious about the train coming because the day was getting on and every few minutes he would be looking out to see if it was in sight. We found some rocks and string and tied a few of these track bombs to the rocks. We dropped the rocks down to the lower part of the bridge foundation to create a loud bang. When this happened old Frank came out to the track – but no train. He went back in and we dropped another bomb. He came back out again – but still no train. The guys were getting quite a kick out of this performance. Finally, the train came and Frank quit worrying about it.

The train pulled our outfit out of the siding and we were on our way to Canford. Just shortly after we got to Canford and started working, the winter set in. Ice on the river, snow, and storms. When Christmas came, the cook put on a wonderful Christmas dinner. This was a few days before Christmas because quite a few men were leaving camp for Christmas holidays.

There were five of us that arranged to go with a local fellow to Vancouver. He supplied the car, and we paid the expenses. We stayed in Vancouver until after New Year's Day. My wife and a girlfriend of her's had already gone to Vancouver on the bus. She wanted to be in Vancouver because her folks had moved there from Princeton. This visit could have been O.K., but when I got there she wanted me to go to work in the shipyards like a lot of people were doing. I said that the shipyards were not for me. She did not want to go back to Merritt. Now we had to give up the house in Merrit and get another place in Vancouver. I didn't have much time, but I managed to get a basement suite on Victoria Drive. I bought a bunch of furniture and when Christmas holiday was over, I returned to Merritt in the car with the other fellows I had come down to Vancouver with.

Now back to work in Canford. Before we could erect the trusses, we had to drive pilings for false work to support the trusses as we erected them. This had to be done on both the upstream and downstream sides of the existing bridge span. This was done by using the same system with the derrick car that we had used on the bridge at Dot. These trusses from the bridge span at Dot were identical to the trusses on the Canford Bridge, both of them being of the old pin and link type. This type of truss was used on a lot of bridge spans in the earlier days of bridge building. The ironwork at the point of connection has to be perfectly aligned. Then all structural members at that point are connected with a large pin, which is threaded on the ends to receive a large nut and washer that holds everything in place.

After the erection of the trusses on the outside of the existing trusses, the two sets of trusses had to be connected together. This was done in the following manner. A short piece of beam was connected between the plumb posts at every panel point. Another floor beam was then placed underneath the existing floor beam and projecting outside the bridge as far as the new trusses on both sides. Now a heavy toggle bar two-inches thick was placed above and below the new beams and connected with two-inch diameter bolts to bring everything into proper tension so that all trusses would be equally stressed when the load of the trains was applied. When all of this work was completed, we removed all the false work and cleaned up the site.

At the camp, all of our bunk cars were heated with wood. At the bridge site there were always a lot of pieces that had been left over after the pilings had been cut to proper length. We bundled up a bunch of these and took them to camp on the hook of the derrick car. One day, when we were making a bundle of these pile butts by picking them up on the side of the track and using the rails for dunnage to have them off of the ground so that a pair of chokers could be placed around them, we almost had a foolish bad accident. These old derrick cars did not have a self-contained power swing. They used a rope swing system. A pair of 1½-

inch ropes was connected to the boom and then into the engine to the nigger head drums. Then the ropes were wound on the nigger heads and controlled by a man who stood between the drums to handle the swing ropes. This job was quite a tricky job. I know this from doing the job a lot of times myself. When the derrick is handling a heavy load you had up to five turns on the rope on each drum. But when handling light loads you only needed a couple of turns. When it was a light load, the engineer would most likely open the throttle more and with only a couple of turns of the rope on the drums, the boom would not swing too fast.

This particular time, Cecil Newman was on the swing job. He had too many turns of rope on the drums. We were using a single whip load line to pick up these pile butts to make a load for camp. This was the last job of the day. Noble Hargin, who was the pusher of the crew, was with me and we were making the bundle on the track. To pick up the pile butts we had a pair of timber tongs on the hook. A piece of piling had been picked up. The engineer opened the throttle. Because he had too many turns of rope on the nigger head, the boom was swinging too fast. Somebody let out a big yell. I was bent down at the bundle getting chokers around it with Noble when I heard the yell. I thought: Holy Jesus!, the tongs had come off the load. But it was the load swinging toward us far too fast. The piece of piling hit me in the ribs. Nobel looked up and it hit him in the face. It knocked both of us across the track and Noble ended up with black eyes.

It was a lucky thing we were not badly injured. When it was all over and we were back at camp, I told Newman what a damn fool he was for handling the swing the way he did. I don't think Noble said anything to him, but he had a hell of a looking face.

At this time we were in the finishing stages of the work on this bridge. We had to move our compressor, welding machine, all scaffold equipment, and rigging and load it on railway cars at our camp. When this was all complete we moved the whole outfit back to Dot to erect the new bridge span there.

Our camp outfit at Canford was parked on the sidetrack, which was actually a passing track. There was no spur track on the railway at this location. The train from Brookmere generally arrived at noon. We came in from the bridge, which was about a mile away. We always brought all rail equipment in and had it in the clear on the sidetrack so the train would go through on the main on its way to Spences Bridge. Well one day, the train was a few minutes early and was sitting on the main track at the south end of the pass track and was waiting for us to come and clear the line. When a bridge company was doing this kind of work on a railway, a railway company man was assigned to the bridge company to make sure everything was always O.K. in terms of railway traffic. He was usually a conductor.

The railway switches were always kept locked for safety. Also, the switches were lined for the main track except when switching for the sidings. Our conductor was a fellow by the name of Bill Mahoney. We were riding on the derrick car together. We could see the train already in and waiting for us at the other end of the sidetrack. The derrick car stopped for the switch to be opened. I said to Bill that I would go and open the switch, just like I had done many times before. He handed me the switch key and I ran and opened the switch. The derrick car started in on the sidetrack. Behind the derrick car, the rest of the crew was coming in on a pump car. I was still at the switch but should have stepped away from it. On the days that were not train days, only the derrick car would take the sidetrack, or the hole as is was known in railway language. The pump car would go on up beside the camp.

Now the pump car was right behind the derrick car. Cecil Newman was on the pump car and he got excited and thought I was not going to keep the switch open for the pump car. He let out a big yell - the damn fool. I thought there was something wrong so I threw the switch again. Well there was the derrick car going in on the pass track, but the rear trucks were on the main track and soon derailed. I realized in a flash what I had done so I threw the switch again for the pass track. I could hear Frank Soucie, our superintendent who was riding on the derrick car asking what the hell is wrong. I snapped the lock in place and stepped across the track where I was standing when they all got off of the derrick car. Bill Mahoney realized what had taken place. Soucie was asking me all kinds of questions. I said it looked like the car jumped the track. He shook his head. Bill Mahoney spoke up and said the trains have had trouble at this switch before. No one else in our crew seemed to know what had actually happened. Now we had to get the train to back up, unhook the engine, go in the side track and remove all of our camp, pull it back out, and then put it on the main track out of the way, then come back on the pass track and using the rail replacers shove our derrick car back onto the rails. This all took about an hour so we didn't get our lunch until it was all done. On another job several years later Frank Soucie came to me and said he thought I did something wrong at that switch in Canford. I replied: "Well Frank, you saw that the switch was in place and the lock snapped shut." He shook his head and said it was a mystery to him. I don't think anyone else ever knew what actually happened except Bill Mahoney and myself.

As soon as everything was cleaned up on the Canford job we moved back down the line to Dot. The steel work for the new bridge arrived on time and we went to work to erect the new span. Here again we could only remove enough of the old floor system of the bridge at one time to replace it with a new section, since we had to be able to maintain rail traffic at all times. We could not remove the false work until the entire structure was erected, pinned, and then bolted in place ready for riveting. We finished all of the work for this bridge in March and cleaned up the site. This was the finish of the bridge work on the Merritt subdivision of the Kettle Valley rail line. When this was over, we all returned to Vancouver.

The history of the Kettle Valley Railway is very well documented in the book *McCullock's Wonder* by Barrie Sanford.

CHAPTER 19

West Kootenay Bridges

THE SAME YEAR THAT I was born, 1911, saw the construction of two of the major bridges in the West Kootenay. Both of these bridges had the same design and measurements for the super structure, but different designs for the piers. The bridge five miles from Nelson over the Kootenay River was three spans of the "through-truss" type, with a wooden trestle approach on the east end. The one at Trail, B.C., had four spans of the same type, with the abutments on the shore on both sides of the river. Both of these bridges were built by the consulting firm of Waddel and Harrington.

The bridge in Trail was the first ever in Canada to use the pneumatic systems to sink the pier caissons. This method of pier construction involves men working under air pressure to keep the water out of the caissons. The men were known as sand hogs. Sand hogs went through decompression chambers to reach the work site. This was done both entering and leaving the work place, and time was limited according to the required pressure. When the caisson was put in place, it was held by cable guy lines fastened to the false work pilings that had been previously driven in. As the men removed the muck from the river bottom, the caisson gradually settled into place until it was either on bedrock or firm ground. Then it was filled with concrete with anchor bolts placed at the top of the pier to hold the shoes that the bridge span rested on.

Sometimes there were also pilings driven inside the caissons before the concrete was poured. These pilings sometimes went a long way below the bed of the river to stabilize the piers. On the Kootenay Landing railway bridge at the south end of Kootenay Lake, where the upper Kootenay River empties into the lake, we drove as many as 44 12-inch by 12-inch steel piles in each pier. We drove these piles 120 feet below the bed of the river. After that, the caissons were filled with concrete and anchor bolts placed to receive the bridge shoes. I worked on this bridge twice for two different bridge companies.

This is the method that was initiated by the firm of John Roebling and Sons when they built the Brooklyn Bridge in New York City over the East River. The West Kootenay district is rather a rugged part of the country with a lot of mountains and rivers running in all directions, creating a need for a lot of bridges to connect the different settlements in the area. For a long time the provincial government had ferries across the major rivers to connect the highways. Since the end of the Second World War, they have built some very necessary bridges to accommodate all the towns and cities in the district.

At the old Castlegar ferry site the government built a low-level continuous girder span bridge to connect Castlegar with Robson on the other side of the river and the Celgar pulp mill and Highway 3. This is the bridge the big chip trucks use now to get to the pulp mill. In the city of Trail, they built a new bridge over the Columbia River to connect Victoria Street with East Trail. This bridge is four spans of the "tied arch through truss" type with three trusses to each span to create a 4-lane roadway with sidewalks on the outside of the trusses – both upstream and downstream. This bridge is about a mile upstream of the original bridge, which is still in use. The structural steel for this bridge was fabricated and erected by the Dominion Bridge Company.

In Castlegar, at the south end of town, they built a pre-stressed concrete girder bridge over the top of concrete piers to connect Highway 3 with a road over the mountain and the village of Salmo and points east, as well as the Castlegar airport and Nelson and points east. This bridge is also over the Columbia River. Also over the Kootenay River on Highway 3, they constructed a nice big steel arch span that connects to the Castlegar airport. As well along Highway 3 there is a steel deck girder span over the Slocan River at Shoreacres and a new continuous girder span over the Kootenay River at Taghum, and a beautiful through-truss double cantilever bridge over the Kootenay River at Nelson at the lower end of the West Arm of Kootenay Lake.

In Creston, where the Kootenay River is split by the reclaimed Creston Flats, a concrete bridge was built on the west, as well as two spans of the through-truss tied arch type over the east crossing of the Kootenay. This occurred after the completion of the Kootenay Pass Skyway to Creston. These crossings are shortly before the Kootenay river enters Kootenay Lake at the place where the C.P.R. Railway crosses the Kootenay at Kootenay Landing.

The completion of the Columbia River Bridge in Trail gave people access to east Trail, Merry's Flats, Columbia Gardens, Fruitvale, Salmo, Ymir, Waneta, and the Pend d'Oerille valley. Today, most people don't pay much attention to the fact that transportation is so easy. But if you think about it and go to a river where there is no crossing and then think how much work and expense goes into the building of a bridge. First of all, it has to be surveyed and measured, then excavated, false work is constructed, piers are erected, and finally the suspension structure and the deck are constructed. But before any of that, all the funds for the project have to be appropriated. The Columbia River in B.C. has no less than 12 bridge crossings, while the Kootenay River, which is the main tributary to the Columbia in the same drainage system, has at least 12 bridge crossings as well. There are also numerous bridge crossings on most of the tributaries. The reason I talk about bridges, I suppose, is because I spent a lot of my life building these structures.

The same year that I was born, 1911, the government built a highway bridge over the Kootenay River at Taghum, 5 miles south of Nelson. This was three steel-through-truss spans and a long wooden approach trestle on the east end of the bridge at the bottom of the Taghum hill. When they built the road out of Nelson it climbed up over rock bluffs, well above the Kootenay River, and then descended the long hill down to the Taghum bridge. After crossing the bridge and the railway, it turned south beside the railway and through the millyard of the Lambert Lumber Company. Then it climbed up and along the Beasley rock bluffs and on up the mountain above Cora Lynn where it crossed Falls Creek on a small wooden bridge, and then on over the Bonnington bench and along the upper part of the village of South Slocan until it reached the Slocan Valley. From there the road was fairly level. It crossed the Slocan River at Shoreacres on a wooden Howe Truss deck span and on down the valley until it reached the rock bluffs at Thrums. Here it stopped until 1919 after the First World War was over. After the war, in 1919, the provincial government installed a ferry on the Columbia River at Castlegar and the road pushed through the canyon above Brilliant and over the bluffs at Thrums. With this, there was a road all the way through from Nelson to Trail – although there were a lot of twists and turns to it, and a lot of places were very narrow and treacherous. With the cars of the day, and the conditions of the road, the trip was about five hours where it is now done in about one hour.

At Blueberry the roadway went down into the creek bottom, then climbed out again on the south side, over a flat for about a mile, then down along the riverbank which was a treacherous sand hill, then wound around the mouth of China Creek and along the rock bluffs above the railway. From here it went across a flat at Birchbank, up another hill and then a winding road around Murphy Creek, and then on again into the valley at Stoney Creek for ¾ miles to a crossing to climb out again on the Tadanac bench, and then down the smelter hill to the town of Trail.

Here is an item concerning travel that a lot of people don't know anything about unless they are about 90 years old or more. When the road stopped at the Thrums bluffs, and there was no road through to Castlegar, some people made a round about trip to get there, but only with horses. Just south of South Slocan you could turn west and go to Crescent Valley on the Slocan River. At Crescent Valley there was a wooden bridge to take you to the west side of the Slocan River and then Krestova, through Goose Creek and then Pass Creek, to bring you to the east side of Castlegar. Pass Creek is also known as Norn's Creek, but because of the pass it became known as Pass Creek. Most of the people that used this road were the people from the Doukabor community. They could travel from Ootechenia over the suspension bridge over the Kootenay River. Also, at the south end of Ootechenia at the place called the Waterloo Eddy, the Doukabors built a water-powered ferry on the Columbia River that would take them across to Blueberry. At this point you would be about six miles south of Castlegar.

There has also been a number of other bridges built throughout the area to connect all of the highways, and also large ferries on the bigger lakes in the district. The old highway bridge at Taghum was dismantled and used at various locations in the Slocan Valley for access to the west side of the river at Slocan Park and also at Passmore. At Crescent Valley they constructed a new deck girder span to replace the old wooden Howe-truss span. It had been planned to use the single span through-truss bridge from the Big Bend on the Columbia River at Boat Encampment, but the job was left too long and the water was rising from the Mica Dam.

Previous to this, while I was working at Mica Dam, the Dominion Bridge Company erection representative, Lou Lessard, came to see me and asked me if I would go to the bridge site at Boat Encampment to look the bridge over and come up with a plan to dismantle it. I did this and submitted a plan. But at this time the logging companies were busy removing timber from the eastern part of the valley and transporting it over the Big Bend Bridge. They still needed the bridge and wanted the dismantling to be held off as long as possible. Evidently it was held off too long. The water from the dam kept on rising and they did not seem to have a plan in place to dismantle the bridge. I am not exactly sure of what took place, but eventually they made some rafts of logs to float the bridge when the water was high enough. The logs lifted the bridge, but it got out of balance and it was drowned – so now it lies forever at the bottom at the Mica Dam Lake. This is now known as McNaughton Lakes and they had to come up with a new bridge at Crescent Valley. The Dominion Bridge Company had asked me for the dismantling plan because I had been a bridge foreman for that company for a good many years. At this time though, I was working for the dam contractors at Mica. General McNaughton was the man in charge of the Canadian Forces overseas in World War two. Later, he had the job to survey the Columbia River system for the projected power sites. The lake behind the Mica Dam is named in his honour.

Double sheave rope block
(sketched by Ila Maber)

CHAPTER 20

Early Trail, Kootenay jobs, and the U.S. Naval gun plant

WHEN I WROTE ABOUT OUR family moving to the town of Trail in 1917 I didn't say much about what the town was like. It was very much like all early day western towns – wooden buildings, false fronts on a lot of them, wooden side walks here and there, and dirt streets that were dusty in dry weather and muddy in wet weather. In the winter, some merchants would shovel the snow from in front of their stores while some didn't bother. There was no snow plowing of the streets and almost all vehicles were horse drawn so they didn't need the roads plowed. In the downtown area there were some street lights, but none in the residential areas. In east Trail, where we lived, there were none – no telephones either. These amenities all came later on. The bridge did not even have side walks and people walking across the bridge had to get out of the way of the horse-drawn rigs, as well as the automobiles when they started running.

The roadway and walkway between town and the bridge was something of an obstacle course. The walkway or path was very narrow so if there was a group of people you would see them all walking in single file. The horses and wagons would struggle through the ruts that were sometimes a foot deep. It was 1924 before the road was paved. When this was done there was a big celebration to commemorate Trail's first mile of paved road from the bridge to Victoria Street, at the bottom of the smelter. There were bands playing, dancing in the streets, and speeches by the mayor and other dignitaries. Herb Clark was the mayor and he was a very forward and progressive thinking man. In later years, at work, I got to know him very well.

Herb became the machine shop foreman and master mechanic for Cominco. After he retired some years later, he came to Riondel as the inspector of the work where I was foreman. At that time I was working for the Dominion Bridge Company. We were erecting the mine head frame ore bins and derrick at the Blue Bell mine. This was the same time that we did the big cable job across Kootenay Lake from the Coffee Creek bluffs to Kootenay Bay on the east side of the Lake. The cable span, we were told at the time, was the longest cable span in the world. The cables were 10,733 feet long and 1¼ inches in diameter. This was the cable span that carried power across Kootenay Lake.

The electric power was needed for the mine and mill and for all of the east side of Kootenay Lake settlements. The steel tower that held the cables on the east side of the lake was 70 feet square at the base and 365 feet high. This cable span and tower was in place for nine years and then the tower was blasted by some of the Sons of Freedom Doukabors. This created the power outage to the Blue Bell Mine and everything else on the east side of the lake. It was also the main reason behind the police rounding up these fanatics who were consequently sent to prison.

As a consequence to this incident, the power line and cable span had to be rebuilt. After the cable span was rebuilt and the power restored, the Blue Bell Mine operated for a number of years, but eventually like all mines, shut down. All the equipment was dismantled and the little town of Riondel became a town of retired senior citizens, but not a ghost town, which happened to a lot of old mining towns.

It was in the process of stringing the cables across the lake we had a rather funny incident happen. For communication with all of the parts of the job, we hired the B.C. Forest Service for their two-way radios. The Dominion Bridge Company rented their service rather than buy a lot of communication equipment to use for only a short time. We had a crew of men on the west shore and a crew in boats out on the lake to look after the pontoons that supported the cables. The crew on the west shore looked after the job of hauling the cables up and over the big Coffee

Creek rock bluffs to the towers. There was a hoist engine we had installed at the west tower site to pull the cables across the lake. The crew on the east side looked after the job of unwinding the 20 tons of cable from each big reel, placing the relieving or damper strands that were placed on both ends for a distance of about 150 feet, hoisting the east end of the cable to the top of the tower, and also hoisting the back or end stay cables that ran from the tower to the back anchors.

All of these connections had to be made at the right time to keep everything in balance. So, being able to communicate with all of the different crews was quite important. Well, something went wrong with the radios. Time was running on and we had to get the crews off the lake before dark. Our engineer on the job in charge of things was a young man by the name of Don Jamieson. I had first known him on the Lions Gate Bridge when he was an apprentice, and we worked a lot of jobs together after that. At this place it is two miles across Kootenay Lake. Everyone was getting anxious. I said to Don: "are we going to get any word to the men?" He said: "I think you had better talk to the Forest Service men." I did this and they told me they had no idea how soon the radios would work. I went back to Don and told him this. I had to get the men off the lake. He asked me how I would do that. Well, I have always had a big heavy voice so I said "watch this". I went to the edge of the beach where we had the east side work taking place. I cupped my hands around my mouth and yelled "COME ON IN!!". I only called once and you could see all the boats on the lake head in for shore. Johnnie Kelly, who was in charge of the crew on the west shore, heard me call. One of his men asked what that was. He turned to him and told him that was Joe Irving across the lake calling in the men.

Years later one day, when my wife and I were waiting for the ferry at the coffee shop on the east side of the lake, we happened to see Corky Evans, a west Kootenay M.L.A. at the time. We had known each other for a long time. He asked me: "Joe, is it true that you could yell loud enough for your voice to be heard across Kootenay Lake?" I answered yes, and that it happened in March 1952 while we were stringing the cables for the power crossing.

One time while we were dismantling the Peace River highway bridge at Taylor Flats, the bridge collapsed. It was October 1957. This was now the spring of 1958 and I was the general foreman on the job. John Prescott, who was the superintendent of all the erection work for the Dominion

Bridge Company, was paying a visit to the job. He and I walked out on the deck of the bridge to the north tower while we were discussing the job. I had a crew working on the tower placing fittings for attaching cables that would be used to pull the north tower back into line. When the bridge collapsed, the north end span fell into the river. Tommy Rhodes was the man I had in charge of this crew on the tower. He had a very squeaky voice but I heard what he was saying. I called back to him to give him instructions – he waved with an OK. Prescott then turned to me and said: "My god, what a voice you have". If old Hi Carpenter had a voice like that every ironworker in the country would be scared off the job. Hi was the general erection superintendent and, at the time, working on the Second Narrows bridge in Vancouver.

Hi had lost his voice by almost being electrocuted on a bridge job years before when a derrick boom came in contact with a power line. He also lost part of his nose and came out of it with a crippled hand. But, he managed to survive it all and supervised many bridge jobs afterwards. Some of the bridges and jobs he was in charge of were the Patullo Bridge in New Westminister, the Lions Gate Bridge in Vancouver, the U.S. naval gun plant in Pocatello, Idaho, the Rosedale Aggasiz Bridge near Chilliwack, the New Alexander Bridge in the Fraser Canyon, and the Second Narrows Bridge in Vancouver. The Second Narrows Bridge is now known as the Ironworkers Memorial Bridge. The bridge collapsed a little before 4 PM on the 17th of June, 1958. It took 21 men to their deaths and injured many more. As well, two more men were killed on this bridge at a later date. Of the 21 men killed in June 1958 there were 14 ironworkers, 2 operating engineers, 2 civil engineers, 2 painters, and 1 diver.

I first met Hi on the Lions Gate Bridge, when I went to work there in 1938. When I got the call to report for work I was told to see "Salt Lake Brownie". I had met him before so when I went to the bridge on a Monday morning and first saw Brownie, he introduced me to Hi. Hi, in his whispering voice, asked Brownie if I was a punk or an ironworker. An apprentice was called a punk back then. Brownie said "no he's a journeyman ironworker". Hi then said "OK" and told me to go see Monte Crab, the rivet gang foreman. Years later when a group of us iron workers went to work for Bethlehem Steel on the huge U.S. naval gun plant that was being constructed at Pocatello, Idaho, it was Hi Carpenter who was the superintendent.

Hi, being an American citizen, had gone back to the U.S. after the completion of the Lions Gate Bridge. He was now in the employment of the Bethlehem Steel Comapany. It was now wartime and work had picked up a lot, making it hard to get capable men. He had a big job ahead of him and he needed men and good ironworkers were at a premium. It so happened that he had a friend from his younger days that now had an important job with the American warboard. Hi was the type of man who, if he needed something, would really go after it. He contacted our ironworker local union number 97 to find out if there were any more men available. He then contacted his friend in the warboard to do what he could about the immigration red tape. Well, in a very short time all the red tape was straightened out and eight ironworkers from local 97 were on their way to the U.S. to work for Bethlehem Steel. This was December 1942, and I was one of the eight.

We had to leave for Pocatello from Vancouver on Christmas day. We arrived in Pocatello on the Union Pacific Train named "The City of Portland" in the afternoon of the 27th of December, 1942. While on the train, some of the guys were talking about the weather we would have on the job. Rummy Croft said he brought his overshoes – you know the kind with the felt overshoes and two buckles. I said I brought mine with four buckles. Rummy then says "My god, if you had one more buckle, you would be a civil engineer." We had a lot of laughs over that one. Bill McGorvan said he only brought four suits with him. Bill was a real dresser. I then said that I brought four suits too – the suit I was wearing, two suits of underwear, and one suit of overalls. Lots of laughs again.

At the depot in Pocatello old Hi met us when we got off the train. Some of the men he didn't know, but he was really glad to see us as he knew about half of us. Rummy asked where the nearest bar was since we needed a drink. Hi took us across the street to a bar where we all had a couple shots of Canadian Club. Hi picked up the tab. Then he took us to where we were going to stay. Some of us were in his car, the rest in a taxi. The place was called the Sunset Auto Court, a very nice place and all first class. He then took us to see the job, which was about four miles out of town. As we drove around the outside of it, I asked Hi how many ironworkers he had on the job. He said he had about a dozen ironworkers and two dozen sheepherders. Lots of laughs. The next day it took about four hours to get all signed up for the job. There was the Social Security office, the U.S. Navy office, the General Contractors office, and finally Bethlehem Steel to deal with.

I had a piece of bad luck the first day on the job. I was sent with Buzz Bickerton's crew. He was erecting the small members of steel following the crew that was making the heavy lifts. I went over and met Buzz. I had also known him previously in Vancouver. Everyone in the Bickerton family was following iron work. He said he needed another man connecting. I said that would suit me fine. Towards the end of the day, we were placing a flat truss bracing section between some of the big crane columns. There were four of us working together. In order to place the truss, we had to remove a diagonal brace between columns until the truss was placed. Buzz was one level below me and he threw me a small choker for that brace. I bent down over the beam to catch the chocker. Just then, one of the men who were the connectors pulled the end of the brace loose. It pivoted from the bolt it was hanging on and it caught my foot against the beam. It was a heavy brace, a 3-inch by 5-inch angle 30 feet long. The angle had travelled about 15 feet when it caught my right foot against the beam. Well, it hurt like hell but I climbed down off the steel. Buzz said he would get me to a hospital.

They came from the Naval Office with a car and took me to the hospital in Pocatello. I remember the doctor, a very nice fellow by the name of Dr. Merrill. They ex-rayed my foot from all positions. The bone of the socket joint was broken about an eighth of an inch from the end. The doctor said he would have to put it in a cast and that I would have to stay overnight in the hospital. The next day, the doctor got me a pair of crutches and then drove me to where I was staying. He certainly was a nice doctor.

That night, when the men came in from work, there was word from old Hi that if I could move at all to come to work. The next morning I got a ride right down to the job. Old Hi came over and said he didn't want me to lose any time or money. He told me to go down to the tool shack and if there is anything there to fix to spend my time there. There are always tools being broken on a job, so I found a lot to do and Hi was quite pleased. This all went on all the time I was on crutches. One morning about a week later Hi came to me and asked if I could drive the front end of one of the truck cranes. The regular driver had the flu. I said if there is a hand brake on it then we'll be OK. We took a look and it had a nice big hand lever for the brake. I checked with the operator about the signals. They were using horn signals. It was a big old Mack truck with a 25-ton crane. I did this for a week or so until the regular driver was back. Then I took over a forge to heat rivots. Another job I was good at.

I will mention here how the signals worked. The horn was used in the same way as the bell signals on a building. When the crane was stopped, one blast was to move forward, then one to stop. Two blasts was reverse or back up, then again one blast to stop. Three blasts was back up to the left, four blasts was to the right, and again one blast to stop. Most of the erection work was done over the back end of the crane. Sometimes the crane sat in one position for sometime. Then it was the job of the front end man or driver to check out everything on the rig: the engine oil, the radiator, keep the rig clean, check the tires, and so on to make sure the entire machine was OK.

When it was about three weeks after the accident, I phoned the doctor about my foot and the cast. He said he supposed I wanted to get back to work. I told him I had been working the whole time. He said he would come and get me and take a look at it. He cut the cast off and looked over the foot and it was OK. He then drove me home again. Now at the job, I could go anywhere again. So I stayed with the rivet gang on the forge and a little later started driving rivets again.

The man on the job who was the general foreman was a man by the name of Bill Thomas. He was about the best man I ever worked for and I learned a lot about ironwork from him. One day when we were on the upper crane run, he came along the crane girders and called me over. I asked him what's up. He said he was going to the office shack where they were having a meeting about the erection of the overhead cranes. He said: "keep your eyes on the shack". If he came out and gave me the signal by putting his hands together, that would mean we would close the building. If he put his hands up and they were apart, it would mean we would leave the building open.

The meeting was between the officials of the general contracting company, Morrison and Knudtson Bethlehem Steel, and the naval representative to discuss the erection of the overhead cranes. If Bethlehem Steel was going to do the job, they would leave the building open to run in a railway track and erect a big stiff-leg derrick for the job. If that was the case, after the derrick was in place, the overhead crane material could be brought into the building and put in place directly from the rail cars. The decision was whether or not Bethlehem Steel would erect the cranes.

Bill Thomas came out of the office shack and waved up to us with his arms open. That meant the building was staying open for the crane erection. He waved again and headed to the parking lot for his car. He would drive to Salt Lake City, Utah, and take a plane to Los Angeles where he would supervise the dismantling and loading out of the big stiff-leg derrick that we would use for the erection of the cranes. For the next 10 days we wouldn't erect any more steel. We would only go ahead with rivet work while we were waiting the arrival of the big derrick.

By the spring of 1943, we had the big gun plant coming along in good shape, so they laid-off half of the Canadian crew and they returned to Vancouver. Four of us stayed on to finish the job with the Americans. There were overhead cranes still to be erected, and a lot of riveting work. These overhead cranes were really something to have had the opportunity to work on as they were a once-in-a-lifetime size of crane to erect. The need for these huge overhead cranes was to handle the huge gun barrels and all of the Allied equipment. Everything was built on an enormous scale for this project.

The building was designed for two of these large cranes – one to run above the other. The lower crane ran on tracks at the 55-foot level while the upper crane ran at the 110-foot level. The supporting columns weighed about 27 tons and were spaced 25 feet apart. The beams from column to column were a set of double beams of about 10 tons each. These were intended to carry double track for the cranes. The track on top of the beams was 100-pound railway steel of 18-inch gauge for the crane trucks. Each crane truck weighed about 18 tons. The pins that connected the trucks to the crane girders weighed 1500 pounds each. The crane tracks were a span of 110 feet apart and the crane girders weighed 70 tons a piece.

The building was 1,200 feet long, so you can imagine the tons of steel in the total structure. The columns that carried the roof system sat on top of the crane columns and were about 40 feet higher with an arm that projected into the building that carried the roof girders. The capacity of the cranes was 275 tons on the big hook and 50 tons on the auxiliary hook. The load block weighed more than 20 tons and was reeved up with 16 parts of 1½-inch diameter wire rope hoisting cable.

To erect and put these large overhead cranes in place, we did not use our ordinary erecting cranes. The Bethlehem Steel Company shipped a big stiff-leg derrick up from California, which we erected on the job site. The mast for this derrick was a 50-foot mast held in place by two big stiff-legs. Each stiff-leg was anchored down with about 50 tons of steel rails.

The boom was 150 feet and it weighed 25 tons. It also carried a 25-foot jib. The derrick could handle 100 tons at a 75-foot radius – 25 tons on the jib.

To erect the big stiff-leg derrick that would be used for the erection of the overhead crane, we used the big Northwest crawler crane. This was a beautiful crane to work with. It carried a main boom of 125 feet plus a 30-ft jib. The main load was reeved with four parts of ⅞-inch diameter hoisting rope for lifts up to 50 tons. The jib could be used with a single whip line up to ten tons. To erect the derrick mast we placed it with the crawler crane and held it in position while we placed the stiff legs with another truck crane.

The boom for the stiff-leg derrick was 150 feet long. The sections were about 4 feet square. The boom weighed 25 tons and was then reeved with 22 parts of ⅞-inch diameter hoisting rope. The boom fall blocks were reeved in tandom. This derrick could handle 100 tons at a 75-ft radius and could handle 20 tons by using two parts of hoist line on the jib.

As soon as we were finished with the erection of the derrick, the general contractor built the railway spur into the building from the north side. We had left the building open on the north side for this purpose. Now the rail cars with the material for the overhead crane could be brought right into the building for unloading and erecting.

To reeve up all the boom and load lines for the derrick, Bill Thomas, the general foreman, asked me if I could take care of the reeving job on the boom fall blocks. I explained to him what I had in mind and he told me to go right ahead. The sheave blocks weighed about half a ton each. They were reeved up in a work ways position sitting close together on timber dunnage. Bill said he would get me some help. It was quite a tricky job to reeve 22 parts of line and have it all in order. I have seen fellows get in trouble with only five or six parts of line, never mind 22 parts. We got it done in good time with out any foul up. To stretch the boom falls out we used the main load line of the crawler crane with three parts of line. We then hung the top block on the mast, hooked the other block to the boom and ran the working end of the line into the hoist engine. At this point we had the derrick ready for the load line, which we took care of next. When this was all done, we started the erection of the big overhead crane.

First we dealt with the crane trucks that the crane would travel on. There were four of these crane trucks – each weighed 18 tons. They ran on double rail tracks of 100-pound rail. The crane girders were connected to the trucks with a big steel pin that weighed 1500 pounds. The crane girders were 70 tons each and the span was 110 feet. The capacity of the crane was 275 tons on the main hoist, and 50 tons on the auxiliary hoist. The main hoist was reeved with 16 parts of 1½-inch wire rope hoisting cable.

The hoist engine for the derrick was gasoline powered. It had three drums for the boom and load lines, plus the swing drums. This hoist and engine weighed 30 tons. The boom was reeved up with 22 parts of ⅞-inch diameter cable with the boom fall blocks being reeved in tandem. The main load block was reeved with 12 parts of ⅞-inch diameter hoisting rope cable. Most of the time the jib was a single whip line for the lighter loads.

For a young ironworker like me – I was 32 years old at this time – it was a real pleasure and a real education in heavy rigging and lifting. Up to this time, the biggest rigs I had worked with were only capable of maybe 25-ton lifts. Actually, heavy rigging is a real science in physics, and common sense as well.

We finished Pocatello that spring in about May. Bethlehem Steel had lots of work, and they wanted me to go to California, which would have been fine with me, but this was during the time of my first marriage and I was having some marital problems at home in Vancouver. So, I had to turn down the offer and go back to Vancouver – a move I regretted for a long time.

CHAPTER 21

Trip back to Vancouver

THE TRIP BACK TO VANCOUVER from Pocatello, Idaho, turned out to be a very interesting one. I left Pocatello in the afternoon on the Union Pacific train "The Portland Rose". When I got my ticket I was asked if I had anything against the number 13. I said no, so I was given number 13, lower birth. Not long before this there had been a murder on an American train and it took place in a lower 13 birth, so a lot of people were leery of the number 13. As evening came on, I was in the diner car eating when a couple of fellows approached me. They were very pleasant and asked me if I was riding in a lower 13 birth. I said I was, so they asked if I had a guitar there. I said yes and that it was on the seat. They said they were going back to the club car to play some music and asked if they could borrow the guitar. I said sure and for them to go ahead and get it. They then asked me if I would join them when I finished eating. I said I would and when I finished my dinner I went on back to the club car to join them.

One of them was playing the violin, and the other the guitar. They asked if I would like a drink. I said sure and they called the porter and ordered some drinks. They introduced themselves as Bob and Doug. I told them my name and Bob started playing again. He was very good on the violin. They asked me to play the guitar but I said no since these fellows were much better than I was. Well, they kept on playing and started to sing. I sang along with them and they seemed to think that was OK. Some songs I knew, others I didn't. The one fellow, Doug, handed the guitar back to me so I played along with Bob. As the evening went on we had some more drinks and kept on with the music. Then Bob asked me if I knew San Antonio Rose. I said that I didn't know it too well, but to go ahead anyway. After he played a few bars I stopped. Bob asked me what the matter was. I said "nothing, but I've heard that before exactly the same as you just played it". He asked where and I said on a Bob Wills record. He then said "that's right, same violin, same man". The song San Antonio Rose was one that was written and produced by Bob Wills. So I said "well then, you are Bob Wills and you have a band called the Texas Play Boys". He said "yes, that's me".

Well, we all shook hands again and we all told each other about ourselves. They were on their way to Alaska to work for the U.S. government. Doug was a soils engineer and Bob was going to be his assistant. Being wartime, you had to do what you were asked to do, and Bob would get back to his band later on. We played and sang songs for quite a while before we all were tired and went to our births. Bob was the best violinist I had ever heard or had the opportunity to meet and play with. We met again the next morning and we stayed together all the way to Seattle. I never met Bob Wills again, but I heard a lot about him and his band. He became quite famous. Years later, when I was on a trip to Nashville, Tennessee, I went through the hall of fame wax works and there was a model of Bob Wills and his violin. He had died some time before that.

When I reached Seattle I had to go to the American War Board office to get permission to leave the United States. At this time, I was under a bond to Bethlehem Steel. It didn't amount to very much, just a few questions about work, citizenship, and so on. Everyone that I met in the War Board Office was a nice person. When I was finished there, I had a free afternoon so I did some shopping. I got some things I had not had time for in Pocatello. Then I checked into a hotel room as my train would not be leaving until the following morning. When I arrived in Vancouver the weather was good early summer weather.

Now that I was back in Vancouver, I had to make up my mind about what I wanted to do. It is sometimes a hard decision to make in your life about which road to take that lies ahead of you. Well, I decided to stay so I notified Bethlehem Steel that they could cancel my bond and that I wouldn't be going to California. Then I called our union hall to tell them I was home and right away I was sent to Vancouver Island to erect a boiler job at Brentwood Bay.

After returning to Vancouver from Pocatello I went to Brentwood Bay on Vancouver Island, near Victoria. At this place the B.C. Electric Company had a steam power plant to supply electric power to the southern part of Vancouver Island. The job here was a new Babcock and Wilcox boiler that would increase the capacity of their existing power plant. The job was inside the building so we had to use a gin pole and a hand winch for power to erect the steam and mud drums to their positions. I went there in the last part of June and I was there until the last part of August.

About this time my wife got the fool notion to move to Osoyoos where her parents had moved to a few months previously. We had been living in a house on Grant Street near Victoria Drive. I drove to Osoyoos on the Labour Day weekend. There was a job there if I wanted to go logging. I thought this might be O.K., so I decided to give it a try. I enjoyed the woods and the fresh air, but the job was not what I wanted. So, about the first week of November I went back to Vancouver where I went to work for old Ed Bickerton again.

This was the Standard Oil Company tank farm project. There were several large tanks to erect, some being enormous. These tanks were second hand tanks from an oil field in Texas. The first tank to be erected was one that had a capacity of 88,000 barrels. It was 120 feet in diameter, at least 40 feet high, with a thickness of graduating from 1" on the bottom to $^3/_8$" on the top.

Now, old Ed did not have a truck or crawler crane, so we had to erect a stiff leg derrick for the job. The first sections of plate for the bottom course at the backside of the tank were set in place with a small ground-based breast derrick with a hand winch. The stiff leg derrick was able to place the rest of the plates on the first tier. When the tier was in place we could use the tank buggies to handle the rest of the plates. The tank buggies were a very good piece of equipment. The buggies ran on grooved wheels and they straddled the tank plate. The buggies were placed on the tier of plates that had been erected with the derrick. Then a plate was hoisted with the derrick and placed in position in the buggies. Then the load was cut loose and the buggy carried the plate to the back side of the tank where it was connected to the bottom tier. The buggies were then returned to the derrick for another plate. As soon as the second course was in place, the riveting could start. The bottom course had 1" diameter holes, the second course had ⅞" holes, and the third course had ¾" holes. The next course had ⅝" holes, and the next ½", and then ⅜". After riveting, all seams had to be caulked. The bottom of the tank was made from ⁵/₁₆" plate and was all welded in place. The roof was built of trusses with a centre post to carry the bottom chord. The roof plates were only ¼" and welded in place.

I stayed with this job until Christmas and then went home to Osoyoos for the holidays. When I returned to Vancouver I found out that there was a tower job starting out near Mission in the Fraser Valley. I decided this would be a better job for me. For one thing, I would receive my room and board because on all out of town jobs, accommodation had to be supplied.

This was another Canadian Bridge Company job. Our rooms in Mission were in the Bellevue Hotel. The towers were for the Canadian Navy radar system. There was to be two towers about 300 feet apart. Both of these towers were 300 feet high and 70 feet square at the base, tapering to 5 feet square at the top. Then, a 12-ft square platform was to be built on the top of the tower.

To erect these towers we used a basket gin pole with a gasoline donkey engine on the ground for hoisting. The pole was hung with chokers from each tower leg for the basket. The guy lines were hung on the tower legs using rope falls so that the gin pole could be leaned to each corner for the erection of each leg of the tower. The hoist line was run through a fair lead block at the bottom of the tower, and then through another block at the top of the gin pole. The second line was used to hoist the gin pole when a tower section was complete. Each tower leg was laid out on the ground and all related bracing was fastened to it with loose bolts and then hoisted to position. Each of these corner sections took roughly two hours of work to complete, then the gin pole could be leaned to the next corner to be ready to hoist another section.

As we erected each section, we had other men following up with permanent bolting. We had a good crew and we made good time throughout the whole project. In fact, Jack Stratford, who was in charge of the job for Canadian Bridge, said that we made record time. As most ironwork jobs go, this one had its thrills too. At quitting time we would get on the load ball to ride down to the ground. When we did this we had a light choker and shackle on the load line to keep the load from spinning. One time, this was not hooked up. We started down the load and were spinning. Joe Lachance told the men to close their eyes. I hollered to the hoisting engineer to let us down in a hurry. We all landed O.K. but it was a pretty wild ride.

When we finished the towers we were all laid off, so we all returned to Vancouver. It seemed that this was a time of odd jobs, one of which was to shim the lifting cables on the old Second Narrows Bridge. The old Second Narrows Bridge was a combined rail and highway bridge. One of the spans was a vertical lift span. The lifting cables had stretched unevenly and had to be corrected. The vertical lift section of the bridge had towers at the north and south ends of the span. When a ship had to go through, the span was hoisted to clear the ship. The lifting cables were fastened to the span on one end, and to the counterweight on the other end. This put the span at the road and rail level. The counterweight would be in the tower. In order to get slack in the lifting cables the counterweight had to be blocked. Then the span could be jacked to relieve the stress on the cables. The span weighed 850 tons so the counter weights each weighed 425 tons. In the top part of each tower there was a built-in girder on each side to be used to support false work to hold the counterweight so the span could be jacked to slack the lifting cables.

For the false work, two 24-inch I-beams were hoisted and placed under the counter weight. Then 12"×12" blocking was placed on top of the beams. When this was all done, the end of the span could be jacked and the lifting cables shimmed. The amount of difference in the cables was only $5/16$", but when hundreds of tons are involved, a fraction makes a big difference. We did this job twice on the old Second Narrows Bridge. Once at each end of the vertical lift span. The old bridge was removed after the new bridges were built. The work on the Second Narrows Bridge was done by the Dominion Bridge Company.

Shortly after this job was done, old Ed Bickerton got a small job to repair a couple of railway bridges in the Kicking Horse Canyon on the mainline of the C.P.R. railway. There had been an accident on the railway and two bridges had been damaged. A big freight train coming down grade from Field, B.C. had one of the box cars jump the track but it stayed with the train. Being down grade, and the freight train being pulled by big powerful locomotives – one of the big 5900 series of engines – no one knew anything was wrong until the freight crossed the upper bridge at a place called Cloister.

The 5900 engine was the biggest and most powerful engine that the C.P.R. ever used in their service. These were a huge engine of the 4104 wheel alignment class. All steam locomotives were classed in this manner. The first number represents the wheels on the leading or pony truck. The second number is the amount of driving wheels. The next number is the number of wheels under the firebox.

Before reaching the bridge at Cloister, the railway runs on the right side of the river. At Cloister it crosses to the left side due to a sharp curve in the river. This is the deepest part of the Kicking Horse Canyon. Also at Cloister, there was a passing track on the railway for half a mile and then another bridge. The passing track ran on the right side of the main track. As the train proceeded down the main track, the switch for the sidetrack forced the derailed box car to the right side and it jumped the track and overturned. Now that the train was broken, the train airline was also broken. This automatically applied the train line breaks. The train came to a stop. Golden was notified on the track phone and the big hook was dispatched to help clean up the wreck.

As soon as the track was serviceable, the big hook was going to return to Golden. But, everyone was excited and in a hurry, and they did not lower the boom on the big hook. Now, as the big hook was travelling west towards Golden, the boom came in contact with the east portal of the west Cloister Bridge and tore it out. The C.P.R. had the B&B crew place a temporary timber brace there. The Western Bridge Company was notified and they immediately fabricated another one. Ed Bickerton did all the erection work for Western Bridge Company.

Old Ed called the union hall for a crew. The foreman picked for the job was a fellow by the name of Cecil Clever. He had quite a lot of experience but had not worked on railway bridges. The CPR set up a camp on the Cloister siding for the job including sleepers, a cook car, a supply car, etc. There was only a small crew on this job and the work was all done with hand rigging. We arrived at the Cloister yard by train on a Sunday afternoon. We had dinner in the cook car and then got our places to sleep. Not too bad for a temporary camp.

The next morning, after breakfast, we went to the bridge at 8 AM. We got our tools that had been shipped ahead to Cloister by rail. To hoist the new portal member in place, we used a hand winch. We fastened this winch to a plumb post and then I was going to hang a snatch block for a fair lead at the top chord level directly above the winch. Clever came to me and told me just to put the block in the middle of the track and lead the line to the top at the portal. I told him that we can't put anything in the way of rail traffic. He said "I'll tell you where to put things". I thought to myself that we were in for trouble on this job.

The other men loaded the new section on the rail push-car and brought it down to the bridge. We hung a scaffold to work on at the portal level. Where the temporary timber was placed, we had to spread the truss with a jack in order to get the new portal section in place. The jack that had been sent for the job was a 25-ton Norton jack. But, whoever loaded the toolbox didn't include the jack handle. At this time, I was now up on the scaffold so I called to Lloyd MacTee to bring the jack handle. He said he couldn't find a handle in the toolbox, so he brought up a handle from a shackle dolly. This was strong enough, but wouldn't fit properly into the jack. I had to use this handle.

In the meantime, the other fellows with the hand winch were getting the new portal section pulled up into place. I kept on with the jacking. By then one end was in place and only a fraction to go and we would have the other end in place also. While I had been doing the jacking with this haywire handle, I had been holding the handle and socket together with one hand. I was sitting on the scaffold with one foot against the plum post, the other foot hooked on the inside of the post for safety. Clever came up on the scaffold. We had the ladder all the way up the batter post, which is the end chord of the bridge truss. I told him I would have it in place in a few minutes. He told me to move out and that he would do it. I moved out and he placed the handle in the jack and with both feet against the plum post and both hands on the end of the jack handle, he was exerting full pressure on the jack. The handle was slipping out of the socket and he didn't notice. About a third pull on the handle it slipped out of the socket. Clever went over backwards and fell to the track 18 feet below. He landed on the rails on his back and hit his head on one of the rails. On railway bridges there are two extra rails on the deck. These are called the Jordan rails. These rails are placed there to help in case of a derailment.

With Clever's head hitting the rail and his back hitting the other rails, he was killed instantly. Then, we could see by the track semaphore (signal lights) that a train was coming. And, here we were with a dead foreman, the iron not in place, and the rigging in the middle of the track.

We called Golden on the track phone. So they sent an engine up. We had a stretcher on hand and placed Clever on this on the pilot on the front of the engine. Rod Morrison was the job steward so he went to Golden with the body.

The west-bound passenger train was now at the east end of the Cloister yard and waiting for clearance. I said we have to get some bolts in that iron and cut the rigging loose so that the train can go through. We did this and the train went through. That was enough damage done, so we stopped everything until we could find out what would be done. It was about 11 AM. We went back to camp and everyone was feeling bad. That afternoon a telegram came for me on the east-bound passenger train. The telegram was from old Ed. He instructed me to take charge of everything and to complete the job to the satisfaction of the C.P.R.

We had to finish the work on this bridge and also repair some damage that had been done to the bridge at the east end of the Cloister yard. One thing in our favour was that we were having good weather. We finished the work and shipped the tools back to Vancouver and then we all returned to Vancouver on the train.

CHAPTER 22

Vancouver-Kootenay Landing Phase 1, 1945

WHEN WE RETURNED TO VANCOUVER we found out that old Ed had picked up some more small jobs. The first of these was to build the new gyproc plant across the Fraser River from New Westminister. One of Ed's sons would be the foreman for this job. His name was Hugie. We had a small truck crane for this job, one that had about a 10-ton capacity. It was owned by Commercial Truck Service. This job would only be about six weeks duration.

After the erection was complete we had to rivet all of the connections. When this was finished there was a small job at the sugar refinery, and another at a paint factory. At this time the Dominion Bridge Company had a small tank job to build at the U.D.L. Distilleries located in Marpole. This lasted for the rest of the summer. When this was over I went back to Osoyoos again and tried logging once again.

Mel Jordie who owned the Osoyoos Saw Mill wanted me to be his woods foreman. That was O.K., but their work system was haywire. They were only producing two truck loads of logs a day. They had a D-4 Cat for skidding and an old truck jammer for loading. I made new chokers for them for skidding, new slings for the jammer for loading, and then mechanical repairs on the jammer. Pretty soon things were running more smoothly.

When winter came I made a snow plow for the Cat. But, even though I more than doubled the production, the outfit was going broke. Mel had borrowed a lot of money for the sawmill and it was not making enough money to cover all of his payments.

In December, our daughter Shannon was born. She had beautiful red hair, just like mine. I could see where there was not going to be much future with this logging job so I quit and returned to Vancouver. Once again I went to work for Dominion Bridge Co. They had more work at UDL Distilleries, as well as an extension to the Lucky Lager Brewery in New Westminster.

These jobs lasted until July 1945. At that time the Canadian Bridge Co. had another contract with the C.P.R. Railway. This was to remodel the railway bridge at Kootenay Landing. This is where the upper Kootenay River empties into Kootenay Lake. I decided this would be the best job for me.

I went to Kootenay Landing just after the first of July 1945. Frank Soucie was the man in charge. We camped right at the Kootenay Landing. The Canadian Bridge Co. had their own camp rail cars there. The project was to build two new bridge piers with one new girder span to relieve the old wooden pier on the east end of the bridge, and then a new pier on the east end of the existing wooden trestle, and then another new steel span to take the place of the wooden trestle.

We started this project by sinking caissons on the east and west sides of the old wooden pier on the east end of the last steel span at the east end of the bridge. We placed guy line cables on these caisson sections to keep them in line. When the caissons were resting on the river bottom, the divers went down to check them to make sure that all was O.K. The divers were a father and son team from New Westminster. This was the Knight team – very good divers.

Once the caissons were in place, we started to drive the pilings. These were all 12"×12" steel beams, all were 75 feet long. We drove one length, then spliced another length to this. These piles were driven to a depth of 120 feet below the bed of the river. There were 44 driven in each caisson. After the piles were in place, the caissons were filled with Tremie concrete. When pouring by this method, a sectional pipe was lowered into the water to the bottom of the pour so that the concrete is spread evenly. As the concrete builds up, the pipe is raised and a section is removed. The concrete was not vibrated in this kind of work.

After all the piles were driven and the concrete in place, the piles were cut to proper elevation and then the cap beams were placed. When these were finished, we were able to place the girders from one new pier to the other. To accomplish this, we had to cut away enough of the old wooden pier to make room for each new girder, one at a time. Now the bridge end shoes were each resting on one of the new girders.

For driving the piles, we used a steam hammer. The steam was supplied from a boiler in a separate car from the derrick car. The derrick car only had to handle the steam hammer. The next job was to build the new pier on the east end of the old wooden trestle. This was a fairly simple job to take care of. It was all in the open, without any bridge trusses in the way of the work. The bearing piles were timbers cut to the proper height with the concrete forms placed and rebar put in place with the concrete poured. Then, the new bridge shoes were placed and ready for the erection of the new bridge span.

To erect the new span, we had to dismantle the old timber trestle as we progressed with the new span. The reason for this was to maintain rail traffic at all times. The old trestle became the false work to support the new steel as it was put in place. Once the floor system was in place we could erect the trusses. This was a 180-foot span and an exact duplicate of the one that we had erected at the place called Dot on the Merritt subdivision of the Kettle Valley Railway in 1942. This ended all the work at Kootenay Landing for that season. The men were then laid off.

I was the job steward, so it was up to me to find out what the disposal of the men would be. To do this I had to hike to Sirdar to the telegraph office at the C.P.R. station. Sirdar was three miles from Kootenay Landing and it was a cold wet day in late November. I hiked to Sirdar and sent a telegram to our union hall. I told the operator that I would wait for the answer. While I waited, I went across the road to the hotel and had a beer with Henry Hornseth, the hotel owner.

I picked up the answer and then I hiked back to camp. I called all the men together to read the telegram to them. Here is what the wire said: "DISPATCH ONE MAN TO KIMBERLEY. ALL THE REST TO VANCOUVER." So, I asked them who wanted to go to Kimberley. No one wanted that job, so I said I would take it. The rest of the men all left for Vancouver. I packed my bags, picked up my time from Frank Soucie, and then caught a ride to Nelson on the next west-bound freight. We could always ride the caboose on the freights. The freights were easy to catch because there was always a slow order in force where a bridge was being worked on.

Before I go on any further, I should mention something about our activities in our off hours. In the hot weather during the summer time we had excellent swimming right at the bridge site. We rigged up a real good diving board with a 2"×12"×16" plank. We also had a big timber float just under the bridge to lie on after coming out of the water. On the weekends we spent a lot of time there, especially on the hot days. We all enjoyed this very much. Also, in the evenings after work, there wasn't anything more refreshing after a hot days work. There was one ironworker drowned at this site when the bridge had first been built back in 1930. But that had been an accident on the job.

For evening entertainment we sometimes hiked to Sirdar to go to the beer parlour for a few beers. Some times we would take a railway hand pump car. There was room on one of these for six or eight men. The first time we went to Sirdar to the beer parlour we went in, sat down, and ordered a few beers. The beer was all bottled beer. After a while we ordered another one, and we wanted to have another one before going back to camp. When we ordered this, the hotel owner told us that there wasn't any more. He said that he was on a quota and could only sell so many bottles each day. We didn't think much of this idea. We went back to camp and the next day after work, I got a sheet of paper from the office and made out a petition for Henry Hornseth, the hotel owner, to take to the Liquor Control board to rectify the situation at the Sirdar Hotel.

It so happened that at this time there was a lot of work taking place in the Sirdar area. First of all, there was the Canadian Bridge Co. crew, then the C.P.R., and B&B crew. Then there was also the Department of Public Works doing a job on the highway, and also the B.C. Telephone Co. working on the telephone lines in the area. All this work in the area made a sudden increase in the population of Sirdar.

I made out the petition and then spent some time after work getting it signed by the men on all the different crews. I took this petition to Henry Hornseth and told him he could take it to the Liquor Control Board. Henry did this and it was not long before there was a lot more beer at the Sirdar hotel. This made the beer-drinking crowd happy.

In August the news came that the war was over. They had dropped the atomic bombs on Japan. It was at the weekend when we got the news, so we all went into Nelson to celebrate. The town went wild, and no wonder after five years of war. Now, as I mentioned before, I was taking the job in Kimberly.

Kettle Valley Railway, Agate
1941

Sullivan Mine headframe, Kimberley, BC
1946

CHAPTER 23

Kimberley Head Frame and the Old Arena, 1945-1948

I ARRIVED IN NELSON, DID some shopping for some winter clothes, and caught the east-bound passenger train for Cranbrook where I was going to catch a bus to get to Kimberley. It was late at night when I arrived in Kimberley. I found out where the Bennet and White employees were staying and I went there. I found out that it was a bunkhouse set up in a former store building. This was Sunday night. I got fixed up for a bunk and went to bed. The crew was eating in a restaurant that was only a short block from the bunkhouse. They had a truck crummy for transportation to work.

The job was to build a head frame and hoist room at the 4380 level at the top of the mine site. The foreman was Bob MacDonald. At one time, Bob had been the business agent for our union, but he had gone back to ironwork. I hadn't worked with some of the crew for a long time, but I knew all of them so I felt right at home. I went into the raising gang and was connecting steel again. I always liked the job of connecting. For erecting the steel, they had a small crawler crane with a real good operator named Lescolter. His brother was the job superintendent. I had not met him before.

When I had checked into the bunkhouse the night before, I found that there were plenty of blankets, but no sheets for the bed. The Bennet and White office was right on the job. So, when I was getting signed up for work that first morning, I immediately brought this matter up. There was no way I liked sleeping without sheets. This is the way I put it to them. I said: "Look, I'm here to work for you people and you will expect the best that I can give you. And I will, each and every day from starting time in the morning to quitting time at night. But when I get to the bunkhouse at night I expect the best from you. Besides, that condition is in the union agreement. I don't want to raise any more hell over this matter. Now, I will go to work to keep up my part of the bargain." I went to work and they did their part of the bargain so everyone was happy.

The hoist room was the first to erect and the crawler crane, although it was a small one, could reach and handle all of the building. The hoist room was a structure 60 feet by 120 feet and 60 feet high. The roof trusses were spaced at approximately 20 feet and connected with lateral bracing and roof purlins. Then this all had to riveted. When I went to Kimberley I thought that it would only be a job for a few weeks. But, it turned out to be much longer. So, at Christmas time I went home to Osoyoos. I didn't like Osoyoos very much anyway, so that was a good chance to leave the place. I sold the furniture when Christmas was over, packed our suitcases, and a trunk, and we left Osoyoos for good. It had not been a good place for us and I was glad to leave.

Our daughter was now just over a year old and the boys were now four and six. On the way we stopped at Tarrys where my mother lived. I talked to her about the situation and asked her if we could leave the boys with her until we could find a place in Kimberley. She said she was glad to do it.

My wife and I left Tarrys the next morning on the bus. It was a slow trip so we didn't arrive in Kimberley until the evening. We took a hotel room and the next day found another room. This would have to do until we could find a bigger place where we could have the boys with us. All of this took a few days to get done, while I was working. However, it all got done and the work was going very well. We finished the hoist room, then the idle tower, and then started on the head frame and the ore bin.

The head frame was to be 120 feet high. The crane we had was only able to reach halfway for the erection. So, we had to erect all of the top part with a gin pole. This all worked out O.K. and we were able to make good time. We had an air power tugger for hoisting. The ore bin was erected with the crawler crane. For the sloping runway between the ore bin and the head frame, we converted our gin pole into a Chicago boom. This we hung from the head frame tower and again used the air tugger for a hoist.

After all the steel was erected we made up another rivet gang. For the next month we all worked at the job of riveting. This continued until we finished the job, which was the middle of March. My son Joe had now started school and I did not want to move again at this time. So, I took a job as a carpenter. There was very little difference in the wages, and there was a lot of carpenter work at the time. My working partner was Walter Olson, a good fellow to work with. Our first job was to place all of the window casings in the existing steel frames. These steel frames were already in all the wall girts throughout the structure. After making up the wood casings, they were drilled and bolted to the steel frames to be ready for the window sash. Then we tackled the doors. This work lasted until about May, at which time Bennet and White got the contract in downtown Kimberley to build the Stedman store.

Lars Paulson was the carpenter foreman for the company. He wanted me to work for him on this job. This building had to have the basement excavated. The store was between two other buildings. The space was only 30 feet wide. There was no excavating equipment on hand or in the area. The basement had to be excavated to a depth of at least 15 feet. The only piece of equipment available was a small dump truck. The company did not have an excavation plan. Lars Paulson asked me if I had any idea of how to take the muck out. I told him that there were a lot of young high school kids looking for work. We could hire them for the job. We also had to get the muck into the dump truck. I told him we could build a platform and a derrick and use the concrete buggies. He asked me if it could work. I told him I was sure it would.

Here is what we did to handle the job. At the rear of the building where there would be no excavating, we built a platform that was high enough for concrete buggies to dump into the dump truck with a small stiffleg derrick mounted and anchored to the platform. The buggies could be loaded by hand by the labourers. The buggies were then hoisted to the platform and then dumped into the dump truck. It took a few days to build a platform and the derrick. Then the high school kids went to work and the dirt started to move. The company hired six or seven kids and they kept the dump truck busy hauling away the muck. The basement kept getting bigger and the carpenters soon went to work on the basement forms. It was while we were on this job that the Bennet & White Co. was awarded the contract for the tunnel job at the 3650 level that would become the main haulage way for the Sullivan mine.

At this time the job at the store was going well. The excavating was going very well, and the forms were following. The City of Kimberley at this time did not have ice in the arena. A number of people had formed what was known as the Kimberley Artificial Ice Society. The people at the head of this society were the city engineer, Stan Shaler, and Phil Barret, one of the Cominco head engineers.

The arena in Kimberley was an older wooden structure and they had the idea that it could be enlarged by moving out the end wall at the east end of the building. Stan Shaler and Phil Barret came to the store job to see me and Lars Paulson to see if their idea was feasible. We went with them to the arena to look things over and discuss the project. I asked what equipment we would be able to get for the job. The answer was none, other than some hand rigging such as hand winches and chain falls. I also asked if we could borrow some steel rails from the tunnel job, which we could. "What about man power?", I asked. Yes, we had volunteers. They asked if the east end wall could be saved. I said it could, and that I could move it in a standing position. They said O.K. and to leave Bennet and White for a while and that I would go on the payroll. Lars would look after the carpenter work and I would look after moving the wall. Everyone agreed with that plan.

Lars arranged for another man to look after the carpenter work at the store, and we started at the arena. To move the big wall we would first of all have to shore up the roof. This required some long timber. I told Stan Shaler I would need some of the city's power poles. He said he would send for some. Then I got some cable and chain falls from Cominco and a hand winch. Chokers I could make myself, which I did.

The help was mostly hockey players in their spare time when they were away form their regular jobs at Cominco. These fellows were all willing workers. Then I borrowed some steel rails from the tunnel job to carry the wall. Next I got the carpenters to cut some holes in the bottom part of the wall and to reinforce the holes on the upper side where the wall would rest on the rails. The existing trusses were spaced at 18 feet, so that would be the distance to move the wall. The first move though would only be far enough to clear the roof. Then we used the wall for false work and scaffold for support, and also as a pattern for the new truss. I placed several sets of guy lines on both sides of the wall with chokers and rope falls.

Then, with a hand winch on the outer side of the wall, a chain hoist on the inside for safety, and a little grease on the rails, we skidded the wall ahead by leaning the wall with the rope falls slightly to the outside and holding with the ones on the inside. Then we placed scaffold brackets on the wall to hold the working scaffold for the building of the truss. The trusses were one hundred feet in length in a horizontal measurement with a depth of 6 feet and built to a curvature of 75 feet in radius. There was only one truss to build and then move the wall out to its final position. This would give them enough room for a standard size ice sheet and room for a grand stand on the east end of the arena. Also, there was room under the seats for dressing rooms. The roof was made to match the existing roof.

While this work was in progress, the carpenters were busy building the ice plant out side the existing curling rink. There were a lot of people around the town that had never seen any construction of this kind and were very surprised to see the wall of the arena in its final position. They were happy to know that Kimberley would have a full-sized arena. Kimberely was a real hockey town. It was the Kimberly Dynameters that first won the Allen Cup for the province of B.C. In 1938 they toured Europe.

It was at this time that the Bennet and White Co. had started work on the tunnel project at the 3650 level. This would be a fairly large project. There was two miles of tunnel to drive. The portal would include a section at the outside of the hill that would be all reinforced concrete poured in place before the driving of the tunnel could start. This would be a job for Lars, and the company wanted me to look after all the freight that was starting to arrive daily. There was material for the camp that was being built for the tunnel, such as the compressor house, etc.

This contract with the Bennet and White Co. also included the construction of the railway grade from the tunnel to the Chapman camp concentrator. This was two miles of railway grade, which included a cut in the hill that would be 100 feet deep and a quarter mile in length. Then, it involved a fill of another quarter of a mile, which would be 100 feet deep – the remainder built along the side of a hill. All together this amounted to a good-sized project. The finished size of the tunnel was seven by nine feet. The first part of the tunnel required timbering for 2,000 feet. The railway track for the tunnel was a 3-foot gauge with 72-lb rail. The timber for the tunnel was all creosoted. All posts were 10"x12". Caps were also 10"x12". All lagging was 4"x12". The spacing between the bents was only eight feet. The lagging is the roof in a timber tunnel. All of this timber and rails had to be supplied in the proper sequence each day and all according to the footage that was being made by the miners that were driving the tunnel.

The tunnel progress was very slow. The ground was very tough and it was often hard to get timbers in place. The main difficulty seemed to be that Bennet and White had taken on the job at too low a price and were constantly going broke on the job. By the time they were into the mountain about 2,000 feet, they decided to call it quits. Cominco took over all of the Bennet and White equipment. The job was taken over by the Northern Construction Co. They absorbed most of the existing labour force. This was the end of the line for Bennet and White in Kimberley.

My job with Northern Construction continued on much the same. Then in May 1948 there was a spell of hot weather and Mark Creek, which flows through Kimberley went on a rampage and was raising hell. I was sent to the creek to help control the flood. What a job that was.

There were hundreds of tons of debris coming down the creek in the form of stumps, trees, logs, etc. The creek started to run wild and ran down the streets. The City of Kimberley had all of their workmen on the job trying to relieve the situation, but it was almost hopeless. Cominco came to the aid of the city. They supplied a couple of D-8 cats and also a crawler crane with a dragline bucket, which could remove a lot of the stumps and logs and other debris.

There were some houses that had been built very close to the creek. These were being flooded and washed away. There was one large house beside the creek just below the Wallenger Street Bridge. The basement of this house was already flooded. The mayor asked me if it could be saved. I said it could, if there was enough help. He told me to take charge and call on any of the men that I needed. I sent a truck and some men to the tunnel yard to get two 40-foot 12"x12" timbers to place under the house. We got these and pulled them through under the house. We then got cables over the roof and fastened them to the timber on both ends. There was a big pile of wood in the yard. I had this thrown into the basement to support the end of the timber when the house would be moved ahead with the Cat that was being hitched to the timber. All of this work was done in a short time because there was plenty of help. I gave the signal to go ahead on the cat and in a very short time the house was sitting high and dry in the yard. Now it could have a new foundation and would be livable again. Everyone concerned seemed satisfied.

At the lower end of town there was a big blockage of large trees and stumps. We were able to remove this with a D-8 Cat. One thing about this job was that there was no shortage of help. Also, we had the use of the equipment from Cominco. The city had just about come to the end of their rope, so it was a good thing that Cominco was there. Cominco had sent down some miners to take care of any blasting that might have to be done.

At the top end of town there was another big blockage of stumps and trees. The dragline could not reach all of this. It was actually forming a dam in the creek. The miners had been trying to open the dam but they had only been using light charges and the dam was continuing to rebuild with new debris. I asked Howard Rainer, the miner in charge of the miners, how much powder they had. He said they had 70 sticks of powder left. I asked him if he had any prima cord. He said yes so I said we should place the powder in 3 bundles and hook these together with prima cord so that we could blow that log jam to hell and out of here. He said OK, as long as I had the authority. I said I did. We sent men up and down the creek on both sides and moved everyone out of the area. The blast was fired. The dam was broken and the creek was lowered almost immediately. After this incident, the remainder of the clean up on the creek was a lot more simple and soon we were able to start repairing the creek bed where it had been washed out with the high water.

We started on this work immediately. But, I found that we were now rather short-handed because a lot of men had returned to their regular jobs. So, some days I had to drive a truck and sometimes run a cat. I rather liked both of these jobs as they were both interesting. This did not take very long and when it was done the creek looked an awful lot better. At this time, the Northern Construction Co. received the contract to build the sink and float plant at the Chapman camp concentrator.

CHAPTER 24

Sink and float plant and underground crushing chamber, Kimberley, 1948-49

THE NORTHERN CONSTRUCTION CO. RECEIVED the contract to build the Sink and Float plant at the Chapman Camp Concentrator. This would be a fair sized job and would be all structural steel. Northern hired a crew of ironworkers from the union hall in Vancouver and when they arrived, I went to work with them. Most of them I had known and worked with before, and there were some new faces among them.

For the steel erection, we had a northwest crawler crane that could handle 20 tons with a 60-foot boom. This machine did not have a jib with it, so we used a piece of 12"x12" timber and with some angle irons, bolts, and some cable we made a good substantial jib capable of handling a couple of tons. It projected over the main boom about 15 feet, which was all we needed for this job. We also had an older model P&H crawler crane that could be used for unloading and yard work.

There was some heavy steel in the building and also some heavy machinery to place. Also, all of the structural steel had to be riveted.

We also placed all of the transit cladding on the steel after erection. Our total crew was about 20 men and the job lasted until Christmas 1948. Then there was something new to tackle. Northern Construction wanted us to go underground to construct the crushing chamber. We started right after the New Year.

The crushing chamber was located 2 miles underground at the end of the new tunnel. To reach the crushing chamber there was a raise of about 400 feet. This brought you to the upper section of the chamber. The first job in the chamber was the overhead crane. When the mining of the chamber had taken place on both the north and south sides of the chamber, they mined out a series of coyote holes in which beams were placed and concreted in to support the crane run. The miners had also drilled holes and driven in eyebolts, which could be used for hanging rigging from the roof or back, as it was called in a mine.

From these eyebolts we hung catwalks along both sides which were our working scaffold for the job of placing the beams in the coyote holes. These beams all had to be set at the exact line and level to support the longitudinal beams that in turn supported the overhead crane. All of these beams were then braced with iron supports and then concreted in, after which we placed the crane beams. After placing the crane beams, which was a rather tricky job working from the catwalk, we hung the rigging with which to erect the crane. This was not an easy job either.

Everything we installed in the crushing chamber had to be loaded on flat cars outside and brought in and up the raise to the top of the crushing chamber. There was a fairly big hoist powered by air in the crushing chamber to haul the cars to the top level. The raise was 400 feet and the vertical lift was 120 feet.

The crane came pre-assembled with the beams, stiffeners, and hoist all in one assembly. A tough job to handle at any time, let alone doing the job in a place like this hole. We did this job on the Easter weekend when it would be quiet and no other work going on in the area. All went well.

The overhead crane had a capacity of 20 tons. When the crusher came it was 17 tons. When the crusher was loaded on a flat car at the outside of the tunnel, it looked like it would be a little too big, but it cleared the tunnel timbers by several inches. But it was hauled through the tunnel on a real slow order and it arrived safely. Now, to haul it up the raise was another time consuming and tricky piece of business. Most of the loads being hauled up the raise could be handled with a single line, but for the crusher we would have to use two parts of line, and the line was not long enough. So, we extended the hitch with long heavy chokers.

We had men following the car with chalk blocks and safety ties. When a choker was removed, the load held safely in this manner. It was a slow trip up the raise but all went O.K. and the crusher arrived in the crushing chamber in good shape. At this point it could be handled with the overhead crane to its final position. Then we had a few more conveyors to build and our underground work would be finished. This was now the end of June 1949.

When we came out from the tunnel on the last day of underground work, Floyd Chase, the project manager, was waiting for me. He signaled that we wanted to see me. I stepped off the train to see what he wanted. He asked if we were all finished. I said yes and that it is all ready for Cominco to take over. He then said he had something else for me.

Cominco had asked if Chase could retain me to take over the townsite job and bring it to completion. I said that would be OK, but first I would like a holiday after being in that hole for the last 6 months. Chased said that was O.K., so I went home. About a week later I went with Chase to look over the job.

There was a lot of work to look after. There were breaks in the water lines, breaks in the sewer lines, roads to upgrade, lanes to grade, yards to be cleaned up, brush to remove, gravel to be hauled, sand to be hauled for the pipe lines, and a hundred and one other things to take of.

This town site project was known as the Lois Creek town site. It was a subdivision containing 170 new houses. Because the tunnel and crushing chamber jobs had come to an end, there were some good men available. I was able to get some of these men for the town site project.

I made up four crews for the job. One crew was for the yards – to take care of the clean up and removal of all brush, but to be careful and leave any good shade trees. Another crew was to look after the streets and lanes. A third and fourth crew was to work on the water line and sewer line breaks. There were a total of 90 breaks in the sewer lines and 120 breaks in the water lines. What a hell of a mess for a brand new subdivision – a disgrace to any man who would call himself a construction foreman or supervisor.

One good thing though, was that we had all the equipment we needed for any part of the project. We had several cats, a good road grader, a power shovel, and all the hired trucks that we needed. We also had good summer weather and good men all willing to work.

When a water or sewer line break was dup up and repaired, it was all backfilled with sand to a good depth before any rough material was allowed to be dumped into the pipe ditch. For streets and lanes, we had the power shovel and about 5 trucks and a grader going steady. The crew on the yards were going steady and doing a good job, as well as the men doing the repairs on the water and sewer lines. As houses became available, people were wanting to move into them.

To give an example of how careless the job had been handled previously, here is one. Syd Smith was the administrator for the Cominco housing project. When a family moved into a house and something was not in order, he would call me to let me know so that the situation could be rectified. One morning he called me to tell me that a family had moved into a house on Fernie Street and that their sewer drain was not working. I went to the house to find that the drain from the basement was not working. I had the men run a sewer snake from the basement drain out towards the street and take the measurement. We did the same from the manhole in the street to measure it. We found a difference of about 9 feet. We dug this area up with a cat to find no sewer pipes for 9 feet. We cleaned out the ditch and placed new pipes and everything worked fine.

On this housing project, there had been a job superintendent, a city of Kimberley inspector, and an inspector from Cominco. There should have been no reason for this kind of careless work. The ditch was refilled and we left the people happy.

We continued with our work making sure of everything as we progressed. Floyd Chase, the manager for Northern Construction, paid us a visit at least once a week to see how the progress was. He always went away satisfied that all was O.K. We worked 5 days a week, and we never work any overtime. We finished the project in early October and shipped out the equipment. We were on time and under the budget allowance. Another job finished!

At this time, Cominco had a job at the concentrator. The job was to build a big settling tank to hold the slush or medium from their new rod mill that had been installed for the new sink and float plant. This was a 120-foot-diameter settling tank with a big hub in the centre on which to mount a big rake for stirring the medium. I worked on this project as a carpenter.

There were some special forms to be made for the hub, for which patterns had to be made. The job superintendent was a fellow by the name of Harold Andrews. He asked some of his regular carpenters if they could do this, and they said no. He came to me about it and I said that I thought I knew how. He asked me to show him what I had in mind. I gave him the idea but told him we would need access to a carpenter shop band saw. He said we could get one on the afternoon shift. I said O.K., and that we could make a platform right there on which to draw the patterns and then send them to the carpenter shop to be cut on the band saw. He said he would arrange for a couple of men to go on the afternoon shift and start the next day. I then told him I would start on the patterns and could have the first ones ready for the shop by quitting time the next day. We proceeded with this and it all worked out fine. When the forms went into place, they all fit perfectly.

This project lasted until the end of the year. Shortly thereafter, there was a call from the union hall to work on some bridges in the Fernie area, which I took.

CHAPTER 25

East Kootenay Bridges, 1950

AT THIS TIME THERE WERE three bridges to build in the East Kootenay district on number 3 highway – one at Natal, one at Michell, and one at McGillivary. The crew stayed in the town of Fernie and ate in the restaurants, but they were not able to have their noon meal at the Michell hotel, because transportation to and from work there was via a truck crummy.

The first bridge we erected was the one at the upper end of Natal, then the one at Michell, then the third one at McGillivray, and the last one down near Creston over the Goat River. For the unloading and steel erection we had a new Loraine mobile truck crane with a real good operator.

The steel all came by rail. It was unloaded and transferred to trucks for transport to the bridge site. The erection work all went well with rivet gangs following along. I worked in the raising gang connecting steel until the erection was complete. Then I took over a rivet forge. It was a surprising thing that a lot of ironworkers never learned the art of heating rivets, while some rivet heaters never learned much else. I learned to heat rivets during my first years of ironwork.

All of these bridges were the through truss type – mostly 180-foot spans with beam span approaches. At this time, I was still living in Kimberley, but managed to get home on weekends. It was on a Friday morning when we were unloading the steel for the bridge at McGillvary. It was the 17th of March. A hell of a snowstorm came in a real blizzard. At McGillvary there was no siding on the railway, so the CPR gave us a hot spot for unloading. That is, they brought the railway cars there with the locomotive and held the cars there while we unloaded them. The snow was blowing like hell and the men worked like hell to get all of the iron unloaded. As soon as the last piece of iron was out of the rail car, the signal was given to the locomotive engineer. He blew the whistle and went back down the grade to Fernie.

The crane operator shut the crane down and the men all jumped into the crummy and headed for the hotel in Fernie. I was going to go home to Kimberley, but the highway was blocked with a snow slide at Elcho so I had to stay in Fernie. That evening, being the 17th of Ireland, there was a lot of celebrating and drinking going on in all the hotels. Our crew was doing their share. There was also a big dance that night.

Late in the evening a fight broke out in the barroom and ended up in the hotel lobby. I am not sure how this fight started, but fists were flying in all directions and a good number of black eyes delivered. After a while they settled down and realized that their fighting was not doing any good, and they all became good buddies again. There is a story told that the ironworkers have a creed: a bottle of blond and a battle – although not always in that order. I don't know what the order was that night, but there sure was a battle.

At the Michell hotel, where the crew always ate lunch, there was a big round table where the raising gang always sat together. The waitress was a nice looking blond girl. The men used to call her dreamboat, which was the name of a popular song at the time. Anyway, on the Monday following the fight in Fernie, the crew all sat in their usual places when they came in for lunch. Dreamboat came to take their orders. When she looked at them, she could not believe her eyes. Among the crew there were five black eyes and one of the men, Jim English, had two. She looked them over again and shook her head. After looking them over again, she finally took their orders and the crew got their meal —then finally a lot of laughs.

On different jobs and different places, there were a lot of men in the ironworkers that at some time in their life had been professional boxers or wrestlers. Some were just rough and ready fighters, so it was wise not to get into too many arguments.

When we finished these three bridges in this area, we had one more to erect down near Creston over the Goat River. For this job we stayed in Creston at some of the hotels there and again travelling to work in the truck crummy. The bridge steel was off-loaded at the rail siding at Kitchener and hauled to the bridge site by truck.

The bridge work lasted until near the end of May and then we were all laid off. I went home to Kimberley to wait for another job. About the end of June a call came for the overpass job over the CPR railway at the east end of Cranbrook to eliminate the level crossing where there had been several accidents. At the same time, a call came for a job in Trail at the smelter for the Dom. Bridge Co. I decided this would be the better of the two jobs, so that is the one I took.

CHAPTER 26

Tadanac Cominco Smelter and the Nordeg Briquetting Plant, 1950-51

THE PROJECT THAT THE DOMINION Bridge Co. had at the smelter was actually two different jobs. One was the new bag house at the lead smelter. The other one was to replace the roof trusses at the No. 2 tank room. Bert Richardson was the foreman on the bag house job, and I took on the tank room job.

The bag house job was all heavy columns and beams for which the company had shipped a guy derrick and a steam donkey engine. The tank room job was mostly hand work, although we had the use of a small derrick on the side of the building with which we could hoist the steel to the working level and then wrestle it the rest of the way into place by hand. The big item here was to be able to keep the tank room production going while we worked above the main tank room floor.

The zinc tank rooms were the places where the zinc was recovered from the zinc sulfate medium. The zinc sulfate ran into the tanks by gravity. The tank room floor was on a slope for this to happen. The tanks were concrete and they were in rows. Each tank was a little higher than the one next in line. There were a large number of these rows of tanks.

In the tanks, the anodes are placed, and through a system of electrolysis the zinc is recovered in a sheet on each side of the anode. It took 24 hours for the zinc to collect on the anode sheets. To protect this working area we covered the area in which we would be working with planks so that nothing would be dropped on the men on the tank room floor. The tank rooms were a rather miserable place to work as there was sometimes a lot of gas from the sulfuric acid in the tanks. Also, the acid in the dust that is on everything eats away at your clothes. On account of these conditions, Cominco supplied the men with woolen clothes because the acid did not affect wool. Cominco had its own tailor shop for this purpose. So, you would see all of the men in gray blanket cloth.

Before any dismantling of a truss could take place we had to support the truss. We did this by placing a system of hydraulic jacks and pipe posts under the bottom chord of the truss at three equal spaces. Then we cut away the pieces of the truss on one side only. These pieces were cut small enough that they could be handled by hand. For the job of cutting the iron, we had several oxy-acetylene torches. When half of the truss was removed, we started to replace it with the new iron. These trusses were 85 feet long and eight feet deep at the centre. The weight of each truss was about 12 tons.

As soon as one truss was complete, pinned, and bolted, we drove the rivets and then moved all the planking to the next one. These trusses were all made from heavy material. Top chords were two 6"×6" angles, and the bottom chords were similar. A lot of cutting had to be done so that the pieces could be man handled. There were 12 of these trusses to dismantle and rebuild. We averaged one a week. This lasted until the third week of October, at which time we received the job to erect the trusses for the high school auditorium in Rossland.

These were also large trusses – 100 feet long with a depth of 12 feet. The auditorium was 100 x 100 feet. There were six of these trusses to build and erect, and they all had to be riveted. For the erection, we had the Loraine mobile truck crane. The crew was still staying in the Cominco bunkhouse at Tadanac. When this job at Rossland was finished, we got another one of the same size to do at the Lloyd Crowe High School in East Trail. By the time all of this was finished, it was Christmas so there were few days of holiday left.

At this time the bag house building was all in place, but a lot of work still remained. There was still work to be done inside and some big gas flues to be built on the outside of the building. This is where I went with my crew when the Christmas holidays were over. The first job I tackled there was the big smoke flues on the outside of the building. These flues carried the smoke into the smaller flues where there were bags that caught the flue dust. The main purpose of the bag house was for the hundreds of bags that were installed there to catch the dust, and at the same time produce cleaner smoke before the smoke reached the smoke stack.

Beside the big outside flues there were smaller ones to be built inside the building and hoppers, and other allied equipment. Also at this time, some of the men were busy placing the bags that would hang under the flues. These bags were the dust catchers. There were hundreds of these bags in place. This work lasted until March. The guy derrick and steam donkey engine were stored in the Cominco equipment yard. The crew all returned to Vancouver.

I also went to Vancouver at this time. Dom. Bridge had acquired all of the structural steel from the old B.C. Electric building that had been dismantled downtown on main street. This was the old gas plant. This steel was erected at the Dom. Bridge plant in Burnaby and became the erection shed for their erection department. We had been working on this job for a couple of weeks when one day John Prescott came to see me about some work.

He said that there was plenty of work ahead but it would be held up waiting for a shipload of steel that was coming from Europe, and it was not due for some time. He also told me that he had a telephone call from the Calgary office asking for a crew of men. He thought because I lived up in the Kootenay country that I would like to go. He asked me to find out if some of the crew wanted to take this job. I talked it over with some of the men and soon had a crew ready to go. By the following Saturday five of us were on our way to Calgary.

When we arrived in Calgary we went to the Dom. Bridge office where we found out that the job was in Nordeg Alberta, which is 120 miles west of Red Deer. We made the trip O.K. but it was one hell of a road from Rocky Mountain House to Nordeg. The job there was to rebuild a coal briquetting plant that had been destroyed by fire. The steel for the job was fabricated at the Dom. Bridge Calgary shops and shipped by C.N. Rail to Nordeg. We stayed in a large boarding house across the street from the Nordeg Hotel —good clean rooms and home cooking.

The Calgary branch had not yet acquired any mobile cranes so we had to erect a 12-ton stiff leg derrick for the steel erection, and another smaller one for the unloading of the steel and equipment at the rail site. Then the material was all trucked to the job site. After erection, all the steel had to be riveted.

The power for the derrick was a steam donkey engine and most of the crew had not worked with steam power. This derrick did not have a bullwheel for the swing, but used the old rope swing system. This was done by fastening a 1.5" rope on each side of the top end of the boom then through snatch blocks to lead to the nigger head drums that were on the outside of the donkey engine. These drums were on the same shafts that power the load and boom drums. These ropes were given a few turns around the drums and the man doing this job was known as the swingman. As the left rope was held tight and the slack taken in, the right hand rope was slackened and the boom swung to the left. Reverse the order and the boom swung to the right. If the swingman knew anything about steam power, he could also fire the boiler and look after the injector to keep water in the boiler.

The foreman was a fellow by the name of Tony Babyak, a good ironworker and a nice fellow. He asked the men if they knew how to handle this swing system. I was the only one familiar with the swing job. This was the same system used on the old railroad derrick cars on which I had experience. I took over the swing job and the erection went at a good rate.

One day some time later, the boiler was acting up. It was hard to keep steam up to proper pressure and some tubes were leaking. Tony ordered some new tubes from Calgary. He came to me and asked me if I knew how to install the new tubes and roll them, since Fred the operating engineer didn't know how to do the job. He said he didn't think there was any part of the job that I couldn't do. We both laughed and I told him that I could do the tube job.

The tubes arrived from Calgary. With Fred the engineer as my helper, we removed the faulty tubes and installed the new ones and had the boiler ready for Monday morning. It was a hell of a cold weekend. We had been getting a lot of snowstorms and a couple of weeks later on a Friday morning we had a lot of it. Some of the crew decided that this would be a good time to have an extra day off for the weekend and go to town. A carload of them did this. But, later that morning the weather cleared so Tony suggested we make up a rivet gang and get half a day in.

"Joe" he said, "I bet you know how to heat rivets." I said yes and that I would handle the forge. Tony said he would catch and stick, Bill Wright could drive, and hammerhead the apprentice could buck up. We went to work and the weather had cleared up. I fired up the rivet forge and the other fellows got the scaffold ready. I took the rivet count for the first point and got the rivets ready. Tony rapped on his catch can for a rivet. The point the men were on was directly across from my forge. I took the rivet out of the forge with the tongs and threw it overhand to Tony. I continued this for several more rivets but Tony waived for a stop. I went over to see if something was wrong and then Tony asked if I would please throw the rivets with an underhand throw. He said that he was deathly scared of the overhand throw. I changed to underhand. He had never caught rivets thrown overhand.

The work continued and the plant took shape and summer was coming on. The briquetting machines were in place along with the conveyors and a lot of work was coming to the finishing stages. This was now the last week in June. I received a message from John Prescott to have the crew in Trail for the first week in July. At this time I was still living in Castlegar and the crew all wanted to go home to Vancouver before going to Trail. I told them to go ahead that that I would catch a ride to Red Deer with the policeman who is going out tomorrow, and then catch the bus there to Trail.

I rode out with the local R.C.M.P. in a jeep to Red Deer. I said goodbye to the policeman and caught the bus and arrived home to Castlegar on the weekend.

CHAPTER 27

Trail Smelter, Sinter Plant Trestle, and Rock Creek Canyon, 1951

I ARRIVED HOME TO CASTLEGAR on the weekend. It was the Dominion Day holiday. After the holiday I went to Trail. The crew had arrived from Vancouver. The job here was to build a railway trestle from an area near the lead refinery to the location of the new sinter plant where the lead concentrate was smelted. This was so that the carloads of lead concentrate could be unloaded directly into the ore bins at the furnace area.

The trestle job was a system of steel bents, bracing, and heavy girders to support railway traffic. For the erection work we had the 20-ton Loraine crane. The steel for the job was all received by rail from Vancouver. We didn't have much working room since we were working between existing buildings of the Cominco complex.

While unloading and sorting, we placed the girders that would be used last, on the bottom of the stack on good solid timbers and stacked several tier deep. After the first set of posts and girders we found that the width of the crane wheels matched the girders, so we could run the crane directly on the girders without using any timber decking. As soon as a couple of sections were in place, a rivet gang started to follow up with the rivet job.

All told, this trestle was several hundred feet long, but everything went like clockwork. When this trestle was complete, we loaded out the guy derrick and the steam donkey engine on trucks to take to Riondel on Kootenay Lake. They would be used at a later date for the erection of the head frame and ore bins at the Blue Bell Mine. For this hauling job we used two big low-bed trucks from the Arrow Transfer Co. of Vancouver.

This job was accomplished in one long day. After we had finished the unloading at Riondel, and had arrived at the Kootenay Lake ferry, we had to wait for the ferry. So, we all had a swim in the Lake, and then a steak supper in the Kookanoosa Lodge where there was a beautiful dinning room. This was the place that if you owned a cattle brand, you could have it burned into the wall by the big fireplace. There were brands from all over the United States and Canada. But, a few years later, the place burned down.

Next we had a small project up on the mountains above Salmo to build a small mill building for the Can. Ex. Mine. This was a small job which only took a about 10 days. When this was finished we all left for the Rock Creek Canyon Bridge. This bridge was the highest bridge in the British Empire at the time.

Then the work in the area around Trail was finished, we went to Rock Creek to build the big bridge over the canyon. By the time I arrived at the Rock Canyon bridge site, it was the 4th week of July. Vic Bratt had already started the steel erection on the anchor span on the west end of the bridge. We arrived on a Sunday. The camp was at the west end of the bridge site. There were several bunkhouses, a cook house, and a separate building for a wash room.

Vic Bratt was the foreman on this job. Vic was a good man to work with. I ran one of the erection crews. We finished the first span and started the next span. The second span had a false work bent on the west side of the canyon, and also secured to the first span with large pins to become part of the cantilever erection method. After reaching the false work bent, we set up the steam donkey at the edge of the canyon. This was used for hoisting the tower steel. On the canyon wall we had a small footing poured that would become the base for the derrick boom that would be used for erecting the tower. The boom falls for this were harnessed to the second span above the donkey engine. The swing was handled with rope falls on either side of the boom. The boom and load falls were each reeved up with four parts of ¾" line.

The steel for the tower was unloaded from trucks and transferred to a big sled we had made for this purpose, one section at a time. These sections were just like a big girder and weighed about 12 tons each. Each section was skidded on the sled down the side of canyon on the road that was made previously for accessing the concrete piers.

There were six of these girder sections for each tower plus the diagonal bracing and the level struts. When erected, the tower was 102 feet above the pier, which was already 185 feet above the creek. All the tower steel was handled by the derrick boom, which was anchored on the side of the canyon. This type of boom was called a Chicago boom.

When the west side tower was complete, the donkey engine and boom and all of the rigging were moved to the east side of the bridge to await the rest of the construction. The west span of the bridge was then built out past the false work to a point that would be two bridge panels west of the tower. From this point we had to place the plumb posts on top of the tower legs, and then connect the bottom chord of the truss to the bottom of the plumb post. This was the most dangerous and tricky part of the bridge erection work. These plumb posts weighed approximately 9 tons. While the mobile crane was working on the bridge deck, we had a smaller one for the yard work to supply the crane on the bridge. This was known as the bullmoose. It was rigged with a very short boom and could carry these heavy loads out onto the bridge where the mobile crane could take over.

To place these 9-ton posts on the tower meant the crane had to reach over 40 feet. Now, this was known as a 20-ton crane, which was true. But, that was 20 tons with a 30-foot boom at a 10-foot radius. For this job, we were using a 60-foot boom at a radius of more than 40 feet. Here is how we handled these heavy loads. We brought the crane as far forward as possible on the deck. Then all the outrigger beams were blocked double and lashed down to the bridge steel. The load was picked up at about a 10-foot radius and then the boom swung around to the position where it was boomed out to set the load. Then we hooked a heavy set of rope falls to the boom gantry. As the boom was lowered to position, the rope falls were slacked at the same time. Everything worked fine. The big plumb post fastened into place on top of the tower. The next one was done in the same manner and all the crew breathed a big sigh of relief. This same operation was repeated twice again on the east end of the bridge. Thousands of people drive over bridges everyday, but have no conception of how the bridges were built or the risk the ironworkers take to build them.

With the plumb posts in place we connected the west span to the tower and got started on the centre span, which was all hung by the cantilever method to the centre of the bridge. When the centre span of the bridge was halfway, we moved all of the operation to the east end of the bridge and erected the east end in the same manner.

The rivet gangs were following right along as there were thousands of rivets to drive. On the tower, the rivet gang set up the heater's forge at the top of the tower and ran a pipe from the forge to the rivet scaffold with a bucket at the bottom of the pipe to catch the rivets. It worked very well.

We erected the east end of the bridge in exactly the same manner that we had used on the west end. Because the side of the canyon was steeper, and a harder place to work, we rigged up a telephone for the hoist engineer on the donkey engine. One morning I was on the phone and I could hear Bobbie Robertson mumbling about these goddamned telephone systems. He sure didn't like them. I called Red Higham so that he could take the phone and give the signals directly to Bobbie. He cooled down and everything went O.K.

An item of interest here when we were ready to start the tower erection. The cat that had been hired for the job of taking the tower sections down the canyon had arrived, but the cat skinner would not arrive until the afternoon bus. But, we were ready to erect steel and we need the first tower section of the tower. In fact, we had it on the sled waiting. We had to get this section down the canyon to the tower site. Our crane operators had never operated a cat. Our construction engineer Don Jaimeson came to me and said he had heard that I had driven cat a lot when I had been in Kimberley. He asked me if I could do it. I said I could if it was O.K. with the hoisting engineers. Together with Vic Bratt the general foreman they talked to Bobbie Robertson and Charlie Guiser, the operator on the Loraine crane. They said sure, "go ahead".

Now, this was an Allis Chalmers cat and I had never driven one of these. I had only worked on Caterpillar equipment. I looked it over, figured out how to start it, checked the oil and fuel, and warmed it up. We hooked on the sled and the machine was running well. This side of the canyon was quite steep, so I took it real easy. I got the sled and the tower section down to the unloading place O.K. The sled was off-loaded and then I made it back up the canyon side O.K. I got a big smile and congratulations from the crew.

We erected this section, then the cat skinner arrived on the bus at noon and everything went O.K. from here on. With the tower in place we erected the remainder of the bridge. The erection work all went very well. The weather held, good rivets were driven, and everything progressed. About the middle of September the government inspector asked me if I had figured out what date we would close the span. The inspector was an old time ironworker by the name of Johnny McCormick. I told Johnny that I would figure it out that night and give him an answer the next day.

That night, in the bunkhouse, I did some figuring and allowing some time for weather machine, hold ups, etc. I had an answer. I met Johnny the next morning on the bridge. I told him the closing date would be the 27th of October.

Well, time went on, and on the 27th of October we jacked the span on the east end. We used two 50-ton jacks for this. We only had to raise the east end 1¼" to bring the bottom chord into alignment and connect the chord. Hurray the bridge was joined! It was 3 pm, October 27th. Not too bad an estimate.

The top chords were a fraction long due to the afternoon sun. Some bolts were placed in one end. The other end needed a fraction to go into place. The men asked "what now"? I said that the chords are safe and that it was quitting time. I suggested we go back to camp and that the chords will fit in the morning. The next morning, with a tap from a sledgehammer, the chords dropped into place. The cool night temperature had taken care of the trouble. The morning temperature was only about 40° F. All bridges expand and contract with the changes in temperature. When travelling over a bridge you might notice some places that look like a big set of fingers. That is an expansion joint where the bridge sits or rests. One end of the span is a fixed end held in place with anchor bolts. The other end of the span is the expansion end where the bridge shoe rests on a roller bed. That allows it to move when the bridge expands or contracts. The span does not get out of line because the anchor bolts are held in a slot in the bridge shoe.

A bridge is slightly longer on a hot summer day than on a cold winter day. The deck of a suspension bridge is slightly lower on a hot day than it is on a cold winter day. Here is a rough rule of thumb concerning expansion and contraction for bridges: the amount of expansion or contraction is roughly ⅛th of an inch per 100 feet of bridge for every 10 degrees change in temperature.

Now, we had to finish all of the riveting, place all of the railings, the expansion joints, and clean up any and all details. The general contractor could then pour the concrete deck and the people would have a wonderful bridge, and the distance between Rock Creek and Osoyoos was then 3.5 miles shorter.

About the third week in November I received a call from Harry Minshall. He was the erection manager of the Pacific Division of the Dominion Bridge Co. He asked me to meet him at the Castlegar airport. He wanted me to go with him and look at the upcoming project at Kootenay Lake.

I met Harry at the airport. We had lunch in Nelson then drove to Kootenay Lake to look at the proposed cable crossing, then to Riondel to the head frame site. He wanted me to start at Riondel as soon as we could have a crew of ironworkers there. I drove Harry back to the airport where he would catch the next flight to Vancouver.

CHAPTER 28

Riondel Head Frame, 1951-52

AFTER LEAVING HARRY MINSHALL AT the Castlegar airport I went home to pack by bags to go to Riondel for the head frame job. I was still living in Castlegar at this time. Harry ordered a crew from the Union Hall when he arrived in Vancouver. Some of these men were with me throughout the Rock Creek Canyon job. This project would last through the winter.

The steel for the job was delivered by railway cars on the C.P.R. barges to the Riondel wharf where we off-loaded the material with the Loraine mobile crane. For the head frame erection and the ore bin, we used the mobile crane and we also set up a guy derrick because the crane was not capable of reaching the top part of the structure. Even then we had to make a jib for the guy derrick boom to be able to place the big sheaves in the wheelhouse at the top of the frame – quite a tricky operation which will be explained later.

All of our meals were supplied at the Cominco cafeteria, which was run by a catering outfit. The rooms for the men were in one of the new houses and quite a nice set-up. My room was upstairs over the cafeteria and very nice. There was a spare bed in my room for special visitors such as machinery salesmen, company engineers, priests, etc. At the Cominco office I was asked how I liked my room. I said fine and that up to that time I had had a United Church minister, a Catholic priest, and an engineer use the spare bed. I then asked when the village nurse would be coming. "Never mind Joe, we will have a room for her if and when she arrives", was the response. Lots of laughs.

The first part of the erection job was the big ore bin. That was a lot of heavy steel, some plate work, and of course everything was riveted. There was a road up around the back of the structure. It was here that we set up the guy derrick to reach the sloping part of the head frame where the structure left the mine shaft and continued to rise on a 39° slope to the east towards the ore bin and over the top of it.

Up and past the ore bin is where the wheelhouse was and where the big 12-ft diameter sheaves were placed. They controlled the hoist cables that brought the ore out of the mineshaft to be dumped into the ore bin. The guy derrick was rigged with an 80-ft mast and a 70-ft boom, but this was not long enough with which to place these large sheaves.

It was the start of the shift at 8 AM. The men were asking me how we were going to place the sheaves. I told them that we were going to get a timber to make a jib for the derrick boom, then, hopefully, we would reach far enough to place them. On the hill behind the job, there was a nice fir tree. I told the men that that was our jib. Some of them looked rather doubtful. The snow was deep, but it was not that far away. We took the cross cut saw and an axe and we soon had the tree down and limbed. Then we cut out a suitable piece and with some rope we skidded the piece down the hill to the job. Then, with some scrap angle iron and some long bolts and cable, we made a suitable jib for our derrick. The mobile crane could hoist the sheaves up onto the top of the ore bin. We then rehooked with the derrick. Everything worked fine. Later on people were wondering how in hell we managed to place these big sheaves at the top of the structure.

It was a mild winter so we made good time with the work. We were also able to make good time with the riveting work. At Kootenay Bay, on the east shore of Kootenay Lake, the big high tower was nearing completion. As soon as we were finished at Riondel we went there to help with the stringing of the 2-mile cables across Kootenay Lake. This was the kind of project that had never been done in this part of the country before.

The cables were 1¼" in diameter and 10,733 feet long and weighed 20 tons each. The towers on the west side were up on top of the Coffee Creek bluffs, approximately 1200 feet above Kootenay Lake. The tower on the east side was 365 feet high. The cables were strung from east to west. The job required three crews to handle it all. There was on crew on the east side, one crew on the lake, and another on the west side.

The big spools of cable were unloaded from a barge at the Kootenay Bay ferry landing, and then trucked to the east tower site on a low bed truck one at a time. They were then unloaded there using a 30-ft boom on the crane. At the tower site we placed each spool onto a stand with an axle ready for unwinding for the trip across the lake. At this time, we also rigged up a braking device with a piece of timber to keep the spool under control while unwinding.

The first job to be done was the west-end relieving strands, which were placed on the end of the cable. This was the first 150 feet of the west end. This had to be done before the cable was placed on the first pontoon and fastened to the hoist line from the west side. This operation took several hours.

The relieving strands consisted of two cables, each 150 feet long, and laid beside the main cable, one on each side and fastened to the main cable with special steel plate clamps grooved to fit the three cables. The relieving strands were placed on both ends of the power cables. Then all of this was bolted together with clamps placed 10 feet apart. All of this hardware was galvanized to protect it from the weather. When this was all done, the assembly was fastened to the first pontoon for the big trip across the lake. The reason for the damper strands was to stop the vibration during a windstorm.

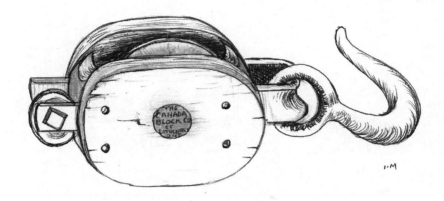

Single sheave 4-inch rope block
(sketched by Ila Maber)

CHAPTER 29

Kootenay Lake power crossing, 1952

BACK TO KOOTENAY LAKE. I have often had people ask me how we strung the cables across Kootenay Lake. People look up at the cables and then the distance across the water and just shake their heads. When we erected the towers on the west side, high up on top of the Coffee Creek bluffs, we did this as the first part of the project. There were three towers with back anchor legs anchored in concrete, all to solid rock. There was an old mining road up the mountain from the village of Ainsworth, so with the help of a Cat D6 bulldozer we took a 20-ton mobile crane up to the tower site. We erected the towers and then we placed a 3-drum hoist in position and put the hoisting cables in place. There were 2 drums of equal size that would be used for the final pull of placing each power cable. This was done by reeving the main blocks at the same time that the cables were fastened onto the drums. This was one cable with the ends of the cable fastened to the two drums and the blocks being in the bight of the line. This was a set of double blocks of four sheaves each to create an 8-part line.

The single drum was a large drum that would spool more than 10,000 feet of cable. The single ⅝-inch diameter cable was pulled down over rock bluffs and hooked to a tugboat to pull the cable across the lake. On the lake we placed special pontoons under the cable to float it. There were 17 of those pontoons. As the cable was towed across by the tugboat,

158

...ed under the cable at intervals of about 500 feet. The
a pontoon was ...de ... two floats about three feet apart with a special
pontoons wer...ecting pieces that had a crank to screw the clamp tight
clamp on t...
to the ...urn trip the ⅝-inch diameter cable was fastened to the big
and as it crossed the lake the pontoons were taken off at the
...d transferred to the east side and placed under the big cable
...cessary intervals. When the power cable was pulled well up on
...re with the ⅝-inch diameter cable, the big set of reeved-up blocks
...nooked on and then these in turn pulled the power cable up over
bluffs to the anchors at the towers. Before the heavy tension came
onto the power cable the east end had to be hoisted and fastened at the
top of the big tower and the back anchor cables had to be fastened. Then,
with these in place, we would give the signal to the west side to go ahead
and also for the pontoons to be cut loose from the cable. It is not hard
to see how handy it was to have two-way radio communication. We did
the center cable first to keep even tension on the high tower. The closing
pull on the west side was a 54-ton pull. You can see the reason for the
multiple set of blocks and parts of line.

There were a few days on this job when we had to stop work for stor...
on the Lake. Kootenay Lake can become a real nasty place to work w...
there is either a north or south wind. The waves can get as high as...
so men could not work on the pontoons. This only happened a...
of times and we never had an accident. When all the work was...
we dismantled the guy derrick at Riondel and trucked all the e...
from there and the cable job to Nelson and shipped it all by...
Vancouver.

The Blue Bell Mine at Riondel was the first in the ...
Country. This is the mine that was staked by Robert Sp...
was jumped and restaked by Thomas Hammil. The ca...
but Sproule eventually lost out. Hammil was murdere...
eventually hung for the murder, though it was never...
well-documented in the book "This was the Kooten...
The story has been told over and over again arou...
and camp bunkhouses.

As I mentioned previously, the tower and...
for nine years. Then the tower was blasted...
of Freedom Doukabors. This created the p...

Mine. The miners were lucky to get out of the mine all their headlamps. When they found out the cause of t by the light of were one mad crew of miners.   ~~ble, they

The Blue Bell Mine goes down under Kootenay Lake and wet mine. I know what the mine is like in regards to water went down into the mine one night with Johnny MacDonald, the foreman. He showed me right through all of the workings. It was one wet place to work. The water seeped in continuously. The mine wore slickers all of the time.

ver crossing
elson on the
to go to Trail
would be the
oment from the
ome equipment
I got from John
Trail so well that
t of all, I kept part
ke. I went to Trail
d Wells. I also had
h had to arrange for
as living in Castlegar

m Vancouver. We got
ted equipment was all
ght on time. Also, a big
lmer – the man who had
and superintendent of all
ratulations on now being a
dge Company. He was now

ains

CHAPTER 30

Sinter Plant, Spring 1952

AFTER FINISHING ALL OF THE work at Riondel, and the pow
at Kootenay Lake, we loaded out all of the equipment in N
C.P.R. rail cars. I got word from John Prescott in Vancouver
to erect a small building on the bench in east Trail. This
Trail Armories building. Because we had shipped all equip
Kootenay Lake jobs back to Vancouver, we would rent s
in Trail with which to do the armories job. In the letter
Prescott he mentioned the fact that I knew the town of
I should be able to find everything I needed there. Firs
of the crew that had been with me at Kootenay La
and hired a mobile crane from the firm of Wade ar
to rent a compressor and a welding machine. I the
accommodation and eating places for the men. I w
at the time so this was easy to take care of.

We received the steel for the job by truck fr
started with the erection right on time. The re
there and the steel arrived from Vancouver ri
surprise for me, the inspector was Hughie Pa
been the Cominco boiler shop superintendent
steel erection for Cominco. He gave me cong
steel erection *foreman* for the Dominion Bri

Headframe for the Blue Bell Mine
Riondel, BC, 1952
The mine is now shut down and nothing remains

Sinter Plant, Spring 1952

AFTER FINISHING ALL OF THE work at Riondel, and the power crossing at Kootenay Lake, we loaded out all of the equipment in Nelson on the C.P.R. rail cars. I got word from John Prescott in Vancouver to go to Trail to erect a small building on the bench in east Trail. This would be the Trail Armories building. Because we had shipped all equipment from the Kootenay Lake jobs back to Vancouver, we would rent some equipment in Trail with which to do the armories job. In the letter I got from John Prescott he mentioned the fact that I knew the town of Trail so well that I should be able to find everything I needed there. First of all, I kept part of the crew that had been with me at Kootenay Lake. I went to Trail and hired a mobile crane from the firm of Wade and Wells. I also had to rent a compressor and a welding machine. I then had to arrange for accommodation and eating places for the men. I was living in Castlegar at the time so this was easy to take care of.

We received the steel for the job by truck from Vancouver. We got started with the erection right on time. The rented equipment was all there and the steel arrived from Vancouver right on time. Also, a big surprise for me, the inspector was Hughie Palmer – the man who had been the Cominco boiler shop superintendent, and superintendent of all steel erection for Cominco. He gave me congratulations on now being a steel erection foreman for the Dominion Bridge Company. He was now a pontoon was placed under the cable at intervals of about 500 feet. The pontoons were made of two floats about three feet apart with a special clamp on the connecting pieces that had a crank to screw the clamp tight to the cable.

For the return trip the ⅝-inch diameter cable was fastened to the big power cable and as it crossed the lake the pontoons were taken off at the west side and transferred to the east side and placed under the big cable at the necessary intervals. When the power cable was pulled well up on the shore with the ⅝-inch diameter cable, the big set of reeved-up blocks were hooked on and then these in turn pulled the power cable up over the bluffs to the anchors at the towers. Before the heavy tension came onto the power cable the east end had to be hoisted and fastened at the top of the big tower and the back anchor cables had to be fastened. Then, with these in place, we would give the signal to the west side to go ahead and also for the pontoons to be cut loose from the cable. It is not hard to see how handy it was to have two-way radio communication. We did the center cable first to keep even tension on the high tower. The closing pull on the west side was a 54-ton pull. You can see the reason for the multiple set of blocks and parts of line.

There were a few days on this job when we had to stop work for storms on the Lake. Kootenay Lake can become a real nasty place to work when there is either a north or south wind. The waves can get as high as 6 feet, so men could not work on the pontoons. This only happened a couple of times and we never had an accident. When all the work was finished, we dismantled the guy derrick at Riondel and trucked all the equipment from there and the cable job to Nelson and shipped it all by rail back to Vancouver.

The Blue Bell Mine at Riondel was the first in the West Kootenay Country. This is the mine that was staked by Robert Sproule. The claim was jumped and restaked by Thomas Hammil. The case went to court but Sproule eventually lost out. Hammil was murdered and Sproule was eventually hung for the murder, though it was never proved. This story is well-documented in the book "This was the Kootenay" by Clara Graham. The story has been told over and over again around Kootenay campfires and camp bunkhouses.

As I mentioned previously, the tower and power line was in place for nine years. Then the tower was blasted down by some of the Sons of Freedom Doukabors. This created the power outage to the Blue Bell

Mine. The miners were lucky to get out of the mine alive by the light of their headlamps. When they found out the cause of the trouble, they were one mad crew of miners.

The Blue Bell Mine goes down under Kootenay Lake and is an awful wet mine. I know what the mine is like in regards to water seepage. I went down into the mine one night with Johnny MacDonald, the mine foreman. He showed me right through all of the workings. It was sure one wet place to work. The water seeped in continuously. The miners wore slickers all of the time.

retired from Cominco and just doing a little extra work.

This was a small job of only a couple weeks duration. On finishing this little project we started on the erection of the New Sinter plant at the Trail smelter for Cominco. This was located in the old part of the smelter in the lead furnace area. There was a lot of heavy structural iron involved in this job: big roof trusses, some heavy crane beams, and some built-up girders. The roof trusses were big and heavy – about 100 feet long, and over 12 tons each. To be able to erect these trusses we needed booms of at least 90 feet long, and to be able to handle 6 or 7 tons. This was really too big of a job for a 20-ton crane with 90 feet of boom. As I explained previously on another job, a 20-ton mobile crane can handle 20 tons with a short boom of 30 feet at a 10-foot radius. To use this much boom on a rig with this much tonnage is asking for trouble. Because the old smelter had to be kept in operation, we were only able to erect about 75% of the New Sinter plant, the remainder had to be done at a later date.

The north and south sides of the building were actually extensions of the main building with the floor beams connecting to the same columns that carried the trusses over the main building. When we assembled the two truck cranes we fitted them with different boom lengths. One was outfitted with 90 feet of boom and a 30-foot jib. The other one was out-fitted with a 70-foot boom. This one was used for unloading steel from the rail cars. These railcars came in on the trestle we had built the previous year. It would also be used to erect the heavy building columns that would carry the steel for the wings and also for the heavy roof trusses. The one with the longer boom and jib could reach all of the steel for the wings, but it was limited to a one-ton load on the jib. Also, the crane beams or girders for the main building could be handled on the main boom. These weighed about four tons each. I was very leery about moving the crane with the long boom and jib, since that much boom creates an awful leverage on the truck that it is mounted on.

Hi Carpenter had returned from the U.S. so he had taken over as the erection superintendent for the Dominion Bridge Company. I had worked under Hi on several projects but I did not like his erection scheme for this building. He wanted to bring in the steel for the roof trusses, then assemble one of them, and carry it into place with the two cranes with 90-foot booms. I told him this would not work. So then he asked me what would. I said we would have to build the trusses directly under the place or columns where they were going to be hoisted. Once a truss is assembled, there will not be any moving of the cranes. The truss would be assembled in a vertical position ready for erection, then the cranes blocked into position, and then the truss could be hoisted into position. Then this same process could be repeated for the next one. Everyone agreed with my proposed method, but something unforeseen changed everything.

John Prescott talked to me about having Bobbie Morell take over one of the rigs to become a pusher (also known as a foreman). I said O.K. and that he could finish the north end for a start. The steel there is mostly light and the crane with the long boom can reach it all. I would erect the rest of the heavy columns on the south side. I told Bobbie that he had a good operator on this crane, but to watch that he never overloads it. I said the jib was capable of a one-ton lift, but no more, and to make sure the rig is well blocked under the out-riggers. This was in the late afternoon.

The next day I was working on the south side of the building. Everyone was busy when all of a sudden...CRASH! What in hell is wrong, I thought. The crane on the north side, with the long boom was laying in a mess of iron and rigging on the ground. First thing to check were the men. No one was injured, which was good. But on the north side some steel had been knocked out of place and was now on the ground. The boom was a total mess...jib and all. As the boom fell, it just missed a rivet gang working in the next panel of the building. I wondered what the hell went wrong. I looked at the load line from the crane and followed it up with my eye to where it was still fastened to a beam. My God, it was one of the crane beams. I asked Bobbie what in blazes he had the jib load hooked up to the crane beam for. He said he was going to move it out of the way. I told him that beam weighed four tons, and that I had told him that the jib was only good for a one-ton load. He said he didn't think that the crane beam was that heavy.

Well, at this point, the erection was at about a stand still. The crane now needed several new boom sections, and we needed another crane to continue the erection. We were able to get another crane from Cominco – big Lima Crawler crane with a 90-foot boom. With that crane we could handle a truss with one crane.

At this time Dominion Bridge had another contract with Cominco – the fertilizer plant in Kimberly. We cleared up the mess and shipped the crane out to Kimberly. It would receive a new boom when it arrived there. Bobby Morell went to Kimberly to be a foreman there on the new fertilizer plant. There will be more about this later in the story. I took over the Lima Crane and erected the trusses and the remainder of the building. I used the other Loraine Crane as a feeder and for all of the smaller parts of the job. The work all went well. The rivet gangs made good time and no more foul-ups. We worked through the summer and cleaned up the job in August. At this time we al moved to Kimberly to work on the fertilizer plant.

CHAPTER 31

Kimberley Fertilizer Plant and Moyie River Bridges, August 1952

WE WENT TO KIMBERLEY. IT was still beautiful summer weather. Since I still had the place in Kimberley that I had built previously I took my wife and kids there as the job was good for a fair length of time. Bobbie Morrell had started the steel erection and all was going well. Cominco still had a camp operating nearby known as Chapman camp, so that is where the crew would stay and have their meals.

On one part of project there were some prefab vessels to erect. These were actually tanks, but they were heavy. These were too big and heavy to be erected with our mobile cranes, and they were busy with structural steel erection. John Prescott wanted me to erect a mobile gantry crane that would be used to hoist these vessels into position. The bases were ready for them. This gantry crane would travel on rail trucks that were located at each corner of the crane. It would travel on rails and have four air-powered winches mounted on it for hoisting.

The rails were spaced at 14 feet. The structure was 16 feet wide by 30 feet long and 35 feet high. The vessels were brought in flat on railway flat cars. They were then unloaded using two cranes and laid in position ready for erection. The gantry was moved into position over the vessel, then the rigging was attached and the vessel was hoisted. As it is raised, the bottom of the vessel came ahead as the vessel reaches a vertical position. In some cases, with a high or extra heavy vessel, guy lines were attached to the upper corners of the gantry to stabilize everything.

After I had the gantry ready for the job, the erection of the vessels was turned over to Bobbie Morrell. I went to the phosphate plant to oversee the riveting. By this time it was October. The weather was still good and all work was progressing well. Bobbie Morrell had now finished the erection of the vessels and was now in the process of dismantling the gantry crane. I happened to be at the top of the phosphate building when I noticed several men looking over at the gantry crane near the vessel location. I asked them if something was wrong. They said yes, there was some trouble over there. I came down out of the phosphate building and went over to the gantry crane. Things were in a mess. Several men were injured. I immediately called the ambulance and got things cleaned up so the injured men could be moved.

Joe Christie was in a real bad way. Louis, a French Canadian fellow, was also injured. The ambulance arrived and we got the men sent to the hospital. I looked at the gantry crane to see what was wrong. The crew had been removing the diagonal bracing and beams from one end of the gantry. The gussets or lugs that held the braces were attached to the top and bottom of the beams on the end of the beams. What happened was that a top beam had been taken out, leaving the braces still connected to the beams below at the next level. Now the next beam was going to have to be removed, but it still had the braces on it. It would be top heavy. As soon as it was hoisted clear of the columns, it immediately turned upside down throwing Joe Christie and his working partner Louis to the ground below where a lot of iron was already laying on the ground.

If the braces had been removed separately, or with the top beam, the braces would have been below the beam where they would be in a safe position. I can't imagine what Bobbie Morell was thinking about to remove the iron in this manner.

Joe Christie only lived for a very few hours, and Louis was crippled for a long time. After this was over, Bobbie Morell went back to Vancouver and some time later he was working on the highway bridge job at Emory Creek, which is on the highway north of Hope, British Columbia. Bobbie was a very tall man – somewhere about 6' 5", or more.

At this time they had finished erecting a set of girders for the highway bridge over Emory Creek on the Canyon Highway. They had been using a crawler crane for the erection, and were now in the process of moving the crawler crane down the road. Bobbie Morell and another ironworker were riding on the crane above the cab to watch that the Gantry would clear any overhead wires. There was one power line that they would come under with the crane. There was plenty of room, and to demonstrate this, Bobbie stepped up on the gantry and reached up to show that there was plenty of height. As I mentioned before, Bobbie was a very tall man. He removed a glove and reached up to hit the wire with his glove. The power from the wire connected with him through his glove. He received a terrible jolt from it and was thrown to the ground a distance of about 20 feet. Between the electric shock and the fall, he was killed. A very sad ending. He was only a young man.

At the fertilizer plant we continued with the erection and riveting of the ironwork. There were several good-sized buildings on this project. There was the phosphate plant, the rock plant, the acid plant, and also the big storage plant. Also, we had conveyors between the buildings to erect. We continued this work throughout the winter.

About the beginning of February 1953, John Prescott took a crew of men from this job to Kingsgate. This is at the Idaho border on the Moyie River. The job there was to erect a highway bridge over the Moyie. This would be a through truss span of 225 feet, and a short beam span on each end for approaches. The crew would have to stay at the Jones Hotel, which was on the American side of the border. At this place there was accommodation for up to ten men. There was no place on the Canadian side of the border.

The Moyie River has its headwaters in the mountains to the west of Cranbrook. It runs southwest for a few miles and then it forms Moyie Lake. Moyie Lake is about seven or eight miles in length and then it forms the river again. For all the river crossings on the highway, it takes nine bridges: two on the upper or Cranbrook end, and the remainder between the south end of the lake and the U.S. border.

For this job they would use one of the Lorraine 20-ton mobile cranes. The bridge steel would come from Vancouver by railway cars and then be trucked from the railway siding to the job site. For this project, John Prescott took enough men for a raising rang. The erection gang is always called the raising gang. He also took a couple men for bolting, and of course, he also took the crane operator. For all of these highway bridges the foundation work and false work was taken care of by a separate contracting firm. When the steel contractor arrived, the job site was ready for steel erection.

By the time this crew would have all the iron erected on this Kingsgate highway bridge, I was coming to the end of the work in Kimberley. John Prescott had sent me orders that when they were finished at Kingsgate to come down there with a couple of riveting gangs. They would be moving to erect the 120-ft through-truss bridge at Hiawatha, which is the place at the north end of Moyie Lake where the upper Moyie River runs into Moyie Lake. We were now getting into early spring weather, which was more enjoyable.

We all got located at the Jones Hotel on the American side of the border. It turned out to be a good place to stay. Good rooms and good food and only a few hundred yards to walk to work. That job all went OK and by Easter time we were coming to the end of it.

Now, in a short while there would be another bridge to erect at the north end of Hiawatha. This is the upper most crossing of the Moyie River. But this would be a different kind of job. This bridge would be a 100-ft girder span. This would be the job that I would take on after finishing the riveting work at Kingsgate and the lower Hiawatha Bridge.

I found accommodation for the crew at the Hiawatha motel. The steel for the bridge will be shipped by rail to Cranbrook. I would have to arrange for a big low-bed truck to haul the steel. I got all of these arrangements made and then took one of the Lorraine cranes for the job. One of them was then returned to Vancouver. These girders were much too big and heavy for the crane to handle, so I took a different approach. It would be a 12-mile haul for these girders and the rest of the steel for the floor at the bridge. The two main girders weighed about 25 tons each.

At the railway yard we placed the low-bed truck beside the railway car and using a short boom on the crane, we lifted one end of one girder onto the truck, then moved the crane to the other end and lifted that end of the girder onto the truck. We then placed shores on both sides of the girder at both ends on the bunks, then tied everything down tight. The girder was in a vertical position. When this was all ready, the truck and crane and crew would all move together to the bridge site.

I had a pick-up truck that I was using on this job. At the bridge site we use the same method to unload the truck. We unloaded the iron on the north side of the river. It was not a very big stream at this place. We had to make three trips with this big low-bed to haul all of the steel: one trip for each girder and one for the floor beams and bracing and railings. All the work proceeded very well.

Now we assembled the span on the site where we unloaded it, but only with a floor beam at each end, and enough bracing to stiffen the structure. There were a lot of pile butts lying around so we made good use of these. We placed them so that they would make rollers to help move the span over the river. After the girders are assembled with some floor beams and bracing, we laid a lot of these pile buts that were left after the building of the bridge piers in front of the girders. Then we moved the crane to the other side of the river to the site of the abutment. The old bridge is still in place today and carrying traffic.

We hooked long heavy chokers to the girders and attached them to the load of the crane. The crane is well blocked. We went ahead on the load and the girders moved ahead on the pile buts, which are now rollers. We kept the girders coming ahead until the south end was close to the abutment. Now, because we were using a short boom on the crane, we could lift one end of the girder span up and onto the pier or abutment. We placed a piece of timber on the abutment for the girders to rest on temporarily. Now we unhooked and moved the crane back to the north side across the river. Although, the river is only like a large creek at this location. We got the crane ready with all out riggers blocked and then we could lift the north end into position and land it on its shoes on the anchor bolts. Then back to the south end for one more lift to place the south end in position on the anchor bolts. Now the girders were in place – more than 50 tons with a small 20-ton mobile crane. Now we could extend the boom and erect all of the bridge floor system. We could also now get busy with the riveting and erection of bridge railings.

When this job was all finished, we moved back to Kimberley. There were a couple of small extra jobs there to be taken care of. When this was all finished the crane was laid off and it went back to Vancouver. I got word from John Prescott that my next job was to be in Williams Lake in the Cariboo area. So, I went back to Vancouver in my pick-up truck.

CHAPTER 32

St. Joseph Mission Church and School at 150-Mile House, May 1953

AFTER ARRIVING IN VANCOUVER I went to the Dominion Bridge erection office to find out the details for the job in the Cariboo. They would be hiring a crew from the union hall. These men would travel there by car as a lot of fellows now travelled that way. There was a camp at the job site where we could all stay. We would have a brand new crane that was being shipped there by rail from Lachine Works in Montreal. I drove to the job. It was at the St. Joseph Mission, which is about 12 miles south of Williams Lake, a mile or so from 150-mile house. When I arrived at the camp I found that the rest of the crew had already arrived. We all got located in the camp.

The first job the next day was to unload the crane from the railway car. The crane was a brand new 25-ton Dominion crane. It was built by Dominion Bridge at Lachine, Quebec. That is the headquarters of the Dominion Bridge Company. The operator of the crane was the son of Charlie Geisser, one of the operators that we had been working with now for several years. He was known as Chic. He became a very good crane operator. We got the crane unloaded, as well as the steel for the job. We had to move all of this about a mile and a half to the job site.

The building was a fairly simple structure. It was a combined church and school for the mission. This is the mission school where in later years there was a lot of trouble with priests molesting students. It all made headlines in the newspapers and T.V. province-wide. The total job only took about 3 weeks, although we were only using a small crew. After some of the bigger projects it was rather nice to work on a smaller job.

We were busy erecting steel and it was late in the afternoon. School was out. We didn't hear anything, but we looked over where a big pile of soil had been left from the building excavation. For about 40 feet along on top of this pile was a row of Indian children. They were all sitting there without making any noise or even talking. They were, it seemed, enchanted with the work and watching the crane lift and swing the iron into position. Generally when kids are playing, there is always a lot of noise and loud screaming. But these Indian kids were all as quiet as a mouse, as the saying goes.

One of the men wanted me to take him fishing. So, after work one day I told him that I think I knew of a good place. We went to Chimney Lake. To get there you take the road by the Onward Ranch Siding where we unloaded our crane and steel. From there the road climbs up a hill. Where you come to the lake, the creek runs out of the lake, and there is a nice big pool there. They had just come out with a spoon hook called a flat fish. I picked up one while in Vancouver. Anyway, this is what we used and between Buster and I, in an hour, we had sixteen silvers, each one 16 inches long. A nice catch.

On another day we were treated to a mechanical rodeo. The manufacturing of concrete buggies had now been made into motorized equipment. This would be a boon to labourers since they were being pushed by hand at the time. The platforms and scaffolds had to be made larger to accommodate them though. But they were faster and more efficient. The labour crew on the job happened to be a bunch of young Indian cowboys. They took over these motorized buggies like ducks take to water. They had some practice runs. They all had a great time doing this and it became quite a show. These young fellows had a lot of nerve, and they were good drivers. I don't remember any accidents, but there were some close calls. It was all very comical to watch.

When the job was finished we took the crane and equipment to Williams Lake and shipped it all to Vancouver on the P.G.E. Railway. We all returned to Vancouver by car.

On arriving in Vancouver in June 1953, I found out that we would next be erecting the big grain terminal at the waterfront on Burrand Inlet. This would come to be known as the No. 3 jetty. An erection crew had already started the steel erection so I would look after the riveting and fitting. For this job, I would be staying right in Vancouver. This would last until the middle of summer at which time we would then go to Sicamous to erect the bridge over the Eagle River at Malakwa. This is a 180-ft through truss span and we would be staying in Sicamous for that job. We would finish that job by the Labour Day weekend and move back to Trail to finish the sinter plant and a few other jobs.

Phase II Sinter Plant and Warfield switching Station, September 1953

THE CREW AND EQUIPMENT ALL arrived O.K. Now we had another job here for Cominco, besides finishing the Sinter Plant. Up at Warfield at the fertilizer plant, we had to erect a switching station for the hydropower that would come from the new hydroelectric plant at Waneta. For the switching station we would use one of the Laraine 20-ton mobile cranes. The steel came in by rail, but in Warfield there was trackage right to the job site.

I moved my wife and family back to Castlegar from Kimberley because it was too much to go to Kimberly on the weekends. The pick-up that I had, an older model dodge, had seen a lot of service. I was afraid that one day it was liable to quit. So one day I went downtown to a garage that was known as the Trail Motor Inn. They had a Chevrolet 6-cylinder for sale. Not a new one, but newer than the one I was driving. They took mine as a trade and I would pay them the difference. We make the deal.

We finished the switching station about the end of September and moved the crane and equipment down to the smelter at Tadanac to finish the big Sinter Plant. That steel could not be unloaded at the Sinter Plant since that rail trestle was being used for the lead furnace. The steel would have to be unloaded in the Cominco equipment yard about a mile to the north of where we would be working. Previous to this, and while I was working in Kimberley, a carpenter by the name of Danny Kemper came to me to talk about a truck. He told me that his brother Kejeld had a big tandem truck in Castlegar and he needed a place to store it. He had used it for hauling lumber in the east Kootenays, but had now moved it to Castlegar, and he had gone to California. Danny and Kejeld were Danish. I told Danny that if he supplied the transportation to Castlegar and back, that I would go with him and find a place for the truck.

We did the trip one weekend. I got his truck stored at a yard that belonged to a friend of mine where there was a lot of room. Both Danny and his brother were very happy about this. Danny asked me if I would like to buy the truck. I told him I would have to find work for it first. Nothing more was said about this at that time. This truck was one of the first tandem drive models in this part of the country. Later, I spoke to John Prescott about the truck to see if I would be able to get some of the hauling that goes along with the jobs. He said there would be nothing wrong with that, but of course I would only be paid for the use of the truck when it was in use. I said yes and agreed with that, because when equipment is idle, it's not earning any money.

This truck was a big heavy one – a tandem drive and a long body with a heavy deck. It was just at this time that Danny's brother Kejeld arrived from California and contacted me at home in Castlegar to see if I still wanted to buy the truck. I said yes, as long as the price is OK, but not otherwise. We agreed on a price and I went to the bank and got the money for him. I then asked him if he would bring the truck down to the smelter at Trail. He agreed and did this. Just at this time, we were unloading the steel for the Sinter Plant at the Cominco equipment yard. I got hold of a local truck driver and we were able to use the truck at the right time. For some time afterwards, we would need the truck almost every day. Also, the truck was big enough to handle the heavy steel.

We got the Sinter Plant done. We had the use of the Cominco Lima crane again for the big roof trusses. This simplified the erection work. After all erection and riveting was done, there was a job to be done at the new Waneta power plant that was nearing the finishing stages of construction. This was a set of towers for the new transmission line. They would be known as the get away structure. When we finished the Sinter Plant, I sent the truck home to Castlegar where it could wait for more work.

When we arrived at Waneta there was a message for me to come to the construction office. The project manager wanted to see me. When I went to the office, I met him. If I remember correctly, his name was Paul Brown. He asked some questions regarding the erection of the towers. I said as far as I can see, we don't have any problems. He said the electricians union was able to claim this work. I told him that the structures would have to be riveted, and I never new of electricians to use rivet guns and drive rivets. He said he hoped I didn't have any trouble but to keep in mind that this type of work is being claimed by the electricians union all over the continent. I told him I was ready to go ahead with the work and I hoped that there would not be any trouble on this project. He said: "good luck, but keep it in mind." We shook hands and I went to the job. We started work and we were never bothered by anyone. It was a short project and everything went fine.

The Waneta power project was, and still is, situated on the Pend d'Oreille River, just before it empties into the Columbia River. This is about 12 miles down the Columbia River from the town of Trail. Now we would all go to Vancouver.

CHAPTER 34

Hastings Park Stadium, Nanaimo Overpass, Yahk Bridges, 1953

OUR NEXT PROJECT WAS THE stadium at Hastings Park that would be known as the Queen Elizabeth Stadium. The steel came by truck from the Dominion Bridge plant in Burnaby at Boundary Road. We used one of the Loraine Cranes to erect the steel.

We had a good crew for the job and all went well. By Christmas time we were more than half complete. We took a few days off for Christmas holidays and then completed the project by the end of January 1954. Afterwards we shipped the tools and rigging back to the erection shed at Boundary Road. The crane, however, had to go over to Broadway Road to do a small job at a school. Since it was only 3 miles from the stadium, we took a chance and moved the crane with the boom in place plus the jib. We put a pilot car ahead and another car following behind with a Dominion panel truck. We were trailing the boom over the back end. Ernie Smith was at the controls of the crane. Frank Hick drove the front end. We had crossed Hastings Street and had gone by way of Rupert Street to Broadway. We were travelling west on Broadway when we were stopped by the city police. They asked Frank where we were going and who was in charge, then finally just said to hold it where we were. They asked me if we had a permit. I told them as far as I knew it was at the Dominion Bridge office. They measured the rig. It was 90 feet long! They asked us where we were going. We said to the school two blocks ahead. They let us go, but gave us a ticket. They fined the company $25. When I got back to the office we all laughed. I told them it would have cost $150 to shorten the boom, truck the boom sections, and then lengthen the boom again. More laughs. But we realized we couldn't do that again.

Now that we were finished at the stadium, the company's work was slowing down. We sent some of the men to Terrace where the company had a bridge job. Some were laid off but I took a small crew to Vancouver Island where we would erect a set of girders for the railway to overpass the highway just south of Nanaimo. This is the branch of the railway that would run down to the salt chuck where the new railway ferry slip would be built. This was the E & N (Esquimalt and Nanaimo) part of the C.P.R. system. This girder span was rather short girders but heavy enough to carry railway traffic. The girders sat on the shelf of the abutments clearing the highway by 14 feet or more. They were only about 40 feet long. The girders came to the site by truck. The weight of the girders was about 12 tons each.

To complete the job, what we did is stop the highway traffic, then line the crane up for the positioning of the girders. The truck with the girder on it was then brought in and the crane lifted the girder. The truck was driven out of the way and the crane was then backed to the site, which was a very short distance. The girder was then guided with hand lines and the girder was hoisted to the proper level. The hand lines guided it into position as the girder landed on its anchor bolts. No more than 20 minutes from hook-up time. We were doing this with a 40-foot boom and working over the back end, so we could do all of this without the use of outriggers. Once done, we drove the crane out of the way and let the traffic clear, then prepared for the next girder using the same method. Finally we placed all bracing, drove the rivets, and cleaned up the site.

Now we would go to Yahk to erect two more highway bridges. One was a through truss over the Moyie River and the other was a beam-span bridge of three spans over the C.P.R. railway to create an overpass. The operator on the crane was a fellow who was an alcoholic and was supposed to be O.K. He had been a good operator while on the job in Nanaimo and had not been drinking. All the moves with the crane there had been very good. Perhaps this made him think he could drink again.

Well, there is nothing wrong with drinking in moderation, but it does not fit in with ironwork. The nature of ironwork means that everyone on the crew has to be in top shape all of the time.

Previous to going to Yahk I had come from Vancouver to Castlegar and stopped at home. There was a local fellow there, Andy, who had driven truck for me. I got hold of him and told him about the job we had ahead of us. We were to go to the smelter at Trail and load a tool shack and a big bundle of 4"x12"x20' planks on the truck. To do this we needed to remove one end wall from the shack, load the shack on the truck, then load the 4x12 planks into the shack from the end. We did this and then Andy left for Yahk with the truck and I went in my pick-up.

The steel was being shipped by rail from Vancouver to Yahk. There was quite a lot of snow at Yahk, but we were able to get a cat there to clear the rail yard for us to work with the crane and trucks. The bridge sites were close together at a place called Ryan, 4 miles east of Yahk. The crane was equipped with two load lines, a single whip for lighter work, and a load block reeved with three parts of line. We had the crane in the rail yard and had started to unload iron from one of the rail cars. The first lift was a short heavy bridge chord, a section for one of the trusses. It was about 20 feet long and weighed about 2 tons. We were using the main 3-part load line for this. Now the crane at this time was about 6 years old. The sheave shaft in the main load block was a little worn so if the load block was descending fairly fast, the sheave in the load block would rattle against the side plates. As I said before, when working in ironwork, you have to pay attention to the job and almost have eyes in the back of your head.

When you load iron or almost anything on a truck, you place pieces of wood, such as 4'x4", under the iron so that chokers can be placed around the iron. There were two men in the railway car and two more to receive the iron at the truck. I walked by the truck on the side near the crane. As I did so, I reached onto the truck to straighten out a piece of 4x4. As I did this, I heard the load block of the crane making the rattling noise. I knew in a flash the load was coming down too fast. I dove under the side of the truck and the bridge chord hit the ground where I had been standing. The men all saw this and everyone was in shock to think of what might have happened.

I went over to the crane to ask Tom the operator what was wrong. He told me he didn't know. I said O.K., and told him to give me the keys and to go over to the hotel and pack his bags because he was finished. The crew was staying at the Yahk Hotel. I said to the men that that was it for today since I had to go to the station to wire for a new crane operator. I did this and the office in Vancouver immediately dispatched another man. He arrived on the next passenger train. He was a fellow I had known for a long time and a very good crane operator: Les Coulter. I never heard of or saw the other fellow again, so I don't know if he ever got another job as a crane operator again. In the back of the crane cab we found a lot of empty beer bottles.

After we got started again, everything went O.K. and we finished the job in good time. I received a wire from the company to move all men and equipment to Savona as soon as I was finished in Yahk. I phoned to the Vancouver office to ask how I would move the crew. They told me I could move them any way I wanted – train or bus or whatever. The train went through there every day, but I asked them what I would use for money. Loyd McWaters, in the Vancouver office, said he would send an extra expense cheque along with the pay roll cheques. I said O.K. and to send this mail in a registered letter to me addressed to General Delivery in Cranbrook. He said he would do that.

The next morning while the crew was dismantling the crane boom and loading the truck with compressor riveting equipment and other equipment such as boom sections and needle beams, I drove to Cranbrook to pick up the mail. The mail from Vancouver would be coming in on the eastbound No.12 train. When I got to Cranbrook I immediately went to the post office and then to the General Delivery wicket. I asked if there was mail for Joe Irving. The clerk came back with "no, sorry". I asked her to check again in the registered mail. She did this and replied "Oh yes, here is one for you". I opened it up, and there was a letter and a special cheque along with the week's pay roll cheques for the men. Although I had lived in Kimberley, I had never done any business in Cranbrook. I walked down the street looking for a bank. I spotted one: The Bank of Commerce. It was 10 AM and the bank had just opened. I went in and went to the teller's wicket with the expense cheque. It was for $350.00. The cheque was not a company cheque, but rather one drawn on a Royal Bank branch in Vancouver (turned out it was an expense account for John Prescott and Loyd McWaters). The bank clerk looked at it and said she would not cash it. She referred me to another clerk. I went over to the other clerk and he looked at the cheque and shook his head and said:

"No, I can't cash that cheque". Just behind me was the bank manager just removing his hat and coat. He asked me if I was having trouble. I told him that it seemed that way. He asked me who I was and who I represented. I explained the situation to him and that this was an expense cheque for travel fares for my crew. He asked me for some identification. I showed him the letter that the cheque came with and also the pay roll cheques for the crew. I had not read the letter yet. I handed the letter to him. He started to read it and then he looked at me. Loyd McWaters was the bookkeeper in the Dominion Bridge erection office in Vancouver. He never called me by my name, and had started the letter with "Dear Red". The bank manager looked at me and laughed and then said that I did indeed have very good identification. He told me to go ahead and cash my cheque an wished me luck with the move. The clerks had been watching so I had no more trouble. I went back to the job and gave the men their pay roll cheques along with the traveling money for each of them. I told them I would see them in Savona.

Andy took the truck with the load. I left in my pick-up and went to Castlegar. At the transportation garage in Castlegar I had some things checked over on the truck. This was before the opening of the Blueberry Paulson part of Highway 3. It was March, so it was warm during the day and cold at night. We had to go over the old Cascade Summit road on the way to Grand Forks. Just a gravel road and two mountains to go over. I told Andy we would travel at night when the road is frozen since we didn't want to get stuck in a mud hole. He said that would be fine with him, but he wanted to know if we could change trucks as far as Rossland. His wife was in the Rossland hospital at the time. I said sure, and told him to go ahead with the pick-up and I would drive the big truck and meet him in Rossland. We did this and Andy took over the big truck when I pulled into Rossland. Now, for a while I went ahead with the pick-up. Shortly after getting over the first summit, I met a couple of fellows walking on the road. The waved me down and I asked them what their trouble was. They told me they had a truckload of machinery and they were out of gas about a mile back on the road. I told them it was about a 10-mile hike to Rossland, but that I had a big truck coming behind me and we had a can of gas onboard. I told them I would let them have that to get them to Rossland. They were very much relieved. They were taking a load of machinery to a mine in the East Kootenay. When Andy came with the truck we gave them the can of gas. Now they were happy. Andy and I continued on and stayed the rest of the night in Grand Forks.

The next day we continued on. Back then, you had to cross Okanagan Lake on the ferry. We did this and reached Vernon where we stayed that night. The next morning we continued on again and pulled into Savona at noon. For accommodation in Savona we stayed at the hotel. There were also some tourist cabins there. Some of the men stayed in the cabins.

The crane arrived, so we had to place the boom sections into it. We were supposed to have another truck and trailer meet us there, but there was no sign of it. The bridge steel was all long beams, and big and heavy. Each beam ran as much as six or seven tons, and up to sixty feet long. The bridge steel was to be all unloaded right here from the railcars in Savona. With no trailer to use for these long beams, we did something different. There was a big pile of railway ties in the yard. So we made good use of some of them. We placed a number of them behind the bull board until they were above the cab. We then held them tight in place with chokers. Then with more ties we built a crib over the rear of the truck. Now these long beams could be loaded with one end over the cab, and the other end over the crib sticking out behind, but was well balanced. The haul was a short one – only about a mile. On some loads we hauled two beams, but on one load we hauled three. We got all of this done in good order. I then sent the truck back to Castlegar with Andy.

The crew returned to Vancouver to the union hall to wait for other work. Frank Hicklenton had been the front-end driver for the crane. I got word from the Vancouver office to have Frank drive the crane to Vancouver. Back then the road through Fraser Canyon had not been rebuilt so a lot of the old wooden trestles in the canyon were not safe to drive the crane over. So, we went by way of the Okanagan Valley and what was Highway 3 at the time, over the Hope-Princeton Road. Frank drove the crane while I was the pilot man with the pick-up. Top speed with the Loraine crane was about 30 mile per hour. The first night we made Kelowna, the second night Princeton, the third night the plant in Burnaby at Boundary Road at 10 PM.

The company wanted me to go to the job at Terrace but I turned it down. I figured that job was all chiefs and not enough Indians. It just seemed to me that all the erection foremen of the company were on that job. I told them I would take a holiday.

CHAPTER 35

Hauling chord wood, May 1954

I STAYED IN VANCOUVER OVER the weekend mostly for a little shopping as I had not had the chance to spend any time in Town for quite a while. Then I left and drove to Castlegar. Now at home, I received a telephone call from Bill Waldie at the Waldie Sawmill. He said he had a little more than a hundred chords of wood in four-foot lengths stacked in the yard at the mill. This wood had previously been fuel for the tugboat Elceho on the Arrow Lakes. They used the Elceho to tow the log booms from up the lake to the mill at Castlegar. The tugboat had now been converted to diesel power so there was no longer a need for the wood. This would also be the end of steam tugboats on the Arrow Lakes.

Waldie had buyers for all of this wood at some of the local Doukabor schools, also the Merry's Wood Yard in Trail, and some in Nelson. Bill Waldie wanted to know if I would do the hauling of all of this wood with my big truck. I told him I would have to find some men for the job and I would let him know. Within the next few days I found a couple of young fellows that were out of work who could handle the job. I called Bill and told him I could do it. We arranged a price and went to work on it.

The fellows I got for the job were two brothers, the Zieben boys, from Gibson Creek. We talked about the job and figured out a price, how much we could haul on a load, how long it would take, and so on. I contacted Bill Waldie again and we arranged to go ahead with the job. We placed two rows of this cordwood on the deck of the truck and a binder row on the top of it. Then by chaining and cinching it down, we could haul seven chords to a trip. It had to be handled by hand for both loading and unloading. The length of the haul to the wood yard in Trail was 23 miles.

Loading and unloading and a round trip would take at least five hours. If they made two trips a day it would mean a 10-hour day at least. The weather at this time of year was in our favour. We took on the job. The Trail haul would take seven or eight days. Now the loads for the school were only six chords each, but they were to be sawed in half at the schools. There were four schools and there would be only one load to each school. Then there was one six-chord load to Nelson. This load was birch. For the schools, we took a gasoline-powered buzz saw with us in the pick-up truck. As we unloaded the wood, we made one cut in each piece of wood before throwing it into the school wood shed.

To get to the schools in Ootechenia and Champion Creek, we had to cross the old Brilliant suspension bridge. The boys were rather leery of driving the truck over this old bridge. So on these trips, I drove the big truck and they followed with the pick-up. The truck with the load would be around 20 tons – a really heavy load for this old bridge. But all went well.

The other two schools were in the Pass Creek Valley – one at Pass Creek, and the other at Gibson Creek. We finished the job, I collected the money from Waldie, paid the boys their wages, paid the garage and gas bill. Then I waited for the Kootenay Landing bridge phase 2, which the Dom Bridge would be starting very soon.

As soon as I received word of the starting date for Kootenay Landing, I drove to Sirdar to meet the crew, since that would be the place where we would be staying. Sirdar is three miles from Kootenay Landing and it was a pusher station where the pusher engines were maintained and ready to help the freight trains up the grade to Yahk.

CHAPTER 36

Kootenay Landing Bridge, Phase II, July 1954

THE WORK AT THE KOOTENAY landing bridge started in early July. This would be the continuation of the job that had been done by Canadian Bridge Company in 1945. I have no idea why the C.P.R. waited so long to complete the project. When Canadian Bridge did the work, the crew was camped in railway bunk cars right at Kootenay Landing. This time the Dome Bridge Company would have the crew stay at the Sirdar Hotel, where they had their rooms and eat in the dining room. They travelled to the bridge on a gasoline speeder. The hotel was run by Henry Hornseth's widow. Henry had drowned in a boating accident on Kootenay Lake on the holiday weekend of May 24th 1949 along with several other people.

This project would be similar to the one we did here with Canadian Bridge in 1945. The work entailed building three more new piers for the bridge spans. All of these piers were built on the west side of the existing piers to move the truss spans 30 feet to the west, to rest on the new piers. The biggest part of the project was driving the piles for the piers. After the caissons were in place and the piles driven, the caissons were filled with gravel and the concrete grout was pumped in under pressure. Those piers would be the same size as the ones we built in 1945, and the piles driven to the same depth and same number. When we had all of the piers complete, we placed steel beams from the old piers to the new ones. This was done by jacking up the end of the span and placing the steel skid beams under the existing bridge shoes. This had to be done at each end of the span and at each bridge shoe. Then the skid beams were greased and made ready to slide the bridge span ahead.

Now, before the span could be moved or skidded ahead, it would require some heavy rigging. With heavy chokers attached to the span at the point where the end floor beam meets the truss, these chokers hooked to a double sheave block and this reeved to another block that would be fastened to the deck of the trestle to the west of the span. The load line of this reeving would be fastened to the coupling of the steam derrick car.

When all was ready and the signal given, the engineer on the derrick car made sure we had a full head of steam. As the derrick car backed to the west on the track, the bridge span would come ahead on the skid beams. All went well with no problems. This operation was done three times for each bridge span. The middle span between the truss spans on this bridge is a vertical lift span to accommodate any lake ship or boat that might have to go through the bridge.

To my knowledge this span had never had to be lifted before, but we lifted the span as part of the project when we renewed all of the hoisting gear for the span. This was quite a novel job. The hoisting gear was a set of cables and sheaves in each tower with the hoist line running to a capstan set in the deck of the span in the middle. To operate this capstan, it was done with four hardwood handles that were placed into sockets in the casting. With men pushing on the handles the capstan was turned and the span was lifted. We performed this operation to make sure that it all worked. It worked very well.

This was one of the last jobs that we had to take care of on this project. We had one sad thing happen while on this job. One of our old time bridgemen got a cold, which turned into pneumonia. Our timekeeper, Bob Minshall, took him to the hospital in Creston, but he died there. His name was Dick Radke. He had worked with ironwork for a long time. He was almost 70 years old. We all went to his funeral, which was held on a Saturday. The pal bearers were all ironworkers.

Vic Bratt was the general foreman throughout this project. Vic was a good man to work with. I had been the erection foreman or pusher under

Vic throughout this job and all of the work had gone very well. For the first time, the Kootenay Landing Bridge was resting on concrete piers for each and every span. We cleaned up the work site and loaded out all of the equipment on rail cars. The crew all returned to Vancouver.

Previous to that weekend, one of the men asked me if I would take him hunting. We took my pick-up truck and drove to Destiny Bay on the east side of Kootenay Lake where the Goat Creek Road leaves the highway. That was good deer country. We were close to the top end of the road and had not seen any deer. I stopped the truck and I suggested we watch there for a while. We sat on some rocks on the side of the road when I saw movement across the canyon. I motioned to Al to keep quiet and soon two huge grizzly bears came into view. These bears were working the rockslide where they were hunting for marmots. Al wanted to shoot at them. I said no, and to just enjoy watching them. If we had shot one, it would have taken more than an hour to get to them, and then how would we have gotten the hide back. I asked him if he had ever seen anything like this before. He said no. So, I told him to enjoy the scene because that doesn't happen very often. We watched them for a while and then found a place to turn the truck around and went back to Sirdar. Al Wilson was feeling better afterwards when he thought about the incident. He realized how far back in the mountains the bears were and what a job it would have been to bring one out.

Then, before I returned to Vancouver, I got word from the company that there was a small-beam span bridge that needed to be built over Kokanee Creek on the West Arm of Kootenay Lake. I was to meet another crew for this job in Nelson. The steel arrived by rail and a truck crane was on the way. I met the crew for this job. They stayed at a hotel in Nelson and got their meals in one of the cafés there. I commuted from home in Castlegar.

We used Kelly Ozelle's transfer to haul the steel from Nelson to Kokanee Creek. The hauling and erection only took a few days. We then drove the rivets and cleaned up another bridge site. At this time, I went to Vancouver to find out what my next job would be.

CHAPTER 37

A very busy year of building bridges and buildings, 1955

THE FIRST PROJECT OF 1955 was the CPR ferry slip in Nanaimo. When I first went to this project I went there with John Prescott to look it over and get things arranged. We went to Nanaimo one morning on the Black Ball ferry. We had our breakfast on board. Next thing we did was to arrange hotel rooms and then we looked over the job site. We would need one of the mobile cranes and also one big barge derrick. John said he would arrange for one as soon as he returned to Vancouver and he would also have a crew come from the union hall. He managed to get the No. 6 rig of Mackenzie Barge and Derrick Co. – a very good rig.

The crew arrived and we started in right away. We all had good rooms. Building a ferry slip is actually building a floating bridge. Part of it was a heavy truss job with one end anchored on the shore and the other end connected to a large girder. The other part was set of towers that could control the height of the outer end of the bridge to accommodate ferryboats at different tide levels. The end of the truss and the end of the girder were connected together by a large pin so that both truss and girder could move as the weight deflected them. At the towers there was also a system of counter weights to counter-balance everything. This was all very interesting because it was not very often that these types of jobs came around.

All of the iron in this job was heavy bridge material because the traffic on this bridge would be heavy railway cars, etc. I did not get to finish this job though. When we were about three-quarters of the way through, the company wanted me to go to Nelson to erect the steel for the new federal building (post office, etc.), which would be known as the Grey Building, in honour of Hamton Grey, a local man who was one of the last soldiers killed in World War II. I left Nanaimo and drove to Nelson with Bob Minshall who was the timekeeper on this job. This would be one of the last riveted buildings in B.C.

The new post office was built beside the old one on Vernon Street. The steel was shipped by rail and trucked from the rail yard to the job site. The company sent one of the mobile cranes up from Vancouver for this job. It was winter, but it was good working weather.

When the steel was being erected we had lots of side walk superintendents watching, and especially when the riveting started. For people who have never seen a riveting gang in action, it must have been fascinating to watch the work. Up on the scaffold, the man who was catching the rivet rapped on his catch can. The heater took a white-hot rivet out of the fire with his tongs and threw it to the catcher. The catcher caught the rivet in his can, and with a pair of tongs placed the rivet in the hole. The bucker-up placed his dolly bar on the rivet and the man on the rivet gun opened up on it. Within a matter of seconds the rivet was driven and operation starts over again. It was very interesting to watch, and also very noisy.

To a lot of people, these jobs look large. But, with good modern equipment they proceed very smoothly and quickly. It also shows the accuracy of the fabrication that is taken care of in the bridge shops, which are a marvel of industry.

This project did not last very long. We finished in March. While in Nelson we also had a one-day job that the Kootenay Forest Products got us to do for them while we had the crane there. We took the crane to the sawmill and erected a steel smoke stack for them. Afterwards, we shipped all of the tools and rigging and the crane back to Vancouver, along with the crew. Back in Vancouver the Capilano PGE railway bridge was ready for erection. This was the next project.

The false work for this project was already placed by another contractor. The steel was delivered by railway cars right to the bridge site. We off-loaded it with the steam whirly crane. This was a railroad crane with a 360° swing. It was known as the Bay City railway crane. The operator was an old-timer steam engineer by the name of Sy Shimmek. He was a very good operator. He was also the same operator we had on the Kootenay Landing job with the same crane.

The bridge was a 300-ft through-truss, which would span the river. This was all straightforward steel erection work. We placed the floor system from pier to pier, then erected the trusses. When it was all erected, bolted, and pinned, the camber was checked. Then the riveting proceeded. We had a good stretch of weather, so all went well. Having this bridge provided railway access to the next bridge along the line, which was Cypress Creek, which was constructed at a later date.

Our next project was to build an extension on to the Dominion Bridge shops in Burnaby. This job started right away. We did all of the erection with one of the truck cranes. This job was a building of columns, braces, wall girts, roof trusses, roof purlins, and sway braces. On the south wall of the building there was a heavy truss placed there to support the place where the two roofs met to form a large open floor area. Otherwise, it was all straightforward work.

We finished this project at the end of May 1955. Then, we went to Salmon Arm to erect the overpass bridge at Tappen, which was over the mainline of the CPR railway. There were three heavy beam spans for this job. Each span was 60 feet long. The steel arrived by rail which we off-loaded at the bridge site. We used one of the Loraine mobile cranes. Ernie Smith was the crane operator.

While working on this job, we stayed in Salmon Arm at the Bellevue Hotel. We finished this project by the end of June and then went to Lillooet to erect the steel on the powerhouse along the Fraser River. This was now July and the weather turned really hot. We arrived in Lillooet right after the July 1st holiday. Since it was summer holidays, I took my wife and kids with me. This job only lasted for about a month. We rented a cabin for much of that time. The kids had a good holiday and they got to see some country they had not seen before.

Back on the job, the steel for the job arrived by rail on the PGE railway. The rail siding was about a mile distant from the job site. The general contractor on the job was The Emil Anderson Construction Co. They had a big low-bed truck that we were able to use for hauling the steel. We used a crawler crane for unloading and erecting. The job went well and the weather was hotter than blazes. The crew all stayed in the contractor's camp.

There were a number of small lakes in the Lillooet area where we went fishing and swimming on the weekends. Most of these are in the higher country where it was a little cooler which was more enjoyable. That year there was a big run of Sockeye salmon in the Fraser River. The local Indians were catching them all of the time. Of course, they wanted to sell them as this was one of the few ways they had to make any money. We bought these fish from them, which they sold for very cheap. So, we had a lot of very nice feeds of fresh salmon. Everyone enjoyed that.

It was the last week of July. We had all the steel in place and the riveting was well on the way when I received a call from the Dom. Bridge office in Vancouver. They wanted me to leave the job in care of someone else and come to Vancouver to get ready to go to Kemano for the big cable job there.

First though, I had to drive to Castlegar to take my wife and kids home before going to Vancouver. We left Lillooet at 6 AM the following morning and drove by way of Spences Bridge, Merritt, Princeton, Osoyoos, Grand Forks, and then home – a long one-day drive at that time. After getting the family home safely, I caught the Kettle Valley train to Vancouver.

Kemano transmission cable
550 feet above the Canyon
1955

CHAPTER 38

Kemano Transmission Cable Way, August 1955

I ARRIVED IN VANCOUVER ABOUT 10 am during the first week of August 1955. I checked into a hotel and then went to the Dom. Bridge office to meet Harry Minshall, the manager of the construction department. I also met Bob Harris, one of the engineers. After greetings, we started talking about the Kemano project. They had both been there to see the place and had also taken some pictures of the job site. They also had some drawings of the proposed project.

We looked over all of these together and studied the pictures of the job site. We also talked over the methods for doing the work and the equipment that we would use, the crew, the hours we could work, and the various other items that went along with a job of that nature. Then Harry asked me what date I thought we could make the pull to hang the cables – not to finish the job, just to make the big pull. I looked over the pictures and the drawings again, did some serious thinking, and then I said: "How does September 17th sound?"

Harry and Bob both looked at each other and could hardly believe it. I asked them why and they said that since I had not even had a chance to see the site, they were surprised that I could come up with the same date they had by only looking at the pictures and drawings for a few minutes. I said "well, that's the way it looks to me". They said they were glad to hear my date was the same as theirs.

We then talked about the crew, the equipment, the tools and cables that would be needed for the big hoist, when we could leave, etc. As things turned out we were delayed for several days because there was a bad airplane accident up in the Kildala Pass almost in the area where we would be working. The plane got lost in the mountains and it was carrying several of the executives from the Kemano project. To my knowledge the plane was never found.

After couple days delay there was more air flights scheduled for Kemano. The crew was ready to leave and we received our flight time and we all met at the sea island airport. The plane that we were going to travel in was an old flying boat that had been built in England in 1928. It was a two-wing job with two engines. We all got on board the plane and it taxied out onto the water, but it couldn't lift-off. On board were 22 passengers and more than a ton of luggage. We taxied back to the dock and all of us got out of the plane.

A couple of mechanics came down from the hanger, but all they had with them was a pair of pliers and some screwdrivers. They took the covers off of the engines and monkeyed around with them for about 20 minutes. They then replaced the cover and told the pilot that it was O.K. to go. We all got back in the plane and this time the plane was able to take off. The thought that bothered me was that if it only took a few minutes to correct the problem, why had it not been taken care of before the passengers were on the plane?

We flew at a low elevation of only a few hundred feet so we had a very good view of the coastline – nice scenery. We were told that the top speed of this flying boat was 90 mph. Our first stop was Kitimat to let off some passengers who would be working there. Then it swung back to Kemano for the rest of us. In Kemano a bus met us, which took us back to camp. This was a huge camp and said to be able to handle 5000 men. We all got rooms although this was only temporary since most of our work would be done from the camp in the mountains in the Kildala Pass.

While we were camped there at the main camp, we unloaded all of our equipment from a barge and hauled it to the campsite in Kemano. At the Kemano campsite we had to reload it for the trip up the mountain as it was required for the job. Also at the Kemano site, was where we placed the sockets on the cables before they were hauled up the mountain to the job site.

The camp up in the mountains was a tent camp, but a good one. There was a large tent for the cookhouse and the dining room. Then there were smaller tents for bedrooms and washrooms. All in all, it was a good camp. The tents all had oil heaters in them and a bull cook to look after them. Bob Harris, the engineer, was my roommate. We found our tent quite comfortable. As well, the food at this camp was first class.

The job however, was a tough one. An awful lot of mountain climbing and a lot of wet rainy weather to contend with, but I guess that is what we were hired for. The first item was to get the big hoist in place. This was a big 3-drum Tyee hoist that was capable of spooling 2000 feet of cable on each drum. This hoist was powered by an 8-cylinder Chrysler industrial engine with lots of power. Next job was to get some lines and blocks (pulleys) up the mountain. We had the use of helicopters when the weather was suitable, but this was not always the case. While getting this part of the job under way, there was also the socket job on the cables to be done. This took place in the yard at Kemano. For this job we had a special tent house set up where we could place the sockets on the cables. In this tent, we were able to work where it was dry, which was important because when we poured the molten metal into a socket, we couldn't have any water around the job at all.

The cables were 3-inch diameter. The sockets were 39" long and each one weighed over 300 lbs. The ends of the cables had to be run through the socket first, then opened up and broomed back and cleaned with an acid solution, then rinsed before pulling it into place in the socket for the job of pouring the molten metal. The metal we used was pure zinc.

Previous to this socket job, while we were working on the mountain getting some hoist lines established, I had a bit of bad luck. We were working on a steep slope and the rock face was covered with moss. All of a sudden the moss started to slide and of course I went with it. I landed on my back and slid down the mountain for about 30 feet or more before I was able to stop. My back was sore but I managed to keep working. However, by that evening I was in a lot of pain and the next morning I could not move.

The next morning, which happened to be a Sunday, I could not even walk to the dining room for breakfast. I asked Bill Wright to take my place, which he did. That night I was not any better, and still the same the next morning. The following night, after work, they put me on a stretcher and then onto a piece of plywood in the back of a jeep and took me down the mountain to the Keman hospital. There I was put into a bed and given some pills.

Early the next morning the nurse came in and said "OK, you can sit up and get washed and ready for breakfast." I told her that if I could move that much, I wouldn't have been there. She asked me what was wrong. I told her I didn't know except that I couldn't move. She said she would help me and she placed her arm around my back and got me into a sitting position where I could wash and eat some breakfast. Later a doctor came in to see me. He asked me what happened and I explained it to him. He looked me over and said he could not say what was wrong. He gave the nurse some more pills for me to take and then he went away. It seemed like I was paralysed because I could not move my legs. I laid there and was wondering what was ahead.

That evening some of the crew came to see me to see if there was anything they could do. I told them they could bring me some books to read to take my mind off of the situation. They did that so I just kept lying there and kept reading. The doctor could not find the trouble. One afternoon I felt that I could move one of my legs a little. I laid there a while more and found that I could move the other one. This was a big relief to just know that I was not totally paralysed. I laid back and went to sleep.

When I woke up I was still able to move my legs, so now I felt better about everything. Some time later I was able to get out of bed and even go to the washroom. The next day I was able to leave the hospital. Bob Harris came in the jeep and took me to my room in the main camp.

At this point, I didn't feel as strong as I would have liked to, so Bob suggested that I stay in Kemano and look after the socket job. It was a very important part of the project and required a responsible person to be in charge of it. I thought that was a good idea and a good way for me to recover my strength. There was a special set of regulations for this work and it had to be done right to the letter. I took a special interest in this socket job to make sure it was all done properly. As I write this now in the year 2005, that cable way has survived for 50 years so I know that we did the job properly.

Our tent house for the job was the only way that the job could have succeeded. We got this all done and then we all went back up the mountain to proceed with the other part of the project. After climbing the mountain a number of times, my back improved and I got stronger all the time. Up on the mountain the miners had been busy drilling the holes for the anchor rods. This was a big project in itself. The anchor rods were 2 ½" diameter by 25 feet. They were power hammer upset for their entire length, which improved their grip in their holes after they were grouted in place.

There were six holes and six anchors for each cable. In order to have a hole big enough for a 2½" rod 25 feet long, the hole had to be collared (started) with a 4½" bit to bottom out big enough for the rod. These rods were all threaded on the outer end and then had a toggle bar placed on the end and held with a nut and washer. These toggle bars were fastened to the large anchor plate by 1¼" U-bolts. There were six of these toggles to match each anchor plate.

To get the anchor rods up the mountain, we boxed two rods together with two 2"×8" planks and then strapped them with steel banding. This package was transported to the anchor site with a Sikorsky helicopter and landed above the anchor site where it could be manhandled to the anchor holes. After placing the rods in the holes they were grouted with embeco grout.

The anchor plates that the cable socket fastened to were triangular plates 5" thick with a 5" diameter hole to match the socket. One of the first things we did was install a telephone system around the job site. We had one installed at the hoist site, one at each anchor, one at the camp office, and one at the hook-up site in the canyon. This cut down a lot of travel.

The big Tyee hoist was located at a spot that was about 1000 feet from the east or right-hand anchor where most of the work would be taking place, and also where we had a roadway for material delivery. There was a lot of material to be delivered to the anchor site. Cement and sand for the grout job, lumber, various kinds of hardware and a lot of rigging were required. On account of the foggy weather, we could not depend on helicopters to deliver all of this material on time, so I rigged up a high line. With the high line we found that we could now get a load of material up to the anchor site in a very short time. Also, as soon as one load landed, the hoist line could return for another load. With this system, we had the material delivery under control. This speeded up the whole project because men should not have to wait for material. Also, it was hard enough for a man to climb up the mountain without having to pack a load on his back.

Because we had the high line for the east side whenever the weather was suitable, we sent up the material for the west anchor with the helicopter. Between these two methods we were able to keep the job on schedule. This was a very important item when working on a project that was governed by weather (winter was approaching). Because we had been delayed at the start of the project on account of the plane accident we had been working seven days a week. We were right on time and by the 17th of September we were able to make the big pull and hoist the cableway into place.

Throughout this project Bob Harris and I worked very close together. Consequently, the progress was very satisfying. Bob notified Harry that we would be making the big pull on the 17th. On the afternoon of the 16th, Harry arrived at our camp to see the job. With him was a man by the name of Palmer Savage, the manager of the eastern division of Dominion Bridge from Lachine, Quebec. They came to our tent to talk to us about the big pull that was to take place the next day.

At the job site we had everything ready for the big pull. After we were introduced, Palmer asked me a question. He wanted to ask me about the power for the big pull. I asked him if they had seen the hoist. They said they had. I asked him what he had in mind. He asked me if I realized that the hoist would have less power when we were near the end of the pull. I asked him if he had seen the snatch blocks and the cutting torch there. He said yes, but he still didn't have the full picture. Then I explained to him that the hoist lines were bought for this job and when we made the first lift the linemen were going to be changing the temporary line. This would take about an hour. During that time we would hold our hoist lines with chokers, which would be at the hoist at that time. Then, we would cut the lines with the torch and pull them off of the drums with a cat that was also there waiting. Then, we would place the hoist lines back on the drums and could go ahead with the closure. Palmer smiled and said "now I know why Harry has you here."

Harry opened up his bag and produced a couple of bottles. He told me to take one over to my men and we can all have a drink. We did this and later we all went for supper. The next day everything went as planned and by 3 PM we placed the pins in the sockets and all breathed a big sigh of relief. DONE ON TIME AND ALL SAFE.

The next important part of the project was hanging the transmission lines under the cableway. The linemen had been busy getting the lines ready while we had been busy with the main cable job. To hoist the transmission lines into place we used a big International TD-24 cat with a 3-drum winch mounted on the rear. This was the biggest cat made by International. They were very good machines – powerful and rugged.

Previous to hoisting the main cable, we placed small structure on the cableway to hoist cables and load blocks, and also a smaller cable known as a straw line. This straw line was for hoisting men to fasten the transmission lines when the time came. Each transmission line was a 10-ton lift. The big insulators were attached to the line and hung on special hardware to the main cable. There were three lines to be hung. The height of the cableway was 550 feet above the canyon floor, where we were working. To send men up to the cableway we used a scaffold float that was 4 feet by 6 feet. We hung this float on the straw line for men to ride up to the cableway.

I realized that when the float reached the cableway that the line would be heavier than the float. To counter act the weight of the line, we fastened a couple of small logs under the float to increase the weight. To control the float from swinging we fastened a long tag line to the float. We had a big coil of this line on the ground and had the tag line running through the bell, or round part, of a shackle. This was in turn fastened with a choker to a small spruce tree close by. I had two men on this tag line job so that they wouldn't have any trouble looking after the float.

For the first trip, three of the crew took the ride: Vic and Cal Shattuck, and Lyle Neilson. Everything went fine and the float was returned to the ground. Then, Bob Harris and me took a trip up on it. When we were about 250 feet above the ground I noticed that we had been pulled a long way off course. I told Bob "FOR CHRIST SAKES HOLD ON!" We didn't have safety belts on, just the ½" load line to hang on to. All of a sudden we were swinging like a pendulum on a hell of a long line. It took a few minutes for the load to stop swinging. When it did stop we went on up to inspect everything and to take some pictures of the cable way for future reference.

We checked with the men to make sure that all was O.K. and that they had everything they needed. Then we rode back down to the ground. When I was back on the ground again I asked the two tag linemen what in hell they had been doing. They said the rope bunched up on them. I said, "You goddamned bastards were not looking after your job. The way this tag line is rigged, there is no way that this could happen if you were doing your job. Do you realize what you did? You could have killed us by not doing your job. There is no transportation out of here until the day after tomorrow. Then you will be on your way and I will do my best to see that neither one of you ever gets another job with the ironworkers." To my knowledge they never did.

Hanging the transmission lines went very well. We were never more than one day on the hanging of one line. There was some work to be cleaned up at the anchors. The big hoist had to be taken down the mountain to Kemano for shipment along with all of the tools and rigging. It all had to be barged back to Vancouver. By the time we managed to get all of this work done, we were into October and there was deep snow at the anchor sites of the cableway. It made us think that it was a good thing that we worked weekends while we had good weather.

At this time, we all went back to Vancouver to find out what our next project would be.

CHAPTER 39

Lulu Island Box Plant, October 1955

BEFORE I DID ANYTHING ELSE, I had told the company that I needed a holiday. That was agreeable to them. So, when we flew out from Kemano and landed in Vancouver, I decided to go directly to the CPR railway station to catch the no.12 Kettle Valley train which left Vancouver every evening about 7:30 PM. Jack Townsend was with me. He also lived in Castlegar. By the time we landed in Vancouver it was almost 7 PM. We got a taxi and went straight to the railway station. We just barely made it on time. It would have been the next evening before we could have gotten to Castlegar.

While on board the train Jack suggested it would be a good idea to take a trip to Spokane for a few days. I agreed providing that my wife could get someone to stay with the kids. When we arrived in Castlegar I told my wife of the plan and she found someone for the job. A day later Jack and I and our wives left in Jack's car and drove to Spokane, Washington. We got rooms in the Cordelaine Hotel, which is right downtown in the shopping district. This pleased the women because they wanted to do some shopping.

We all went to a couple of shows and spent a few relaxing days in Spokane, then drove back to Castlegar. After a couple more days, Jack and I returned to Vancouver to work on the Lulu Island box plant. This was a straightforward job of columns, beams and roof trusses with long span steel joists from truss to truss for the roof support. Altogether there was a cover of 11 acres. About 9 acres of these would be one building. When we had this project 75% complete we had to wait for more foundation work, but we had another job to go to.

This new job was in the Peace River country in Dawson Creek, BC. This was one of the stations on the mid-Canada line, or what was known as the Pine Tree Line. Except for the cold weather this was a simply one story project. They had a camp right at the site, which made everything handy. Yes, it was a dry cold, but dry or not, it was cold. For instance, an oil heater was going steady in the shack where we kept our bolts and tools, etc. The bolt sacks in the bottom of the storage pile were always frozen until you broke them open for use. The night temperatures were going down to −50° Fahrenheit. During the day it would warm up to −20°. This was cold work, especially for ironwork.

The men would stop now and then for a hot cup of coffee. We were planning to finish before Christmas and we finished on the 22nd of December. There had been a crew of ironworkers on another part of the Pine Tree Line project working in the woods east of Dawson Creek. They finished their part of the project at the same time.

It was in the evening and we were still loading tools for shipment when their crew arrived at our camp. They had made arrangements to stay at the camp. These were all ironworkers who we knew. They had been travelling in a winterised jeep (it had side covers). When they left their bush camp and were travelling down the bush road, they came across a woman lying on the road. She was almost frozen. They picked her up and took her to the little trading post further down the road. At the place where they picked her up there was a stalled truck. When they reached the trading post her husband was there. The story was that he was a woodcutter and they were heading for the trading post but their truck stalled. He told her that he would walk to the post to get help. But, in a very short time, she was too cold and decided to follow him, and collapsed on the road. The cold was too much for her and she died shortly afterwards. This is an example of dry cold....cold is cold. When we reached Vancouver, the crew said they had never been so glad to see rain.

After the Christmas holiday we finished the Lulu Island job and then started the Cypress Creek Railway girder span on the P.G.E. Railway. This was located in West Vancouver. At the time, the P.G.E. rails had reached Cypress Creek in West Vancouver. This was the end of the steel until such time as the Cypress Creek bridge was built. The bridge was a heavy girder span about 85 feet long and weighed at least 45 tons each. For this project we used the big 2-boom steam derrick car. This derrick car was a special old-time railway derrick car built with two booms to handle railway bridge girders. This rig had plenty of power and also power swing. But, in handling heavy loads you did not swing the booms very much off of centre. The rig was capable of travelling with a 50-ton load, but you would do this only with the booms tangent to the derrick car. Also, before swinging the booms the least bit sideways, the front end of the car had to be well blocked to avoid any tipping of the car. If you followed this method there were no troubles.

The girders and the other steel for the bridge were shipped by rail to the site where we off-loaded it. We had a short rail siding for this work. Great care had to be taken when unloading girders because of the swing from the derrick track to the spur track. After placing the girders, the bracing and struts were all placed and then all points were riveted. This finished the railway span. Then we had another girder bridge to build over the same creek up-stream from the railway bridge for the upper levels highway. But we did not have a derrick car to handle the girders. This is a different story.

The Cypress Creek Highway bridge was a lot bigger job than had been planned for. One big difference was the method for bridge girders with trucks and mobile truck cranes compared to handling them with railway cars and derrick cars. When large heavy material is loaded and shipped by rail, it is not subjected to sharp curves and supper-elevated curves, as is the case with trucks on a lot of the old-time streets and roads. Also, the mobile truck cranes of the 1940s and 1950s did not compare with the handling capacity of the railway derrick cars. This meant that you used a different approach to a job of this nature.

The Cypress Creek highway bridge was a 5-span girder bridge. The centre span was a brute of a job to handle. This set of girders was at least 10 feet deep and 115 feet long. Not the easiest pieces of iron to handle. There were two girder spans on the east and west ends of the bridge. These girders were much smaller than the centre ones. The trucks didn't have any trouble hauling them and a mobile crane with 25-ton capacity handled them and put them into place.

There was a road already built to both ends of the bridge project. This meant that we could erect two spans on the east end and then move to the west end and erect the two spans on that end. For the centre span, Dominion Bridge fabricated a large steel gin pole. This pole came in sections to the job site where we erected it with the mobile crane and placed the guy lines on it. We also used it for the hoist line, which we reeved to a 4-part line to handle the centre girder. For power on this gin pole we used one of the company's big gasoline hoists. We also had the mobile crane for a helper. At this point, the job was to get the girders to the job site, which was a different matter.

One of the big truck companies took the contract to haul the bridge material to the job site. I think it was the Commercial Cartage Co. They didn't have any trouble with the first four spans. Then they came to the job of hauling one of the big centre girders. That was a different story.

By this time it was well into spring, about the end of April. The first girder had been loaded at the Dom. Bridge plant. The hauling was done early in the morning to avoid the morning traffic. Don Jamieson, our engineer on the project, told me that the truck company planned to haul these girders the same way that I had hauled the ones for the Hiawatha job out of Cranbrook. I told him that it wouldn't work. He asked me why not. I told him that these girders were a lot different. He said, "Well, they took the contract to haul them". I told him that it wouldn't be easy for them.

The roads and streets in West Vancouver have a lot of uphill curves and slopes to them. It was a bad place to haul a bridge girder that was 115 feet long and about 11 feet above the truck. As I mentioned before, they were going to haul the girders in an upright position. When we were driving to work that morning I mentioned to the men that we were likely to see some trouble on the road when we would be climbing the hill from Marine Drive to the Upper Levels Highway. We had only gone about one block up the hill and there on the corner, on the lower side of the road, was the big bridge girder laying flat on it side in some flowerbeds. It wasn't long before a lot of officials were on the site. The task then was to get the girder loaded again.

We had our crane come down from the bridge, and the truck company had a couple of cranes come to help as well. Now, the problem was that the truck company still wanted to haul the girder in a vertical position. I told Don Jamieson that they were crazy to do that, but at this point they were still in charge. Well, the girder was loaded and fastened to the truck and trailer. When the truck started moving again it only moved a very short distance when the girder fell sideways again and almost tipped the truck along with it.

There was a big discussion and Don asked me what I would do. I told him that the girder had to be hauled laying down, but that it would need to be stiffened so that it wouldn't get any kinks in it. Don sent to the bridge shop for some bailey bridging which we fastened together and placed along the centre of the girder to stiffen it in the flat position. This all took time, but we finally got the girder loaded. People were glad to see all of us out of their flowerbeds and on our way.

At the bridge site we unloaded the girder using two cranes. We also used the cranes to help get the girder to the position where we could get a hold of it with our big gin pole. We got this one into place. When they shipped the next one, it was shipped laying down and braced. We handled the next girder in the same manner. After the second girder was in place, we had to dismantle the big gin pole, then place all of the floor system, drive all of the rivet connections, place the expansion joints and bridge railings, clean up the site, and then we were finished.

The next bridge project was the Mamquam Girder Bridge in Squamish. The railway grade from West Vancouver had been completed some time before and the rails had been laid while we had been building the Upper Levels highway bridge.

Two-boom steam derrick with a 50-ton load
at Cypress Creek on the P.G.E. railway
1956

CHAPTER 40

P.G.E. Railway Girder Bridge, Squamish, May 1956

ONCE THE CAPILANO AND CYPRESS Creek railway bridges were in place, railway bridge equipment could be moved to Squamish and the Squamish railway bridge could be built. By the time we arrived in Squamish the bridge piers were all in place and ready for bridge steel. We travelled to Squamish on the Bonnable, a small ship that worked the Howe Sound area, a nice little ship. We had rooms at the Squamish Hotel, as well as our meals. The distance to the job was only a few blocks so we didn't require any transportation.

We had the use of both Dominion Bridge Co. railway derrick cars for this project, along with the two boom rigs for the girders, and the Bay City whirly for all of the rest of the work. Both of these rigs were steam powered. The girders for this bridge were all of the through-girder type. That is, the floor system is carried by the lower part of the girders, whereas with a deck girder, the floor system is carried on top of the girders. The reason for this is due to the difference in the elevation of the grade. When there is plenty of clearance, the deck type is used. When the grade is close to the water, the through type of girder is used.

The shore spans for this bridge were about 50 feet long and about 30 tons each. The centre spans were 100 feet each with a weight of close to 50 tons each. The bridge steel was delivered by rail from Vancouver shops. There was a siding beside the track where we could store the cars of steel until they were needed. Also, we could take the girders directly from the rail cars to their positions on the bridge. When all of the steel was in place, everything could be riveted.

One day while on this job, I received a phone call from John Prescott. They had a job at the Standard Oil plant in Port Moody to place a big vessel. They were going to use the gantry crane that we used in Kimberley when there was a bad accident with the crane. This gantry had also been used for another job on Vancouver Island, again, with another accident. A lot of the ironworkers were therefore leery of using this rig. You could hardly blame them.

John asked me about the bridge job. I told him all of the iron was in place and that we were driving rivets. He then told me about the job at Standard Oil and wanted me to leave the Squamish job in care of someone else, and come to town and look after the gantry job. I told him that I would be in on the next boat. I left Tommy Rhodes in charge of the bridge and caught the next boat for Vancouver. I told John that I would go to the Standard Oil site and be there at 8 AM the next morning.

Here's what I found: The gantry crane was about three-quarters erected and about 200 feet from where the vessel would be placed. The gantry was sitting on a track that was on a curve and also not a level track. I phoned John at the office to ask what the plan was. He told me that old Hi had planned the job. I told him that I was going to change the plan all together. He said, "O.K., you're the boss there now".

I went to see the engineer of the Standard Oil Co. to ask him about the erection plan for the vessel. He was a man about 6'6" tall and he said the vessel would come in on a truck and trailer, be unloaded with cranes, and then stood up to a vertical position with the gantry. The gantry would then move the vessel to its final position. I told him that plan wouldn't work. He asked why. I asked him if he wanted to blow the plant all to hell? He said no, of course. I then told him that is why I was there and we had to change the plan or else I wouldn't be there. He asked if it could be done safely. I said yes, but not the way it was planned. He asked me what my plan was. I told him we would finish erecting he gantry and move it to the site empty. Then we would place guy lines on it and take out that haywire track. When the vessel arrived, we would take it from the truck and trailer and place it in position. Then we would dismantle the gantry. He told me to go ahead since I seemed to know what I was doing.

We finished erecting the gantry and moved it to the position where the vessel was to be placed. Then we placed guy lines on each corner to stabilize the gantry. Next we removed all of the haywire track system that had been placed. The next morning the vessel arrived on a truck and trailer, which we guided into position with the gantry. With the help of the crane we unloaded the vessel so that the top end of it was entering into the gantry with the bottom end on some skids, which would help during the raising of the vessel.

As I explained in a previous chapter, the gantry was powered with an air hoist on each corner. We got the air hoses all hooked up and the lifting chokers in place. The crane was rigged to help at the bottom end. We then went ahead with the lifting. All went well and we had the vessel in place in short order. The anchor bolts were a good fit, so it wasn't long before the vessel was standing on its own feet and we could cut the rigging loose.

This happened to be a Saturday so I asked the men if they would mind working some overtime. They all said that would be O.K. So we went ahead with dismantling the gantry. By 8 PM we had it down and ready for loading on a truck. Since the gantry was in place, I could then go back to my job in Squamish on Monday. So, I appointed one of the men to be the foreman on Monday for loading out the gantry steel. Everyone was in good spirits since the vessel was in place. It is a good feeling when a job has been done successfully, and especially with a rig that has injured and killed men. I spent Sunday at home in town and returned to Squamish on the Monday morning on the Bonnabelle.

When I arrived back in Squamish, I found everything in good shape. At the bridge, rivet work was proceeding well. The only rigging work left to do was to get the derrick cars ready for travelling. There were enough men on the job to take care of this work while the riveting was taking place. The weather was holding well so the rivet gang was making good time and everything was being cleaned up properly.

In a little over a week we were finished and all of the tools and rigging were loaded out. The crew then went back to Vancouver. Before we left the Chinese fellow that ran the dining room in the hotel put on a special dinner for the crew. There were plenty of drinks and by the time we were on the Bonnabell we were a real happy gang.

Back in Vancouver I went to the Dominion Bridge Co. office to find out what the next project was. The B.C. Electric Co. was going to erect a cableway for a power crossing from Lang Bay on the sunshine coast to Nelson Island as part of the electric transmission system to some of the islands in that area. This was a very similar project to the one we had done across Kootenay Lake several years previously.

John Prescott said to me that I had the experience on the Kootenay Lake project. So, this would be a good job for me to handle. Bob Harris would be the engineer. John said Bob and I would get along well together. However, John said that there would likely be a union jurisdictional argument over this work. So, they didn't know where we would finish the job. But we had to start because we had the contract.

CHAPTER 41

Jarvis Inlet Cable Crossing, June 1956

PREVIOUS TO THE SQUAMISH JOB I had moved my wife and kids down from Castlegar to Vancouver. We were living in south Vancouver in the Mount Pleasant district, a very nice area. It was now summer holidays for the kids, so I decided that they could all come with me and we would rent a summer cabin at Lang Bay. They were all happy about this move because there was a very nice beach at Lang Bay right close to the cabin.

We got well started with the job. The steel for the towers arrived and we unloaded on the Lang Bay side and ready for erection. Nelson Island would be different though. Nelson Island is actually a small mountain. We had a small boat with an outboard motor for the job, which we needed at different times for crossing Jarvis Inlet. We also had a logging camp on Nelson Island where we stayed while working that side.

The steel for the towers on the Nelson Island side needed to be delivered by barge and tug boat, and being on the salt chuck, needed to be delivered at high tide. This meant that a barge could come at some ungodly hour of the night and someone needed to be on hand to meet it when it arrived. I remember getting out of bed at around 2:30 AM for this job. All mobile equipment was required to come to the island by barge also. To get to the tower site there was a roadway of sorts, which climbed over the mountain to the tower site. Part of the grade was up to 35% grade.

To haul the steel we had the use of some cat crawler wagons and pulled it with a cat. In some places we had to use two cats in a tandem hitch because it was almost all that one cat could do to pull itself up the hill. Going down the other side, the loads had to be held back or they would have run away. All of this made for slow progress. But when you hire out on a job you expect that it won't be all roses.

Here is an example of what you might run into on a project like this. Bob Harris had to go to the tower site on the island to take the levels at the foundations. On the Nelson Island side we had a small jeep for some of our transportation. Bob and Stan smart and myself went over the mountain in the jeep. While there, a storm came up and a lot of wind. We went to the tower site and Bob took the levels. Stan was the rod man. We got back in the jeep and headed back to camp. Before we got to the top of the hill, we were stopped by a big fir tree that had come over in the windstorm while we were at the tower. The tree was at least two feet through and a big portion of it was on each side of the road. There was no way to get around the damned thing.

We didn't have any tools or rigging of any kind with us. We would have to either cut the tree or walk all the way back to camp. At the tower site while Bob and Stan had been busy with the level instrument I had looked around the job site. The only thing that I had seen in the way of tools or rigging was an old double bit axe and an old choker. I told Bob and Stan about these and said I would go back down to the tower site and get them. Then we would have a chance to get the tree out of our road. But, it would be a lot of work.

I back the jeep down to a place I could turn around and went down to the tower site and came back with the axe and choker. We started to chop through the tree. We had to make two cuts in order to get a chunk out of the tree. We took turns with the axe, so that made it a bit faster. Within no time lost between turns we were winning the battle. Finally, when the second cut was about three-quarters of the way through, with the old choker hooked to the cut end of the log and hooked to the jeep and a downhill pull, I managed to break the log and back down the hill with it. It was long past dark when we arrived back at camp, but the cook gave us some supper. We were three tired men.

Well, this was one job we didn't get to finish because the electricians union won the trade jurisdiction dispute over transmission lines. We had to leave the job to them. Our crew all returned to Vancouver to find other work. As it turned out, the company had a lot of work in Prince George, so this is where I worked next.

They had two jobs there. There was the PGE Railway bridge across the Fraser River and the Hudson Bay building up town in Prince George. Both were good-sized jobs. I worked a few days on the bridge job and then the steel arrived for the Hudson Bay job. This is where I spent the rest of the summer.

The building was situated between two existing buildings. The structure started in the basement and then rose three stories above street level. For a store building it had fairly heavy steel. We had access to the basement from the alley at the rear of the building. So, that is the way we moved our crane in, and also the steel for the job. We erected the street end first and worked form there to the rear of the building.

It was summer and good weather, so working conditions were good. We also had lots of sidewalk superintendents watching the progress. On this job, I think it was a first on a building in B.C. that we fastened it all together with high strength bolts instead of rivets.

We worked five days a week on the job, so that gave us plenty of time on the weekends for fishing and other activities. I remember taking the kids fishing out to McLeod Lake and River. I told them that the water they were fishing in would empty into the Arctic Ocean. They asked why so I explained to them that we were on the north side of the height of land and that the drainage of the country is now all to the north. So, when they got back home, they could tell their chums that they had been fishing in Arctic waters. My little daughter Shannon could hardly believe me.

We finished the job about the middle of August and returned to Vancouver.

CHAPTER 42

Kicking Horse Canyon, September 1956

WHEN I ARRIVED BACK IN Vancouver John Prescott told me the next project would be the park and the Yoho bridges out of Golden. I had a few days to get ready so I spent some time getting the tools and rigging ready. I started on this, but then I received a phone call from old Hi Carpenter at the Oak Street Bridge. There had been a bad accident there and Bill McGowan had drowned. Hi wanted me to come there and help out because the Golden job had been set back a few days and he wanted me as soon as possible.

I went to the Oak Street job the next morning. Murray McDonald was the engineer. I had worked with Murray on several jobs and enjoyed working with him. The first job was the girders on the north end of the bridge. There was a big crawler crane that had come in off of a barge. This was used along with a truck crane to erect these big girders. Murray explained the job to me. I started to think about it. The big crawler would take more than half of the load, and the truck crane would take the rest of it. That would have been O.K. if the job could be done with a short boom. But, to reach the piers with the girders we would need more than 80 feet of boom. It is very doubtful if the truck crane boom could have handled that much load with a long boom.

I told Murray that we were in trouble. He told me that Hi thought it would work. I told him that I didn't think it would. But, we put the long boom together and got everything ready. We did all of this and made sure the rig was level and well blocked under the outriggers. We hooked up the chokers and took the slack out of the load. I explained the deal to all of the men and told them to stay alert and not get too close to the load. We checked with the crawler and they were ready. I gave the signal to the operator and he went up on the load. The load was hardly a foot off the ground when CRASH!, the boom folded and everything came down. The boom was all smashed. Murray came over and said, "well Red, you were right".

Now some other arrangements had to be made for this part of the job. I got the word that the golden job was ready. I left on the 1st of September and that was also the morning that my son Michael was born. Right after I left my wife at the hospital with young Michael, I had to drive to Golden. This was before the Rodgers Pass was open, so it was a long drive with a detour through the United States and through the East Kootenay.

I arrived in Golden in the evening, but some of the crew did not arrive until the following day. We were supposed to stay at the Dawson and Wade camp, but it was a haywire camp so we all got rooms down in Golden. We started work on the Park Bridge, which was about 10 miles from Golden. The steel for this job came by rail on the C.P.R. We off-loaded it at the Leancoil Siding about 10 miles above the bridge site. We also received our cranes at this siding. One was a brand new truck crane with a 25-ton capacity built by Dominion Bridge in the Lachine shops in Montreal. This was the crane that we used for erecting these two bridges. The second crane was a Dominion crawler that we used for unloading. The operator on the truck crane was Jimmy Metcalfe. The operator for the crawler crane was Ernie Merkel. For hauling bridge steel we were able to get trucks in Golden.

We received several cars of steel and worked on the hauling job. We couldn't start the erection because the steel we needed first was not there. I phoned Vancouver and found out that it had been shipped. But, where was it? It seemed to be lost. I obtained the railway car number from the Vancouver office and started a search for the car. I did this by having the C.P.R. send telegrams to different places along the line. We finally found that the car was sidetracked in the Coquitlam yard. I notified our office and the car was soon on the way.

Now, as soon as we had the steel that became the first part of the Park Bridge, we were able to start the bridge erection. But, another problem came up from the design office. This bridge was to be erected by the cantilever method. So, the truss chords that fastened to the posts were to be fastened with a large pin. To insert the pin, the steel had to have perfect alignment or the pin had to have a tapered pilot end. The pins that we received were blunt so there was no way that we could enter them through the holes in the bridge chords. I had to phone Angus McGlaucklin in Vancouver to explain the problem. He said it was an over site on his part and wanted to know if I could get the pins tapered at the machine shop in Golden. I told him that could be done. So, he said to take care of that and that he would make sure the pins for the other end would be taken care of before they were shipped.

I took the pins to Golden where I had them tapered, so we didn't lose much time. At this point the erection went ahead very well. The local people were all wondering how the bridge held itself up. It is a little mind boggling to see a bridge structure hanging out over a river without support under it.

A number of the men were hunters so they had rifles in their cars thinking that they might get a chance to get a moose or an elk. One day, when we were heading out on the bridge with a chord on the crane, a car stopped and told me that there was bull moose about a mile back up the road. Ernie Merkel, the operator of the yard crane, was free so I asked him if he wanted to see if he could get it. He took Jimmy Metcalfe's gun and went up the road. We were busy placing the bridge chord. When he returned he said that he had killed it with one shot. At quitting time about six of us went with Ernie to get the moose. I had a company station wagon so we dragged the moose to the road and stuffed it into the station wagon. In Golden we left the moose with Ernie. He butchered it and some time later we all had a moose dinner that was prepared by his wife. Now back to work to build a bridge.

The weather was good so we were making good time with the bridge erection. When the halfway point was reached, we moved to the other side of the river for the second half of the span. This meant that we had to cross the old wooden bridge with the new crane. This was a risky undertaking. But, by removing the counterweight and shortening the boom, we made the crane a lot lighter. To make the old wooden bridge a little safer, we laid 4"×12" planks where the wheels of the crane would run to strengthen the deck. The crane was now much lighter. I asked Jimmy Metcalfe how he felt about the crossing. He said O.K. I told him not to change gears while on the bridge and not to hit the brakes. He said O.K and started across. We were a little anxious at this time but the crossing went very well. We replaced the counterweight and boom and resumed the erection.

On this end we did not have any trouble with the bridge pins as it had been taken care of in the Vancouver shop. Again, the progress was very good. It was an exceptional fall and was enjoyable weather for working. We finished the erection of this bridge in the middle of November and moved down the line to the next bridge. This bridge would be known as the Yoho Bridge.

The Yoho Bridge was also a cantilever job, except that the approaches were girder spans, and also there was a slight curve at each end of the bridge. We used false work bent at each end for the start of the truss. Again, we erected the east end of the bridge first. The steel was again hauled from the siding at Leancoil. But, when the erection moved to the west end, we moved the unloading work down to Golden, along with the crawler crane. There was one thing in our favour. There was very little highway traffic because the Rodgers Pass had not yet been built. But, then we had something else to contend with: WINTER.

The Kicking Horse Canyon can be the meanest place in the country to work in the winter. Or, maybe that was an exceptional winter, but the Kicking Horse was kicking us with everything it had, and then some. First of all, we had a lot of snow. Then the cold weather hit with a bang. Also, the wind can blow like hell down the canyon. The weather was so cold it gave us a lot of trouble with starting engines in the mornings.

We moved our tool and lunchroom shacks to the west end of the bridge site. We also placed them about 10 feet apart so as to have a place to run the crane between them at quitting time. This space could also be covered with planks and a tarp from the roof of one shack to the roof of the other. We then had a place to start the crane in the morning that would have a little protection from the weather.

This set-up worked very well, but one evening an oil heater in one of the shacks plugged up and started a fire. The crew was eating supper in the café when a man came in and told us there was a fire up at the bridge. We immediately ran out and into our cars to go to the bridge. At the bridge site we had the toolboxes all lined up on the side of the road. We also had the snow shovels right on top of the tools to always be ready for snow. When we arrived at the bridge, one shack was completely on fire and the fire was spreading to the other shack. The snow was about 2 feet deep. So, with several men shovelling snow onto the fire we were soon controlling it. But, the fire had reached some oilcans inside the second shack and one of these exploded. The spray hit some of the fellows in the face. We got them into the station wagon I was driving and I took them to the hospital in Golden. They were cared for immediately and I drove back to the bridge. When I arrived back at the bridge the men had the fire almost out. They soon finished this, but the crane had been damaged on the front end and would need some repairs.

I notified John Prescott in Vancouver. Fred Shaw, the mechanic from the erection shed, was sent up to repair the crane. We were lucky that there was not much damage and Fred had it repaired in a short time. The following week the weather turned milder, so the work improved, and by Christmas time the west approach was all in place. We were just about to shut down for the Christmas holiday when I received a phone call from John Prescott. He wanted to know if I could ship the crawler crane to Vancouver before we shut down. I replied that I would do it if there was a suitable rail car available. I went to the station to ask the C.P.R. agent about this and he checked it out. It happened that they had one car in the yard that was suitable. I sent John a wire and got some of the men onto this job. We had the crawler loaded and checked out that same day. Afterwards we all caught the afternoon train for Vancouver for the Christmas holidays.

We all spent Christmas holidays with our families and returned to work after the New Year. But, the winter weather turned colder with a lot more snow. It is hard to realize just how much cold winter weather slowed down a job. But the pace of work on a bridge of this nature was sometimes slowed to a crawl. We could have everything work ways at quitting time, and the next morning everything was covered with a foot of fresh snow. When this happens, before any work can take place, everybody had to shovel snow. Where the bolting work was taking place, the connections had to have the snow cleaned out with an air hose. Sometimes the steel had to have the ice thawed out with a propane torch before bolting could take place. Also, it seemed that the men worked much slower when it was so damn cold. In fact, the weather was so dam cold, I was afraid that due to the men having their faces half covered with scarves, that someone was going to stumble off the bridge and be killed.

I talked to John Prescott about this. I said it would be better to shut the job down until the weather changed. He agreed with me, but he also said that the company cannot pay wages unless the men are working. The men agreed with this and the shut down did not last long before the weather changed.

We started on the west end of the centre span. Due to the face burns that some of the men received during the fire, they had returned to Vancouver. Among the replacements were two French-Canadians from Montreal. They were both good ironworkers, but one of them didn't speak English. So, the other one was the interpreter. They were brothers, so a good job for them was to connect together. These were the Poriere brothers. They were both good men. They also had good appetites. Every night they would have either a porterhouse or New York steak. Maybe they never had steak before, but this was their supper every night. But, they earned it during the day.

Also at this time, John Prescott asked me if I could release Jim English. He needed him to run a raising gang at the airport job at Comox on Vancouver Island. I did this and I had Jack Townsend push the raising gang.

Little by little the weather started to improve. The snowstorms eased up and the progress was better. The bridge took shape and everything was work ways. When it came to closing the span, the west end was a fraction high. To overcome this problem, we backed the crane onto the span. The hinge on the west end worked perfectly and the connection came into line, and bolts and pins were placed. We had a bridge. All there was left was finishing the remainder of the bolting, place the drains and expansion joints, clean up the site, ship the equipment and tools to Vancouver, and finally the men too. That was the end of the Yoho Bridge.

CHAPTER 43

Garibaldi Bridge Girder Change, April 1957

THIS PROJECT WAS THE RESULT of the power project north of Squamish for a powerhouse at Cheekye. The Chakamus River was diverted so the water flowed into a huge depression that became known as Daisy Lake. This water flowed through an old creek bed under the P.G.E. railway. The creek bed had previously been bridged with a deck girder span, but would now have to have more clearance for a much larger water flow. This entailed the removal of the deck girders and the replacement of them with a set of through girders. This was another job for the big two-boom derrick car. The Emil Anderson Company had a construction camp at this site for part of the power project. So, this is where we stayed while working here.

Before a girder could be moved, all of the rails, deck ties, and bracing and struts had to be taken out. When this was all out of the way, we hooked into a big girder for removal. The original plan was to scrap this bridge. But, the plan was changed because the P.G.E. was going to be built further on to the Peace Country, and a place had been found for this particular bridge.

The engineering department of the Dominion Bridge Co. was unable to obtain the proper measurements of the anchor bolt location for the shoes of the new girders. This meant that we had to take care of this job in the field at the time of the girder erection – not the easiest thing to do out on a bridge job. The new shoe plates were 2½" thick. It is a hard job to cut a hole through iron this thick with a torch, unless you have a relief hole for a starting hole.

Our engineer was Don Jaimeson. He asked me if we could do this job with the cutting torch. I said yes, if they didn't mind a sloppy job. He asked how else we could do it then? I said we could mark out the holes the same as if we were in the shop, and drill them with the air drill. Then we could enlarge them with the torch and we would have an acceptable and decent job. That is what we had to do.

To do this kind of drilling in the field we used an item called an "old man", which is a type of drill press. It worked very well and allowed us to perform a good job. With the pilot holes in place, the torch could do a decent reaming job. One of the main things is that when you leave a job, you want to leave with the idea that the job was done properly.

We took care of this particular job on a Sunday. All went well. When we placed the girders, everything fit as though it had been done in the shop. From then on, it didn't take long to complete the project. We loaded the old girder span for shipment north. Then we loaded out our equipment and tools and returned to Vancouver. The Emil Anderson crew seemed to take a lot of interest in the job and was fascinated by the way the old steam rig could handle the tonnage of girders.

CHAPTER 44

Phil Gaglardi's Penticostal Church, Kamloops, June 1957

SOME TIME AFTER WE FINISHED the Garibaldi railway job, John Prescott came to me and said he had a new kind of job for me. He wanted me to go to Kamloops to build a church. I asked him who it was for. He smiled and said it was for Phil Gaglardis. I asked him "why me"? He smiled a little more and said that some of these jobs take diplomacy, and that he thought I was the man for this one. He told me that I would have to hire a crane and whatever I needed in Kamloops. And, that I could make arrangements for the crew at one of the hotels, and also a café for eating. He asked me if I could leave on the next day's train. I said O.K. The train left in the evening.

John called the union hall for a crew. I went home to get ready to leave. I was unable to find a suitable crane in Kamloops, but I was able to get one from Vernon. The steel arrived by truck from Vancouver. We only needed a small crew for this job. I arranged for rooms for the men at the Leyland Hotel, which was only a block from the job site, and also a restaurant close by.

The crane arrived from Vernon and also the steel from Vancouver. But, the crane was a small one so it was not able to reach far enough to place the trusses. Also, the anchor bolts were still not in place. To reach the trusses and place them in proper position, we had to get the crane closer to the centre of the job. The carpenter foreman was a brother to Phil Gaglardis. I asked him if there was any timber that I could use. He said he might be able to get some from the Public Works yard. I then got the idea that Gaglardis was the minister of Highways, so I went to the Public Works yard to look for suitable timber for some falsework. I needed this so I could bring the crane into the building and be above the basement at ground level. I picked out the necessary timber and told the yard foreman that it was for Phil Gaglardis's church and that it was only on loan. They loaded the timber and sent it to me at the church. We soon set it up and had the crane in the church where it could reach all of the iron and place everything.

Then there was the anchor bolt deal. Because the anchor bolts were not in place, I told the carpenter foreman we would fasten the columns to the trusses and stand them up together. He could place the bolts later. I had the guy lines on the trusses until I had several of them in place and braced together. This took some worries off my mind, and the work all went ahead.

When we had enough of the steel in place that we could back the crane out of the building again, we loaded out the timber again and sent it back to the yard like we had promised. Then we raised the remaining steel from a position on the ground outside the church. We finished all of the bolting job, and made sure that all of the iron was plumb. We then cleaned up the site and said goodbye to the Phil Gaglardis church.

Maybe this is the only way that ironworkers get to see the inside of a church. But then again, they don't have to listen to a sermon.

CHAPTER 45

Harrison River Highway Bridge, July/August 1957

I ARRIVED IN VANCOUVER ON the weekend of the July holiday and reported to the Dominion Bridge office. I received the news that I was to go to the Harrison River Bridge to relieve Al Wilson. He had to go to the Peace River to help out on the new P.G.E. railway bridge that was now under construction. I arrived at the Harrison River job the morning after the holiday. Al Wilson was there to meet me and show me what work remained to be done. He had it written down on a little piece of pocket notepaper. He told me of the remaining work. He said it would take me a little over a week to clean up the entire job. He then left for Vancouver and then on to the Peace River.

Most of the crew was staying at the Sasquatch Inn. I looked the job over and I didn't agree with the finishing time that Al had given me. The more I looked around at the job, the more work I found that remained to be done. In fact, there was still A LOT of work remaining. I phoned Murray McDonald, as he was the engineer in charge of this project. I asked him to please come out to the bridge job. I wanted him to go over the job with me because I knew that the news at the office was that the job should be finished in another week. I didn't want the office asking me everyday when I would be finished.

Murray came out and together we went over the job and made a list of the remaining work. I also told Murray of Al Wilson's time figure. He laughed about this and said that is the way some people are. I said yes, but when the bridge is turned over to the government, every detail has to be complete. He agreed with me and said that Al didn't have my experience.

I can't imagine what Al was thinking about when he said that the work would be all cleaned up in a week. The bridge railings had to be placed yet, along with all of the deck drains and expansion joints, plus other odds and ends of details that always seem to crop up on a job when you think that you have everything done.

I needed some kind of rig to handle this work, so they sent out the bull moose – a handy rig for these bull cooking jobs. At this time we had beautiful summer weather, so I rented a summer cabin and brought out my wife and kids to enjoy the summer holidays. They could also go to the Harrison Hotsprings. I did this because I could see where the work was going to last until some time in August. It was the second week of August when we finally cleaned up the site and loaded out.

Then it was back to Vancouver to find out what the next job would be. As it turned out, the next job was near Revelstoke – another highway bridge job at a place known as Wood's Crossing. For this project we stayed in Revelstoke. It was a three-span bridge over the Eagle River and the C.P.R. railway tracks. This would be become part of the Trans-Canada Highway system.

The steel for the project was shipped by rail from Vancouver. We received it at the Clan William Siding. The bridge was a continuous beam span of three spans, and the beams of each span were about 60 feet long. It took a truck and trailer to haul these beams. We were able to get the equipment in Revelstoke. The beams each weighed five or six tons each. The mobile crane with 60 feet of boom was able to handle the job O.K. The Rodgers Pass was not yet built and the traffic was light, so this was in our favour.

Because it was still summer holiday, I had my wife and kids with me. We had no trouble finding accommodation in Revelstoke. In fact, Revelstoke was a nice little town and we enjoyed living there. The job only lasted until the second week of September. The steel was all fastened with high strength bolts so the bolt-up job followed right behind the erection.

I had a brother, Ben, living down the Arrow Lakes at West Arrow Park. On the Labour Day weekend I drove to Arrowhead and caught the ferry to Beaton. I then drove to Trout Lake where we (my wife and kids) stayed over night. The next day we drove to Kaslo, then Nakusp, and then to Arrow Park to visit Ben and his family. We spent the night there and the next afternoon caught the ferry again fro Arrowhead and Revelstoke – an enjoyable weekend. There was a lot of country that was just then becoming accessible to motorists for the first time. So, this was an enjoyable way to spend a weekend.

Soon the holidays were over and the kids were back in school. The wife and kids had to go back to Vancouver for school. We finished this job by the middle of September. I returned to Vancouver for our next assignment. We did that and found out what it was. I was another trip to the Yukon to build more bridges and the powerhouse on the Yukon River at the Whitehorse rapids.

CHAPTER 46

Bridges and Powerhouse on the Whitehorse Rapids, Yukon Territory, 1957

AT THE OFFICE IN VANCOUVER I received the information about the Yukon project from John Prescott. I flew to Whitehorse where I met with Hi Carpenter. Together we went over the jobs that were ahead of us. I was able to rent all of the required equipment from John McIsaac Construction based in Whitehorse. They became allied with our work.

I went home and again packed my bags for another job. When I arrived at the airport I met Don Schook, one of the junior engineers of the company. He told me he was on the way to the Peace River Bridge. We were sitting together waiting for flight calls, but he had a different flight number than mine. When his number was called he said that he would see me in Fort St. John. I waived goodbye and when my flight was called, I boarded the plane. But, when the plane was air borne it flew out over the ocean (Georgia Straight), so I knew something was different. I asked the flight steward the reason, but he didn't seem to know why.

We were flying into the sunset. After a while we landed in Sand Spit on the Queen Charlotte Islands. The plane was serviced and refueled. When the plane took off again, there was a stewardess on board who looked after the remainder of the flight. I asked her why we were flying the coast route. She said that the reason was that Captain Dewar was in charge of the flight, and that he was licensed to fly the coastal route. I asked if that would be Ken Dewar. She answered yes and asked if I knew him. I told here that I knew all of the Dewar boys when they lived in the Kootenay.

We were flying in a D.C.3. Afterwards I saw her go into the forward cabin and shortly the captain came out. He came down the aisle and I stood up as we shook hands. It was a surprise for both of us. After all the small talk Ken asked me if I had ever been up in the forward end of one of these planes. I said no, so he asked me come and have a look. It was a beautiful moon-lite night and we flew over the Taku Glacier. What a site. Ken was the oldest of the Dewar boys and said he was going to retire soon. I was in the front end the rest of the way to Whitehorse. I said goodbye, and as it happened, never saw him again, although he did make it through to retirement.

When I landed in Whitehorse I met Hi. He had just come in on a plane from Fort St. John. We still had to fly to Mayo to see about the two bridges we were going to build in that area. When we arrived in Mayo we got rooms in the Mayo Inn. I also made arrangements for the crew for when they arrived. For a small town, there seemed to be a lot of activity in Mayo. Some of it was due to our work.

The engineering for these jobs was handled by the Poole Construction Company of Edmonton, Alberta. We met their engineer and together we went over the projected work. The Mayo Bridge was only a mile out of town, so transportation was simple. The Crooked Creek Bridge, however, was a different matter. The Crooked Creek bridge was on the south side of the Stewart River by about five miles. The Stewart River had a ferry crossing and there was living accommodation there at a roadside lodge. I made arrangements there for the crew.

The most important thing at the time was getting a rig to erect the steel. There was a crawler crane at the Crooked Creek job, but if we used it for Mayo it would have set the Crooked Creek project back. We didn't want to do that. At Mayo there was a D-6 Cat with a small derrick on the back end of it. The Mayo River was shallow, so this cat rig could do a lot of work by working right in the River, but we needed more boom than what the rig had. This cat belonged to John McIsaac Construction

Company. So, when I got back to Whitehorse I was able to get an extra boom section made at John McIsaac's shop.

Hi Carpenter and I spent a day with the Poole Construction engineer to look at both jobs. The Crooked Creek job was a 50-mile drive plus the ferry across the Stewart River both ways, so it was a long day. The Poole engineer had doubts about getting the job done in time before freeze up. But, after spending some time with us in the bar at the Mayo Inn, he could see that we knew what we were doing and seemed to be satisfied.

The next day we drove with the Poole Engineer to Whitehorse. On the way we had another look at the Crooked Creek Bridge. Back then it was a long drive from Mayo to Whitehorse – 256 miles and four ferries to cross. It was after dark by the time we crossed the last ferry at Carmacks. When we were 20 miles or more out of Whitehorse we ran out of gas. There was a small hole in the gas tank caused by some of the rough roads the car been over recently. Now what? Wait for help we thought. We waited for a while and as luck would have it, a freight truck came along that was a gas burner. We managed to get some gas from the driver. The engineer fellow who was driving found some gum which he stuck over the leak. It held, and we made it into Whitehorse O.K where we got rooms at the Whitehorse Inn and got some sleep.

The next day, Hi Carpenter left for the Peace River and my crew arrived from Vancouver. I then made arrangements for them to go to Mayo where we started the Mayo River Bridge. Some of the crew went with me in the jeep that I had arranged to get from John McIsaac Construction Company. McIsaac also fabricated the extra boom section for the Mayo job. While we were waiting for the boom section we started the bridge with the machine the way it was.

The steel for the job was trucked in from Whitehorse, from the White Pas and Yukon railway. We also got hold of an old army truck with a short boom to use for the yard work. This was a big help. We got the job started and after a few days our boom section arrived. We placed it in the rig. Then we could make good progress. The cat was able to work in the river quite well as the water was low at this time of the year. For the equipment we had, we made very good time. The weather was holding so we made good use of it and worked six days a week. This was only a 100-foot pony truss span. Even with a slow start, we finished the job in the first week of October. Afterwards, the crew returned to Whitehorse to erect the powerhouse.

For the crew, we found a good rooming and boarding house right downtown in Whitehorse. For transportation I had the McIsaac Jeep. For the steel erection at the powerhouse, we had an almost new American hoist and derrick truck crane. This was pleasant to work with after the little cat.

This was not a very large powerhouse in comparison with some of the other ones I had worked on. The steel arrived by truck from the railway. With the long boom on the crane it was easy to sort out the material for the proper erection sequence. This building was also fastened with high strength bolts. The general contractor, Poole Construction, supplied the compressed air for our needs. We worked six days a week on the project. When this job was finished we had to go north once more for the Crooked Creek Bridge.

There was a man on the crew by the name of Bill Falk. One day shortly before the end of the job, he came to ask me if I could take him into the drug store. He had severe pain in his arm and needed some kind of painkiller in the worst way. He had injured his arm while on the Oak Street Bridge. I think the cold was giving him trouble. I told him it was better for him to go back to Vancouver. I could take four men north with me for the Crooked Creek Bridge. So, along with Billy, I sent my son Joe Jr., who had been working as an apprentice. That left me four men to take north for the Crooked Creek Bridge. Also, there wasn't much accommodation at the Stewart Crossing Lodge, where we stayed.

We finished the powerhouse by the middle of October and loaded out our tools, etc., for the trip north. This was the last truck convoy of the season. After we crossed the ferries, they were pulled out and the rivers then froze over to have ice bridges. The day we headed north was the 17th of October.

That was an enjoyable trip. A long string of trucks all loaded with various types of equipment for the various industries that were working throughout the northern part of the Yukon. Between Whitehorse and Mayo there were four rivers to cross on ferries. First, the Yukon River at Carmacks, then the Pelly River, then the McMillan, and then the Stewart River. For our job, we would be staying on the south side of the Stewart River.

We left Whitehorse at 8 AM. It was late afternoon when we arrived at Stewart Crossing where we stayed for the Crooked Creek Bridge job. The fellow who ran the lodge at Stewart Crossing was a person I had known in Princeton in 1937. He had gone north and acquired property at the Stewart River crossing. He had married an Indian girl and they were running the lodge. The meals they supplied were good, but our room was a log cabin at the back of the lodge. The cabin was heated by a big wood stove, which they kept well supplied with wood. Our beds were all around the wall area and the toilet was outside. All in all though, it was not too bad for the Yukon. I arranged to have a truck at the river crossing for transportation to Mayo since I had to go there once a week to send in the time for the men and do whatever business had to be done, and also pick up the mail.

For the erection of the steel on the job we had the crawler crane, which I mentioned earlier in the story. This was a good rig, which had 50 feet of boom. So, this would be adequate for the job. The bridge truss was the same size as the one that we had erected in Mayo. The days were getting increasingly shorter, so we worked every day. Even then, before we finished the bridge, it was dark before quitting time. There was no time to lose.

The creek was now frozen and the whole country was tightening up for winter. The men were producing as much as possible. Every Friday I crossed the river in a rowboat and fired up the truck and drove to Mayo to take care of business needs. There was out-going mail, the mail to pick up in Mayo, and always a list of things for the men – mostly to remember to pick up some liquor for the evening happy hour. While I was gone into town, one of the men drove the jeep to bring the men in from work. I always made it back by suppertime.

Johnny Hunter had purchased the book of Yukon stories by Robert Service – The Rhymes of a Sourdough. So, in the evenings the guys would say "Come on Red, read a story to us." We would have a shot of rum and I would read. After a while I would look around to see them all asleep. A good supper and a good drink is very relaxing. I always enjoyed Robert Service poems too. This was the only entertainment that we had while in the Yukon.

By the time we came to the finish of the bridge job, the daylight was down to seven hours. We were not sorry to finish the job. We had to leave our tools, etc., to be trucked out later since the ice bridges were not in place yet. On our last day, we all rode the truck to Mayo, left the jeep at Stewart Crossing, and caught a plane to Whitehorse to make connections for Vancouver.

We travelled from Mayo in a DC-3 airplane. After we were airborne the stewardess asked us if we would like some lunch. We all said yes. I was sitting in a seat next to the isle. Thomy Rhodes was sitting by the window. Just then, the plane hit an air pocket and the plane took a big sudden drop. The stewardess landed across me right in my lap. I said "I don't need any lunch, just stay where you are and I will be quite happy." After the plane levelled off and she was able to recover herself, she was blushing like a rose. I told her not to feel bad. That was all of the excitement for that trip.

We landed in Whitehorse where we changed planes for the flight to Vancouver. On the way out to Vancouver we made a stop at Fort St. John to pick up more passengers. When we arrived in Vancouver I reported to the Dominion Bridge office. There I received the news that I had to go to a place called Tank Creek in the Thompson River canyon to erect a set of bridge girders for a highway underpass for the Trans Canada highway.

CHAPTER 47

Tank Creek Girders and Savona Bridge Remodelling

I WAS ONLY ABLE TO spend a couple of days at home before I had to leave for Tank Creek. I had to take one of the Dominion Bridge trucks, which could be used for a crummy on the job. The general contractor had a camp built out of mobile trailers, which is where we stayed during this project. The camp was tucked into one of the little side canyons of the Thompson River. The trailers were clean and neat, but very cramped for room. So, they were not the most comfortable of buildings for a crew to live in, but they were O.K. for a short job like this one.

The general contractor had a heavy North West power shovel with the dipper stick and shovel removed from it. This was our crane for the job – plenty husky but not much reach. This place was on the main line of the C.P.R. railway, so when it came time to place the girders it had to be done in the minimum amount of time so as not to hold up any trains.

The general contractor looked after the highway road-flagging job. The crawler crane could handle the girders with ease. The railway company gave us a specific number of hours to perform the job. Then, it was up to us to do the job without any hitches. We made sure everything was in order, and when the girders came, everything went according to the plan. Another girder job done safely. This place was just about the most cramped place to work in all of the Fraser and Thompson River canyons. But, we did the job without any trouble.

As soon as I finished the Tank Creek job, I returned to Vancouver where I went downtown and bought a used GMC panel truck. I then made arrangements to store our furniture, loaded up the wife and kids and our luggage, then drove to Kamloops. In Kamloops we rented a furnished apartment in North Kamloops. The crew for the Savona job stayed right in Savona.

At Savona, the government built a temporary bridge and roadway to handle the traffic while the bridge was being remodelled. For the steel erection we had one of the mobile truck cranes. For the unloading and handling at the railway yard we had a small crawler crane to unload the rail cars and load the trucks. The plan was to dismantle the end spans of the bridge and completely rebuild them, to reinforce the centre span, and replace all of the bridge deck with new floor beams and stringers and new steel decking. This decking was known as Irving grating. Some of the men asked me why it had that name. So, I told them that it was patented by one of my uncles. Of course, no one believed me. But, it was good bridge decking.

The weather was still mild with a fair amount of sunshine, so we were making good progress with the work. We did the north end span first then moved to the south end and rebuilt that one. Then we worked the centre span from the bridge deck.

The floor beams and stringers for this project were all made from castellated beams. That is a method where the beams have a series of holes cut at regular intervals and then the web of the beam is cut lengthways. When joined again, the beam is several inches deeper to become a stronger and lighter beam. Now, these all have diaphragm stiffeners for lateral bracing. The trusses of the centre span all had to have some extra bracing and stiffening members as well.

Just before Christmas I received a call from John Prescott to see if I could send the crawler crane to Kelowna because it was needed there for the Kelowna bridge, which was just starting. Just at this time there was a lot of bad winter weather with reports of trucks off the road in the ditch. So, I ordered a rail car for the shipping of the crawler crane. We shipped the crawler by CPR rail and then there was no worry about a truck going in the ditch.

After the Christmas holiday most of the remaining work was the bracing and stiffening of the centre span. By this time the crew had been reduced in size, and we had colder winter weather. By the end of January we were almost finished with the Savona Bridge when I received a call from John Prescott that I had to leave for the Peace River. The bridge had collapsed at Taylor Flats and now had to be dismantled.

CHAPTER 48

Dismantling the Peace River Highway Bridge, 1958

I ARRIVED AT THE FORT St. John airport on the 10th of February. I went to Taylor Flats where we all stayed during the dismantling of the bridge. The bridge was in one hell of a mess. The north end suspension span was lying in the river. The centre span was in a big deep sag of about 18 feet. The north tower was leaning almost 10 feet to the south. Jim McNaughton was the field engineer at the time. He was a good man to work with. The first job was to get rid of the concrete deck. There were several ideas for cutting the concrete, but the only one that worked worth a damn was the old jackhammer, and letting the pieces of concrete fall on the ice where nature would take care of it when spring arrived. After some wasted time, this was the method we used.

One of our biggest and toughest jobs was cutting out all the rivets in the centre span. These were ⅞" diameter rivets. Some of the crew had never been on a rivet-busting job before. We only had one Long Thom, which was one of the best tools for this job. Although, it takes at least two men to handle it. We did have busting chisels for the rivet guns, but some men need a lot of practice to be good with these tools. The only access to the work was from the south end of the bridge, which was at least 10 miles by way of the PGE railway bridge over the Peace and Pine Rivers.

I have often been asked what was the reason of the bridge collapse, because it was not a very old bridge. I also wondered a lot of times why it should have happened. As close as I can remember, the bridge failure took place on 17 October 1957. I was in Whitehorse, Yukon Territory, when it happened.

A few days previous to the bridge collapse, I had been invited to dinner to the home of John McIssac – the owner of the John McIsaac Construction company with whom we were doing business on the Yukon projects. After dinner was over we sat in the living room discussing bridge jobs. John asked me if I was familiar with the suspension bridge at Taylor Flats over the Peace River. I replied that I didn't know much about it. He then said there was going to be trouble there. I asked in what way. He told me how they had hauled the big vessels for the Petroleum plant over the bridge at the time of the plant construction. The bridge had been designed for a live load of 25 tons. The vessels for the plant were in the neighbourhood of 100 tons, plus the weight of the two trucks used in transporting the vessels. From the reports on this work, two such trips were made.

The bridge had been built on a grade so that the north end was higher than the south end. The north end anchor was only a dead weight, and not pinned down with anything such as pilings. The petroleum company had also been allowed to excavate and build a big pipeline in front of the anchor to deliver water to their plant, which was located on the bench above. According the weather reports, this was the wettest season in years, which saturated the hill where the bridge anchor was placed. Now, the pipeline sprung a leak and was washing out much of the ground in front of the anchor. The anchor, being pulled by the bridge cables, then started to move out to the south. This in turn caused pressure on the cable bent through the short deck truss, which was located between the anchor and the cable bent. Then the short deck truss lost its fastening to the cable bent, so it fell to the ground. The cable bent failed and then the suspension cables snapped so the north end suspension span fell to the river. The north tower then leaned towards the centre and this is the way the bridge was when we arrived.

At this point, a labour gang went to work with jackhammers to bust out the concrete. The ironworkers started the job of busting the rivets and replacing about 30% of the holes with bolts and pins. It was then decided by the engineers that it would require an anchor on the north end to place cables from the top of the north tower to the anchor. This would allow us to pull the tower, which in turn would bring the bridge deck level for a crane to be able to work on the deck for the dismantling of the centre span. The anchor was constructed in the roadway to the north of the old cable anchor site. This required a number of steel fittings on the top of the north tower that held the cables from this anchor.

Our engineer, Jim McNaughton, had to leave for other work so Bob Harris took his place. We were still travelling to work the long way around by way of the railway bridge. I asked Bob what he thought about a catwalk from the north side to the tower so that the crew could walk onto the bridge from the north side. He thought it to be a good idea, so he ordered the cables and U-bolt clamps for the catwalk. We used 1"-cables to support the catwalk with ⅝" diameter cables for the handrails with 2"×6" for the deck. These were fastened with the U-bolt clamps. When we received the cables, it did not take long to build our catwalk bridge, which eliminated an hour travelling time in both the morning and night.

The forms for the anchor were now at the stage where the reinforcing bars had to be placed. Also, snow was melting and running down the roadway. We diverted this runoff with a big steel pipe, which carried the water past the work on the anchor. Now, there was something of which we did not have any knowledge. Up at the petroleum plant a tank was running over on account of a faulty valve. The gasoline, or whatever it was, was running off with the snowmelt and running down to the river by way of the old roadway where we were building the new anchor.

There were several ironworkers placing rebar rods and tying them into place in the anchor form. There were also some labourers working there. The crew was working overtime to finish the job. At this time we were expecting some truckloads of equipment from Vancouver. This was in the evening after supper. One of the trucks arrived and the driver asked me if we could unload him. I asked him if he knew how close the other trucks were. He said they were only a half and hour behind him. I said O.K. and that I would get the crane operator and a crew. We had just arrived at the anchor site when someone yelled from inside the anchor form "Hey something is wrong! There is a hell of a smell of gas here!" The labour foreman yelled for them to get the hell out of the form. They got out and just then there was some kind of an explosion and fire. The men all ran for their lives. There was fire all the way up and down the stream where the water was running on the side of the road and all the way to the petroleum plant, and also down to the river. Some men tried to run up the bank on the side of the road. One of them fell back into the stream, which was now a stream of fire. This was one of the labour crew, a man by the name of Art Wills. The crane operator was burnt about the face and hands and some of the others had similar burns. The crane and welding machine was damaged, and also one side of my truck. Some of the men lost work clothes that had been in the change shack. We never did get to know what started the fire. Pacific Petroleum also suffered. When the fire reached the plant eight tanks burned. It was not fully extinguished for another 30 hours or more.

When a tank farm or storage place is built to hold volatile liquids, it is supposed to have a dyke built around it to contain the amount of liquid that is in the tanks. When the dyke was built in this case, it was only built around three sides because freeze caught up with them on the dyke project before they could finish. So, the dyke was not finished but the tanks were filled. When the trouble developed the liquid gas ran away with the snowmelt and we were in the trap.

We were lucky that there was only one man who lost his life due to that goddamned fire, and that there was not a lot more damage. There was no doubt a lot of controversy over this in a good many offices before everything would be settled.

Well, we managed to get the anchor finished and the cables run from the anchor to the tower and all fastened in place. The anchor was then back filled so that we could tighten the cables to straighten the tower and lift the suspension span to a position that would be near level. When the anchor was built there were 4" pipes placed in the concrete through which the cables could be run for the job of pulling the bridge tower back into line. The ends of the cables were fastened to 3" diameter steel rods, which were threaded on the end with an acme thread. On the backside of the anchor where the rods came through we placed heavy steel plates over them. When the rods came through the anchor, the nuts on the bolts could hold the load. With another steel plate the power jacks could be placed between the plates and pressure applied. As the rods came through, the first set of nuts would be tightened against the first plate. Then, the jacks were reset for another pull.

We used four jacks for this job so that altogether we could take a tension strain of 1000 tons. The tower came back to a vertical position and the span was in a normal position ready to dismantle. For the next month the rivet-busting job proceeded to be ready for the dismantling work.

It was after the fire, but previous to the job of pulling the tower to the vertical position that the second narrows bridge in Vancouver had an effect on the Peace River job. The second narrows was running low on steel due to delayed shipments from the steel mills. So, the bridge was shut down for a spell. This gave Hi Carpenter a chance to visit the Peace River job. He brought his raising gang foreman with him, Jim English. As I noted before in this story, I had been with Hi on several jobs. Jim English had spent a lot of his apprentice time with me and also worked for me as a raising gang foreman. There had been some difficulties on the Peace River job that were hard to put a handle on, some of these being poor tools or not the proper tool for the job, and sometimes inefficient men. But, when you are a thousand miles from home base, these matters are sometimes hard to correct.

Jim took on the job to run the rigging gang and very soon some of the men were leaving. I talked to Hi about this. If someone did not suit Hi he would fire him right away. I told Hi that was probably O.K. when we were in town, where we could hire more men from the hall by just using the phone. But, when you are 1500 miles away it is a hell of a different matter. I also told him that besides, a new man might not be as good as the one you fire. He did not agree on this.

A short time later Hi and Jim left to return to Vancouver. On Tuesday afternoon at quitting time, the crew had al stopped at the Taylor Flats hotel to have a beer. This was 17 June. Johnny Le Piere had gone home where he was living in a motel. I was sitting facing the door when in came Johnny. His face was white. I knew that something was wrong by the look of him. He came to the table but he was so nervous he could hardly speak. Finally, he said, "Holy god, the Second Narrows Bridge collapsed." The news was on the radio when he arrived at the motel.

Now, everyone was making phone calls because all had friends or relatives on the project. This would take some time. I walked into the hotel lobby after supper. Arnie Moffat was there. He was in tears. I asked what the trouble was. He told me that his brother Percy had gone down with the bridge. He had not even known that his brother was working on that job. Arnie was feeling terrible and he said he would have to leave for

Vancouver in the morning, but he was short of money. I told him not to worry and lent him $100. I felt bad too because I knew Percy very well.

This was a terrible shock to all of the crew. The ironworkers are a close-knit group of men, mostly due to the kind of work they do. So, something like this really hit them a hard blow. Now, as I mentioned before, we had some problems on the job that had been hard to overcome. But, the company thought that a new foreman would be the answer, so this is what happened.

Well, that was fine with me, so I left and decided that the best thing for me was to take a good holiday and forget other people's worries. So, I went back to Castlegar.

CHAPTER 49

Celgar Pulp Mill and Other Jobs, 1958-63

AFTER ARRIVING IN CASTLEGAR WITH my wife and kids, we rented a house on the west Robson Road. This was an older house but a fairly good one that I thought would do us for some time because I had no idea what would be ahead for work. This place also had an old barn, which I fixed up for a workshop. At this time there was a lot of talk going on about the proposed pulp mill and other various jobs that were coming up in the area. The old big truck that I had left in Castlegar needed quite a bit of work. So, this would be a good time to work on the truck in case work for it turned up. The old barn came in handy for this.

My small truck was getting some work done on it. One day as I was walking down the road from town, the Government Road foreman stopped to give me a ride home. He asked me if I was working. I said "not right now". He asked me if I would come work for him. I asked him what he had. He said he needed someone to look after the compressors and equipment that they would be using to drill and blast out the rock bluff for the road to the Celgar Mill. This job was very close to where we were living, so I said "O.K." This was not a hard job for me to handle – service the machines, fuel them, clean them, and make sure that they were all

O.K. This was a big rock bluff to drill and blast so this job lasted for some time. When this was finished the road to the new Celgar mill could also be finished. Then mill construction would start. I stayed with this job until the rock bluff was finished. As soon as the road was ready, some of the pulp mill contracts started. But of course, it was some time before any of these jobs were ready for steel erection.

The first small job to turn up was the new Woolworth store in Nelson. This was done by the Chinook crane service from Calgary. This was a very short job as it was mostly a one-story building built on the corner of Baker and Ward Streets.

A little later on another job turned up in Nelson. This was the Notre Dame college building out in Fairview. This job was several weeks duration. This was done by the Dominion Bridge Company. They called me from Vancouver to ask me if I would look after the job. I agreed and the job went very well. At this time the ironworkers went on strike so all work was held up for some time.

One of the first jobs to be done at the Celgar plant was the steel fence around the perimeter of the area. There were some contractors that were not involved in the ironworkers strike. The fencing contractor was one of them. When the fencing job started I received a call to work for them. This turned out to be an O.K. job.

When this job was finished I found time to work on my big old truck. This was time well spent because later on there was plenty of work for the truck on the Celgar project.

Some time later the strike was over and I received a call from the Dominion Bridge Company. They had the job to build the dry kiln at the pulp mill. I was asked to do this job, which I did. This was a good job. Heavy drum sections to handle and place. For this project we had a North West crawler crane – a very good crane for this work. This was a big dry kiln, so even with the North West crane we could not handle all of the sections. For these sections we had to build false work and roll these from the railway flat cars all the way into position above the roller nest, and then jack them down to their final position. The lighter sections, which weighed about 25 tons, could be placed with the crane. Also, the tires could be placed, which had to be done carefully and welded to the kiln tube or body. These were large items to handle, and also to set to very fine tolerances.

When the dry kiln project was complete, the Dominion Bridge

Company did not have any more contracts with the pulp mill. Most of the ironwork erection went to the Arrow Steel Erectors, a branch of the Arrow Transfer Company.

The big steam powerhouse was their most important building on the project. I went to work for them on this job to push the raising gang. There was a large amount of steel in this building. Some of it was at least 100 feet high. Also, some was heavy iron to support to the steam boilers. The erection crane for this job as a 25-ton mobile – a good crane, but not enough reach.

For the high steel on the building Arrow did not have a guy derrick so they used a different method, which was not a very good one. They hoisted the crane body off of the truck and placed it on the third floor of the building. Then it could reach high enough, but the machine would be on its own way to dismantle and lower down to ground level again, actually a hell of a job. Some of these kinds of ideas soon show the difference between the tried and true methods, which have been proven over the years of erecting steel into high places. On most multi-story buildings, a gang of ironworkers jump a guy derrick four floors in a four-hour period, and the same from dismantling – some difference. I suppose it is a matter of live and learn.

While on this powerhouse job we had one real sad experience. We had been erecting the steel on part of the east wall of the building. It was shortly after the lunch hour. The connectors had just reached the top to connect the top strut in that area, when Kevan Dugan slipped and fell. He hit the top of a tank about half way down and then fell the rest of the way to the ground. We got him into an ambulance in short order, but he died in the Castlegar hospital later that same day. It was very sad.

When the powerhouse steel was all in place, Arrow had a few smaller jobs. But, they wanted to leave and not take on any more work on this project. Horton Steel from Edmonton was building the digester. The Flanders Installations were installing a lot of the pulp mill equipment.

There were still a lot small jobs to be done throughout the mill. Hughie MacDonald was the engineer for the Simonds Engineering Company. They were the consulting engineers for the entire project. Hughie came to me one day and said that he had a proposition for me. I asked him what that could be. He went on to say that there were a lot of small jobs to be cleaned up on the project, and it seemed that these jobs were not getting done. He then asked me if I would want to take on these jobs as a contractor. This was such a surprise to me that I found it hard to answer. I asked "why me?" He said, "Because we know that you can be trusted to do the job right". I told him I would have to think about it. I knew I could do the work O.K. But, there was bookwork to take of, wages to be paid every week, and then I would have to take out a withdrawal card from the union. Everything had to be done fair and square.

One o the biggest problems would be the wages for the men every week. Although, Hughie said that if I turned in my paper work as soon as a job was finished, he would see that the money came through. I told Hughie "O.K." and that I would talk to the bank about it. We shook hands and I told him that I would let him know very soon. I went to see the bank manager. I had known him for some time. I explained the situation to him. He didn't hesitate and said he would open an account for me and call it your construction account. He then made the first deposit.

I then went back to Arrow and drew my time. Then I told Hughie that I would take the deal. He showed me the first jobs. Then I called the union hall for a couple of men and also arranged for their accommodation at the Celgar camp. I named my company "J.A. Irving Construction".

CHAPTER 50

Celgar Pulp Mill, and J.A. Irving Construction

IT WAS EARLY SEPTEMBER. THE jobs could be done with only a couple of men. But soon, I need more men so I called the union hall again and hired more. The work was all progressing well and more work was coming almost every day. I knew that I would need some help with the bookwork, so I hired my brother for the job. He as two years older than me and he had done a lot of book keeping, so this worked out fine. I also needed a place on the job to keep some equipment, as well as a tool shed or shack. Arrow wanted to get rid of their tool sheds and shacks, so I managed to get all of them at a bargain price. And, they didn't even have to be moved. A few days later Coleman Electric needed a shack. Since I had more than I needed, I sold one of them and recovered the purchase price.

We were kept busy with all of these "small jobs". Some were not so small. I made sure all of the bookwork was up to date. Ben was a good book keeper, and I have always had a good memory so everything went along O.K.

As soon as any work slacked off and men were not needed, they were laid off. It was a surprising thing that after the pulp mill was built, how many small jobs still had to be done. For most of the winter we were able to get by with only a small crew of about four men. There was a lot of welding to be done. I rented a welding machine almost steady. I was in the process of buying one when the news came of the Pacific Steel Erectors bankruptcy sale.

I received the catalogue in the mail so I showed this to the bank manager and said I think I can make a better deal than buying this other one. He agreed and told me to take in the sale. I did that and for the price of the one welding machine, I got a good welding machine, snatch blocks, comealongs, drills, and many other items of small rigging. Now I didn't have to rent one.

The Horton Steel Company from Edmonton was building the pulp mill digester plus some other jobs. They were always in need of moving bolts, pins, cables, and other pieces of boilermaker's equipment. They rented my old truck for this work. The truck suited them for the job and they were using it a lot of the time. So, the truck was earning money too.

The Boundary Electric Company advertised a hand winch for sale. This was one thing I could use on the job, and I didn't have one. It was a bargain price so I bought it. The electricians who had been using it said it was no good. I took it home, cleaned it thoroughly, greased it, and found nothing wrong with it. It worked first class. At the time, we didn't have any material that could not be hoisted with a hand winch. Then I made up another tool to go with the hand winch. I needed a good drill on a lot of different jobs. So, I purchased a no.3 Morse taper electric drill. Then I welded a no.3 broken drill bit to an extra drive gear for the winch, and, we could then use the winch with power.

We also made an old man out of some scrap shafting and iron for the drilling jobs. The drill, being a no.3, was capable of drilling and reaming holes up to 1¼" in diameter. Also, one of the tools I had managed to get at the bankruptcy sale was a no.4 corner air motor. With this we could drill almost any hole required. We also had to do quite a lot of fabricating for some jobs, so I purchased a couple of good acetylene cutting torches. We were then equipped good enough for small jobs.

The A.I.M. Company of Vancouver had been doing a lot of the steel fabricating for the pulp mill project and still had some erection work to be done. So, then we did this work. But as I said, before they were small jobs. Well, time went on and the pulp millwork gradually came to a finish. There were other jobs to bid on in the area, but some other outfits were bidding on these also, sometimes with some foolish low bids. I could not see any sense in working unless a job was making some money, so I shut the business down and decided I would go back to work for someone else.

CHAPTER 51

Kimberley Fertilizer Plant Extension, 1963-64

When I decided to shut down the business I turned in my withdrawal card and let the union hall know that I was available for work. In a short time I received a call to go to Kimberley to work for the Kootenay Engineering Company. When I arrived in Kimberley I found the project well started. There was a camp for the men right at the job site. The construction superintendent was a fellow who I had known previously. He had been a carpenter foreman on other jobs. He seemed glad to see me and said that he had lots of work ahead for me. Then we had a lot of small talk about other work and a few laughs and jokes.

He said that he needed a foreman to look after all the work and that he knew I could handle it. I said O.K. Most of the work ahead was extending the existing buildings. I had worked on these buildings when the Fertilizer plant had been erected back in 1952/53.

For the steel erection we had some of the same cranes that had been there at the time of the original construction of the plant. There was the same Lima Crawler and also the same Northwest crawler. These were still good cranes and husky enough for most of the work. The plant was built on a flat bench land so there was no trouble to move the crawler cranes from one building to another. Since the high strength bolt was being used at that time, there was no riveting to be done.

There was a rail trackage into the job site so most of the steel and equipment was shipped in by rail. There was also plenty of yard room for storage. Most of the work went ahead in an ordinary manner, but a few jobs required some rigging inside the buildings. This would be a different deal altogether.

We had quite a few men on the job who were new at the trade and therefore did not have hardly any rigging experience. So, when some of these jobs had to be done, we had to keep a close eye on all the details of the work to keep everything safe and proper. The iron plant was one of these jobs. Building the big furnace was all inside rigging work. This was a 100-ton per day furnace. For a lot of men, building a furnace like this was a once in a lifetime job. It was an electric furnace so it required a large transformer to be placed within the building. This was the heaviest rigging job on the project.

The transformer room was about 40 feet above the ground floor. This was where the transformer had to be hoisted and placed. The transformer was equipped with small railway wheels that matched the rails that had been placed on the transformer floor on that level. On this level, the floor had sections that could be opened up and moved for the hoisting of the transformer. High above were lifting beams on which to hang the rigging for hoisting the transformer.

Then came the job of hoisting this big, heavy, and very expensive piece of equipment. Kootenay Engineering did not have a suitable hoist for the job. They suggested using the load lines of the two cranes. I told them that would not work worth a damn. So they asked what the answer was. I said that we needed a good 2-drum hoist or donkey engine. They asked where we could get one. I said most likely from the Dominion Bridge Company. They asked me if I could arrange that. We were in the construction office at the time, so I asked them if I could use the phone. I picked up the phone and called Dominion Bridge in Vancouver. I asked to speak to Bob Harris. He was surprised to hear me on the phone, but after some small talk I told him what I was doing and what I needed. He then told me how much the rental would be and that the hoist would be shipped without cables. I told him the company would send him a purchase order and we would await shipment. The company was surprised that it could be arranged so quickly.

We continued with the work of preparing for the big lift. For example we made sure that all of the hosting blocks were in good shape, greased, and cleaned. We had new hoisting cables for the job and good snatch blocks for fair leads. When the transformer arrived on the rail car we had the railway track extended to the plant doorway so the transformer could be lifted by the crawler cranes, and the rail car could be pulled out from under it. Then it could be lowered to the ground and rolled into the building on its own wheels where the rigging was waiting for it. Then the hoist could be brought into place and unloaded and the hoist lines connected. Then the load blocks could be hooked to the transformer and everything was ready for the big lift.

The operator for this particular job was Bill Frolick. He was usually on a truck crane but he was a very good operator – careful and attentive. I had picked out the best crew for this job. It was shortly after lunch when we were ready for the lift. When the transformer was above the floor level the men had to work under the load to replace the floor under the load. The transformer weighed at least 60 tons. No wonder I wanted everything perfect for the job. Well, all went as planned and the transformer went into place without a hitch of any kind. All of the high-priced help from the office came to watch the proceedings.

Then, at the building that was known as the rock plant, we had another problem. Ed Green, the superintendent, said we had to get the rigging ready to set the rock crusher in place. He told me to take a look and see what I needed for the job. The rock crusher weighed 30 tons. But, there was a big heavy beam overhead that could be used for the job. I looked at the beam to see the size of it and the span of its bearing points. I then looked this up in the AISC book to check all this out for strength for the proposed lift of the rock crusher. I found that it was not near strong enough for the weight with its existing span. I told Ed Green of this. When he told them in the office about it, they did not believe it until they went over the beam strengths in the AISC book. We had to make other arrangements.

The rock crusher wasn't too big of a problem. There was plenty of room to build false work and the crusher could be handled on the outside of the building with one of the crawler cranes. The false work was built and the crusher was set on the false work on a crib. Then with rollers it was moved into position above the crusher base. Then with good hydraulic jacks it was lowered down to its final position.

Most of the remaining work was straightforward ironwork. A few problems regarding jurisdictional disputes came up, mostly from the pipe fitters union. Most of the time the work went on without too many problems.

It was on this job, or rather while I was on it, that I had a different problem develop. My wife had always complained that I was always going away from home. But this was not the case since I had brought my wife and kids to Kimberley on this project, the same as I had done before. But, this didn't suit her either. Anyway, we were having a lot of trouble and by the spring of 1965 we were in divorce court. I obtained a divorce. The work was finishing and the High Arrow Dam was starting, so that is where I went. I worked on that project from start to finish.

Previous to this I had taken my wife and kids whenever I could to different places in B.C. to be with me while on various jobs, such as Kimberley, Peace River, Lillooet, Vancouver, Revelstoke, Harrison River, Sicamous, Kamloops, and Castlegar. We also lived in Victoria and Osoyoos. All that moving seems to show that a man wanted his family close to him.

CHAPTER 52

High Arrow Dam, Castlegar, 1965-68

After leaving Kimberley I called our union hall and I was told to report to the High Arrow project in Castlegar. I did that and found that I was the first ironworker there. At that time, the equipment was just starting to arrive, and there was a lot of it. To handle the work, more ironworkers were needed. The first part of the job was to assemble the machines as they arrived. There were crawler cranes, power shovels, truck cranes, and various other pieces of equipment to unload and assemble. A large camp had been established right on the site.

This was a B.C. hydro project. The contractor was an American outfit. To build the dam they had a Canadian Company as an associate, but this seemed to be in name only. It was known as The Foundation Dravo Corporation. Everything on the project, including all of the supervisors, was American. It makes one wonder why the Canadian Partner was necessary. After working for contractors for so many years and doing work in a safe and economical manner, it was hell to see work being done in a manner where material and time were wasted to get the job done. But, it seemed that was the goal of the project.

The project had been bid by Canadian contractors but the bids were thrown out with what was known as a target price – some target. In later years I often wondered why I stayed with the job. I suppose part of the reason was that the pay cheques were good and the work was steady except that the politics of the job were rotten.

The material that came by rail had to be unloaded over at the siding at Brilliant and reloaded onto trucks to be hauled to the job site. This was a five-mile haul.

At this time, mid 1960s, there was a lot of construction in various parts of B.C. As a result, there were a considerable number of inexperienced men on permit from the union hall. A number of the men on the work force left a lot to be desired as tradesmen. I was not one to bellyache about conditions and hard work, but I always believed in fairness, and fairness is a two-way street. Workmen have to be fair, and the employer has also got to be fair. But these goddamned dam jobs were really something different. A white hard hat, a cigar, and a two-way radio in a pickup truck seemed to be the ingredients that constituted a supervisor – and maybe a loud voice with a southern accent. At least that was the way it was on the first part of the project until they came to realize that Canadians were capable of construction work also.

One of the cranes we had was a brand new 110-ton Bucyrus Erie truck crane. One day it had been working where it was unloading some material for a barge. At quitting time it had been left there on fill with the out-riggers extended and in a safe position. Of course, this job was operating on two shifts. One night, somebody decided that a roadway was needed on the side of this fill where the crane was sitting. They thought it was needed to get down to the river. A big cat was sent there to cut the roadway. The cat undermined the crane outriggers and the crane toppled over – very good supervision.

These were the kind of booboos that seemed to take place throughout the project. On the north end of the project they had a washing plant for the concrete gravel. Close by was a big pond of waste water. A D-8 cat working there somehow got stuck in this pond. I was at the rigging shack and was notified about the cat. I took some men and some heavy chokers and shackles in a truck to the site of the trouble and called for another cat to pullout the one in the mud. To place the rigging on the cat we were in water almost up to our knees. All of a sudden a loud voice from the roadway above started yelling at us "Come on, get that thing out of there!" I stopped work and said the men "Hold on". I also have a hell of a big voice so I answered, and I was also mad as hell: "Look you goddamned assholes, if you are so goddamned good, come down here and do the job yourselves." This loudmouth happened to be the project manager. He must have been surprised because he called back "O.K. Red." Then he and the rest of the white hats left and we got the cat out of the mud hole. I never heard anything more.

Throughout the project there were, at times, jobs that were interesting, but a lot of jobs that were a pain in the backside. There were some real good cranes to work with, but sometimes for small jobs it was like pulling teeth to get the proper tools to work with. For instance, if there was iron that had poor holes for connection, they did not have anything in the line of air tools for drilling and reaming. It was hard to understand an outfit that owned million-dollar cranes, power shovels, cats, etc., but could not buy some simple hand tools. When we asked for this kind of equipment they looked at us like we had come from Mars.

In some cases there was waste that was unbelievable. A big crawler crane with a 7½ yard bucket could break a drag cable right close to the bucket and be replaced with a new one. The old one, which could be used for a smaller machine, would be buried and left. Cost plus projects? B.C. taxpayers had lots of money.

There were two divisions for the work on the project. What was known as stage one handled all the incoming material and assembled all the cranes, shovels, and general equipment, and placed all iron that was concreted in place. Stage two erected all cranes and equipment that became part of the dam.

Here is a job that was handled by the stage-two division. When some of the head works had been built to the level, which was to be the top of the dam, stage two erected the crane that would eventually be used for lifting the gates over the head works. For this job they used the 110-ton Bucyrus truck crane. The material had all been hauled and unloaded at the east end of the dam site. There was a slight grade on the way up to the dam level. The crane was equipped with at least 100 feet of boom, not very good to travel with, but fine when the outriggers are used. The crew assembled the crane legs with the top sections on this grade. Then they intended to retract the outriggers and travel up the grade on to the dam level with the assembled section. To hoist the section to a vertical position, the boom had to swing and this put the crane off level. The crane started to tip over. The operator got excited and dropped the load just missing some of the crew. Not much damage but some nervous people. Another time, with the same crane with a different operator with a long boom on, the crane swung the machine when the boom was in a low position and the outriggers not extended. That tipped the crane over.

On the upstream end of one of the sluice piers w were installing the iron known as the nosepiece. This had to be placed and lined before the concrete could be poured. It was braced with pieces of rebar that were embedded in the concrete. I was on the scaffold with the crew. Without any warning, a piece of 2"× 6"× 12' lumber came down from the top of the pier. It hit me on the top of my head and knocked me down to my knees. The end of it hit one of the men on the side of his ribs. He was falling but I came up off of the scaffold and caught hold of him before he fell from the scaffold. He seemed to be in bad shape. We had him placed in an ambulance and sent to the hospital. It was later that I felt the effects of the blow to my head. My neck was plenty sore but I didn't do anything about it. Later on I was awarded the gold hat award for my hard hat saving my life. Some of the engineering crew had been working on top of the pier and had kicked a loose piece of 2"× 6" which slid on the icy deck of the pier and came down 45 feet. The middle of the piece hit me on the head.

As I mentioned before, we had at different times a lot of green men. The hiring of men was all done from the Hydro office. I don't think they knew the difference between an ironworker and a gospel missionary. One morning when we were unloading a carload of equipment at the rail siding, there was a new young fellow on the gang and an incident happened that I could hardly believe. We had only been working for about an hour when this young fellow came to me to ask if I could send him to a doctor. I asked him what was wrong? He told me he had cut his finger off. I asked him how it happened. He showed me. There was a piece of shafting about 6" in diameter and about 30" long which he had attempted to lift from the rail car to place on the truck. The shafting slipped and caught his finger against the edge of the steel car, which cut his finger off. I asked him where his gloves were. They were lying on the car. They were a new pair of welding gloves. He had been hired as a welder. He had been to welding school in Vancouver. But of course, he had never done any work. Now he had been sent out on a big construction job and he didn't know his ass from a shotgun. Poor guy. A piece of shafting should have a rope chocker placed around it and lifted with the crane.

We had a small bus for transportation so I called the driver and he was taken to the hospital. I never saw the young fellow again. Somehow, even with the job being manned with green men, there were no fatal accidents. This was due to luck more than anything else. Once when a tugboat was pushing a barge loaded with gravel, the tug was travelling too fast and the water was coming over the top of the barge. The whole works capsized but somehow all the men came out and were rescued.

Well, time went on and the job was finally finished. This was early in 1969. I for one was glad that the job was finished. It was after I had gotten my divorce, and while working on the Arrow Dam that I met another woman and started to take her out for evenings. She had lost her husband to a heart attack. We seemed to get along together so in May 1967 we were married. This year, 2005, we will celebrate 38 years of marriage.

CHAPTER 53

East Kootenay Coal Project, 1969

IT WAS SOMETIME DURING THE winter of 1969 that we were finished on the Arrow Dam. I had worked steady while on the dam project so I was glad to have some time off. I had only been on unemployment insurance once, and that had been for a very short time. So, I thought that this was a good time to sign on and take things easy. This is what I did, and as it turned out, the work situation slowed down, but would pick up later that year – so nothing to worry about.

I had been building a shop on the old Irving family place at Tarrys. So, this would be a good time to try and finish it. This is where I spent most of my time for the next couple of months. Then a call came from the union hall to work for Coast Steel. The first job was a conveyor change over at the Celgar pulp mill. Then from there another at the East Kootenay Kaiser Coal project. The part of the project that we worked on was the big repair shop that was situated up on the mountain above the old coal town of Natal on the Harmer Ridge.

The structural steel for this shop was erected by another contractor. Our job was to install various pieces of equipment, such as roof ventilating fans, etc. This didn't last very long and we were finished in early October.

I had been dealing for a piece of land in Crescent Valley, B.C., for some time. As it happened, on the 21st of September 1969 I was able to complete the deal.

Now another job turned up which was also on the Kaiser Coal project. This job only required two men since it was a series of small steel sheds for protection over various pieces of propane equipment. We erected these small sheds by hand and then did the metal cladding on them. This job was for the Boundary Electric Company. My working partner was Zeke Mazeppa, one of the best men you could get for the job. We finished the job just before Christmas when the miserable weather was setting in.

About the middle of February I received a call to go to Kamloops for a short job to help clean up some small odds and ends of unfinished work on the cement plant. The plant had been constructed the year before and was situated about seven miles east of Kamloops on the north shore of the South Thompson River. The job consisted of a lot of details to finish various parts of the plant. Why these details were left undone was sometimes a mystery, but this seemed to happen on a lot of projects. Sometimes several little jobs can be done in a day, and others take a lot of time.

Well, we were only about six weeks cleaning up the project with a small crew of about six men. I never could figure out why all these small jobs had been left undone by the contractors, but there must have been some valid reason. We finished by the end of March. Then I had a little time at home, so I used it to get more work done on the place at Crescent Valley.

The next call for work came that summer. The call was to work on the booze plant which was being built at Winfield, northofKelowna in the Okanagan. It was reported to be the most modern booze plant in North America. The construction work was being done by the Flanders Installation Company. There was a camp right on the site – a good one.

Tom Essery was the general foreman. Al Sharon was pushing the raising gang. A lot of detail work had been missed in the shop fabrication of the structure, such as the layout of holes for stairway erection, ladders, doorways, etc. Tom said to me, "You are just the man I want". He then asked me to take over all of the detail work. I said O.K., and got some men together for the work. That was actually one of the better jobs of ironwork. The first job was a stairwell. It required us to layout and drill holes, and hang the stairs in one of the main buildings which was at least 100 feet high. The floor levels were about 10 or 12 feet apart.

This turned out to be a good job—five days a week and no overtime, which meant I could get home every Friday night since it was only a 4½-hour drive home. The field fabricating work went really well and the weather held out nicely.

Later on in the project there were pipe fitters on the job and some of these men were from Nelson too, so we pooled the driving between us by alternating our cars. This worked out well and we were able to work this way right through to the end of the project. When we got caught up with the field layout and fabricating, Tom got me to take over some of the erection work.

One day, a group of us was waiting for a crane to come and unload some trucks and we were passing the time by peddling the bull. The subject of missing fingers came up. Each one of the group was showing his hands to show where he had lost a finger or thumb. There were seven or eight of us in the group, and everyone except me has lost a finger or thumb or an eye. I was the only one to still have all of my appendages. Two had lost thumbs, two the index finger, one the little finger and a piece of the hand, and one had lost a thumb plus he had lost an eye. This gives an idea of some of the hazards of ironwork. It also shows how useful are a good pair of work gloves and eye protection.

I had worked on the construction of a number of plants for the manufacturing of various products, but I had never seen one as modern as this one. The claim was that everything could be run by computers from the office with hardly any man power. And, I believe that statement to be true.

The work carried on throughout the fall of 1970 and we finished about Christmas time or shortly thereafter. With the exception of a highway overpass bridge in later years, this was the only construction job I ever worked on in the Okanagan Valley.

CHAPTER 54

Quenelle Pulp Mill, February 1971

BESIDES IRONWORK, I HAD ALWAYS been interested in electrical work. I was living in Nelson at the time and night school courses were being offered in this work. I signed up for the course. The instructor was a man that I knew so I thought here was my chance. But after only two lessons, I received a call to work on the new pulp mill to be constructed at Quesnel, B.C. I went there to work, so I had to let the electrical study go for a while.

I drove to Quesnel in my pick-up. Jim English was the general foreman on the job. Dominion Bridge was the contractor. The work had already started with some steel erected. Jim asked me if I would look after some of the bolting up and the plumbing. I said O.K. and got some men together for this work. Then we had a brand new crane come in so we helped getting it unloaded from the rail car and assembled ready for work. The crane was an 85-ton Link Belt. A nice job. This crane was able to reach the top of the powerhouse job, which was going to be over 100 feet high.

The plumbing job was going along very well, as well as the bolting. Mell Alexander was running the raising gang. With the new crane the powerhouse steel was going up quite well. Dominion Bridge now had a new erection superintendent named Lew Lesard. I had known him since he first came to Vancouver several years back. He showed up one day at lunchtime and we had lunch together at the camp. He told me of the railway bridges that were coming up on the railway line to the Fording Coal project in the east Kootenay. I said, "my god Lou, that is right in my backyard." He said he would give me a call as soon as the job was ready. It wouldn't be very long. I said I would be ready for it. It was only a couple of weeks later when the call came. I left Quesnel, went home to Nelson, and then to Sparwood for the bridge jobs.

For these bridge jobs we didn't have a camp, but had rooms in a motel and had our meals at a restaurant. For transportation the men used their cars and were paid mileage. The cranes for the project were rentals.

These bridges were all deck girder types. One of the cranes was a 100-ton capacity, which was used for the heaviest lifts and the longest reach. Most of these girder spans were shipped as a complete span. That is, the two girders together with all of the bracing, struts, etc., in place. For hauling them from the railway to the bridge site we had a very large low bed truck. To be able to place these spans we had to build a fill out into the river in order to get the crane close enough to handle the lift. We also had a 50-ton truck crane, so in some cases we used the two cranes together in order to place these spans. We also had a 25-ton truck crane for the bullcooking jobs such as the assembly of the big cranes.

Bill Jelleveneskis was the erection foreman on the project. The first bridge we tackled was the Elk River Bridge. This was close to the old town of Natal. The second bridge was over Cummings Creek. This one was a completely new bridge. It was also of the deck girder type, and had to be completely assembled on site. These were large 100-ft girders. To be able to place these girders we had the 100-ton crane partly in the water of the creek.

The East Kootenay country can be a mean place for men and working conditions. The day we had to start the Cummings Creek Bridge, the weather decided to turn nasty. About 4 AM it started to snow and by mid morning we had at least a foot of fresh snow on the ground. Fresh wet snow – what a hell of a mess. Well we worked in the damned stuff, and it sure was miserable. It was hard to believe but it was the 12th of June. It was tough going, but we managed to get the Cummings Creek job done. We were all soaking wet and dirty, but then the weather improved and we soon forgot the bad days.

The Elk River Bridge was a total of five spans, but these were short spans – some only 50 feet long. These spans had all come complete with two girders, struts, and bracing. With the crane power that we had, the erection work proceeded smoothly and fast.

When these two bridges were complete we moved further up the valley to a place known as Grave Creek for a three-span girder job. This was the worst place of all the project sites to get the cranes and girder spans to the bridge site. To reach the Grave Creek site we had to go by way of the road to the Fording Coal project, which included the long Fording hill, and then the back road to the Grave Creek site. For the cranes and the big trucks with the girders, it was almost half a day's travel. Those kinds of hills were all low gear deals for heavy equipment, so the trips were naturally slow.

We left one of the big cranes at the railway yard to finish the unloading and took one big crane and the 25-ton crane to the bridge site. The weather turned wet. We also had a breakdown with the small crane, which we had to repair on the site. We had to remove the starter and take it to a repair shop. This didn't hold us up too long, but it was a miserable job to get under a rig in the mud and the muck to monkey wrench. However, we got the repair job done and did not lose much time. Everything was work ways again, and the weather improved, and the work proceeded in a normal fashion. These bridge spans were second-hand bridges from an abandoned railway branch in the Adirondack Mountains in new Brunswick.

We finished all of the work on these railway bridges to the Fording Coal project during the month of June 1970. That was the last time that I would work in the East Kootenay.

CHAPTER 55

Similkameen Copper Mine, Princeton, 1971

NOT LONG AFTER COMING HOME to Nelson from the East Kootenay bridge jobs, I received a call from the union hall to go to Princeton where the construction work for a new copper mine was starting. The accommodation there was in a camp. Princeton is about 280 miles west of Nelson, and the mine was located 10 miles west of Princeton. The company that I was hired for was the Britain Steel Company. The Commonwealth Construction Company also had a part of the project. When I arrived there I was asked if I would take over a gang to be the foreman. Don Geldard was the general foreman on the project so I said O.K.

There was a mine building already constructed which needed some details to finish. Then they expected more material for another job. That was the reason for hiring the extra crew. Now, a queer thing happened. Britain Steel received word that the steel order would be held up for some time. So, that meant that the new crew would have to be laid off. Now, Commonwealth Construction had another job ready to start, so they wanted to take over Britain's new crew. This was arranged and we all signed on with Commonwealth.

The job that we did was to build some corrugated large pipe tunnels about nine feet in diameter, in which conveyors were built to carry the ore. These tubes were each a couple of hundred feet in length, and ran from the mine to the concentrator. Where we were working was where the rock had been excavated. And, as this was July and August – was it ever hot! The camp was also placed where there was a lot of rock so it was also a hot place.

One day near the end of August we had a visitor on the job. It was a fellow who I had known when I worked for Dominion Bridge in Alberta. He was now in a manager's position for Commonwealth Construction. We shook hands and then found a shady place to relax and talk for a while. His name was Tony Meshinsky.

One day some time later, the project superintendent asked me to come to the office when I had a chance. I said O.K., I will come a little later. It was some time after lunch and all was going well on the job. So I went over to the office to see what the superintendent had on his mind concerning me. When I went into the office he thanked me for coming and offered me a chair. Then he said "Joe, you have a wonderful record as an Ironworker Foreman. We have something different to offer you." I had never known him before so I was wondering what he knew about me. Then I remembered about Tony Meshinsky visiting the job. Then he said "Joe, we need a general foreman up at the Gibralter Mine project and we would like to have you take the job, but only if you would like to go, because we also like the work you are doing here, so it's up to you. You think it over and let me know." I thanked him and told him I would let him know in the morning. He thanked me and I went back to work.

I gave the offer some thought that evening. I decided that if I was away from home I might as well be making the best money possible, so I decided I would take the job. I gave Chris my answer the following morning and packed my bags once again. I drew my time and headed home.

When I arrived home I found out that I should make a trip to the east Kootenay. One of Syvlia's (my new wife) boys (Doug) was working on a ranch in the Bull River area and he wanted to bring home a couple of calves to raise on our place in Crescent Valley. One of these calves would be for himself, and one for us. The next morning I went out to our ranch and put the rack on the pick up truck for the job of hauling the calves. Then I went back to Nelson, picked up Sylvia and we drove to Cranbrook where we spent the night. The next morning Sylvia and I picked up Doug at the Glen Bower ranch and also the two calves, which at this time were five months old. Then we went to the Brand Inspector's place to have the calves inspected before heading home. By the time we had done all of this, it was about 11 AM. Then we could drive home.

It was about noon and we were maybe 15 miles east of Creston, so I turned on the radio to get the noon news. Holy Mackeral – what a shock! There had been a bad accident on the new bridge being erected at Kamloops by the Britain Steel Company. The bridge steel erection foreman had been killed with the collapse of the high line. I knew right away who it was and said to Sylvia and Doug "holy..., that is Ronnie Dyson." What a shock. I had Ronnie on my crew for a long time during his apprenticeship. He was only a young man. After I was at home I received more details of the accident. The bridge is over a dry gulch to the southeast of Kamloops, and quite a high bridge.

We were then into Labour Day weekend so I had one day at home before I left for Gibraltar, which is 40 miles north of Williams Lake, up in the hills. I drove to Williams Lake by way of Rock Creek and Kelowna, then Vernon and Kamloops, Cache Creek and Williams Lake, and finally up the hill to the job at Gibraltar, where I got myself settled in the camp. It was a good camp located on a small hill just above the mine project.

The next morning I went to the office where I got all signed up for the job. Then the superintendent, Dan Bandola, showed me all around the project and showed me the work that I would be in charge of. He then showed me the pickup truck that would be the one for me to use for the job. Then I went around to meet the men, some of them I knew, and some were new to me, but they all welcomed me to the job.

CHAPTER 56

Gibraltar Copper Mine project, September 1971

THE PROJECT HAD BEEN GOING for some time so a lot of work had been done. The big concentrator building was well on the way. The secondary crusher building was just starting, and this amounted to 50% of the work. Then, there was the primary crusher and the waste disposal, and all of the conveyors.

The material for the project came mostly by rail to the siding known as Gibraltar, which was about a 12-mile haul. We also received a large amount by truck. The cranes that we had for erection were all fairly new and all truck mounted cranes. Some of the crane operators were knew to me, but from observation they were handling the cranes O.K. At this time there was a lot of construction work in B.C. Some men never stayed very long on a job, so there was a lot of men coming and going most of the time.

The fall weather was very good so we were working a lot of Saturdays, and this was an enticement for a lot of the men. When you get a good crew together you don't like to see it broken up. When there are several crews on the job, the problem is multiplied. However, there were some good men there for the job of foreman or pushers as they were known. The one that I picked for the main raising gang was Eddie Keneuph, a very good man any time anywhere. Also, there were some other good men that made good at the job of being a pusher.

The secondary crusher building was quite large and would contain a large amount of equipment such as screens, crushers, conveyors, shakers, etc. Also, there was an overhead crane to handle installation, and later on to handle repairs. The primary crusher building was smaller in size but the crusher was to be a very large one. The base of it alone weighed 75 tons, one solid chunk of iron – a real handful. This big crusher however was done much later on. The main thing at the time was to get the buildings erected so that the cladding could be placed and the buildings could be roofed, etc. The Cariboo winters can come early and can also be very severe.

In the fall, when the weather is good, there was more work done in one day, than sometimes in three days in the winter when it was snowing and blowing. As it happened, the weather was very good most of the fall, so the erection of the buildings proceeded at a very good pace. Also, the management of the project was being handled in a very good manner. Dan Bandola was the general superintendent, and Mel Smailes was the project manager. They were both good men and had a good knowledge of construction. Also, the camp was a good camp – good rooms and good food. All of these conditions made for a good job.

The waste disposal was a fairly large erection project by itself. The building was erected on a concrete base about 12 feet above ground level, 40 x 60 feet by 60 feet high, carrying conveyors on both sides. One conveyor came from the secondary crusher, the other one for rock disposal was cantilevered out from the building for a distance of 150 feet. The outer end was 70 or 80 feet above the ground. This was a tricky erection job.

There had been a very similar one constructed at the Fording Coal project where the steel erectors had a bad accident while erecting the conveyor. I received the news of the accident and therefore made a study of the erection method. I worked out a method for the erection and explained it to Eddie Keneuph. We went over the method together. When this type of conveyor was erected at the Fording job, a man lost his life and we did not want any accidents here. Dan suggested that we use the two cranes on opposite sides of the conveyor structure. I said "no" to this proposal. Then Dan asked me how I thought it should be done. I explained to Dan that when two cranes are working on a big lift together, they should be working in unison so that they both swing in the same direction at the same time. After I explained it to him, he agreed.

The conveyor structure was built out from the building and supported by the building for the first 50 feet. Then the remainder of the truss section of the conveyor was assembled on the ground in one section and loaded on a truck and trailer for transport to the erection site. At this place I had a cat level a place for two cranes to be able to work together on one side of the conveyor. The two cranes were placed in position. Then the truck and trailer came into place and the load hooks of the cranes were hooked to the truss with spreader chokers to divide the load evenly. When connected, this truss would be on a slope and the crane on the outer end would be required to hold his load while the other crane hoisted the underneath supporting steel into place. Everything worked as planned so all concerned were happy with the project.

Now, another job was placing the conveyor belts. Some of these belts were big heavy belts up to 6 feet wide and ¾" thick, and more than 1500 feet long, and weighed 20 tons or more. After pulling a belt into position with a hoist, the vulcanizing crew went to work on vulcanizing the belt joint. Before the belt could be placed, all of the conveyor idlers and return rollers had to be placed and lined. There were hundreds of these to place. A good portion of the ironwork was done before the bad winter weather arrived. The cladding was placed on the buildings so the work on the conveyors was under cover. This was a good thing because it was one hell of a cold winter.

The primary crusher was quite a job because of the weight of the crusher base at 75 tons. This base was shipped by rail to the Gibraltar siding, where we then took it to the job by truck. For this hauling job we had a special heavy low bed truck. This truck had an extra axle that could be jacked into place to help carry the load by placing more tires on the road.

The crusher base was much too heavy for any of the cranes we had on the project. So, when it came to unloading it from the rail car and reloading it onto the truck, we had to make use of cranes, jacks, and rollers. Also, this job came when the cold weather was with us, so everything was moving slower than ordinary. When we finally got that big chunk of iron unloaded and reloaded onto the big low bed, the tractor unit under the low bed could hardly move the low bed. We happened to have a road grader there, so we hooked the grader on for more motive power.

At the MacLeese Lake junction, where the Gibraltar road left the highway, we had a D-8 cat waiting to help pull up the hill. From there to the mine it was almost all uphill. With the aid of the cat we made the first hill O.K. Then there was a level road for a little way. We had one pick-up in front of the parade, and I was following the load in my pickup.

I noticed sparks coming from the rear end of the truck tractor, so I called to the lead pick-up to stop. The trouble was a burned out bearing on the first rear end of the tractor. This meant that we needed a different tractor to finish the trip up the rest of the hill. By this time it was long past dark so we left everything where it was for the night. In the morning we needed a different truck tractor for the remainder of the trip.

The truck outfit arranged for the change and the next day we got the tractors changed. But then there was another problem. The tire chains were breaking and coming apart. Also, we had to put a bucket loader behind the trailer to help up the steeper grades. It was a slow trip, but we finally reached the primary crusher building at quitting time. To unload we brought the load as close as possible to the big door. Then with a crane lifting on one side only of the crusher base we managed to slide the load from the low bed right to the door of the building where we could handle it.

The overhead crane that we erected in the Primary crusher building was of 100-ton capacity. So, with the crusher base at the doorway, and using a mobile crane on one side of the base, and the overhead crane on the other side, we could move the base into the building without any further trouble.

Along about this time we were having a lot of bad winter weather. So, there was trouble in a good many places in B.C. Some places had real bad snowdrifts, while other places were cut off by avalanches. There was winter trouble in general all over the province. At the Gibraltar camp we were running low on propane fuel because the fuel trucks were held up with snow slides, etc. If the situation did not improve, the camp would have had to have been evacuated. This was a serious situation.

Also on account of the winter weather, the project was almost standing still, or so it seemed. Everyone was complaining. So, one evening after supper, I went to my room and composed a poem about the job. I called the poem "Cool Gibraltar". I was in a hurry, so I wrote the poem in the same style as the old "The Night Before Christmas". The poem was printed at the office the next morning and most everyone asked for a copy.

Not long after this, the weather changed and everything got moving again, and the project was coming to completion. The erection of structural steel was all complete, and the conveyors were all in place and working. The crews could then be laid off. As it happened, there was a short job for me right at home. The Kootenay Canal project was starting and the first thing needed was a bridge across the Kootenay River for access to the project. It was a concrete bridge, which came under the jurisdiction of the carpenter's union.

CHAPTER 57

Kootenay Canal Bridge and Mica Dam, Spring 1972

WHEN THE LAY OFF CAME at the Gibraltar job, I was not in the lay off, but was asked if I would work on the erection of the high line for the bridge job. This job was already under way with Bert Knox being the foreman. I had known Bert for a good many years, so I said O.K. This job was right at home, so that suited me fine. I travelled home on the 3rd of March.

This was only a very short job. When we were finished, I didn't look for another job since I wanted to spend as much time as possible on our new place in Crescent Valley. I had no end of work there. There were fences to build, the old log house to remodel, pipe lines and pumps to install, and a hundred other jobs to take care of. We were living in Nelson at the time. Because I didn't contact the union hall, I didn't receive any call for work.

I was busy at the Crescent Valley place and it was late in August when I received a call from the union hall to see if I would take a foreman's job on the Mica Dam. I said O.K. and I went to Mica late in August. The job there was the penstock in one of the tunnels. When I arrived at Mica I found they had a house trailer for me to live in, and my meals would be supplied at the camp. I also had a pick-up truck for my transportation to work, etc.

This penstock work was the first job at Mica that I was foreman on. The Mica Dam was at this time well advanced. It had been in progress for several years. The tunnels under Mica dam were quite large – 50 feet in diameter. There were two of these large tunnels. At this time, one tunnel was taking the flow of the Columbia River. Of course, at this time, the high water was over. The second phase of our work was the big trash racks on the upstream side of the dam.

On the downstream side of the dam, and directly above the tunnel was a very wide roadway leading to the west side of the project. It was on this roadway that we had a crane for the work of unloading trucks of equipment and then lowering these loads down to the tunnel level.

First of all we needed equipment in the tunnel to handle the penstock sections and the gates that would eventually handle the flow of the water. The first piece of equipment was a hydraulic crane capable of a 10-ton load. Then we needed a truck to transport these loads from the portal to the work site. The equipment had to be lowered from the roadway to the tunnel, which was at least 60 feet below the road.

The hydraulic crane was handled in two sections. The crane was small enough for the boom to swing 360° in the tunnel. The truck had to back in with the loads and then could go forward coming out. The truck travelled on the floor of the tunnel. A sidewalk was built on one side for people. Near the penstock worksite, on one side of the tunnel, a small lunchroom was built for the work crews.

The ironworkers built the penstock and placed the gates, but the fitting and lining of the gates was done by the machinists. One of the main items of this work was to see that all the sections of the entire job arrived in the proper sequence. The workspace was limited so there was no room for storage inside the tunnel. Every section had to arrive at the right time or there would have been be a foul up. The work went well and by the middle of October we were finished our part of this project. So, we moved to the upstream side of the dam to tackle the big trash rack job. That was all heavy steel with 24" I-beams. These beams all had to be assembled into large sections to form the trash racks. This was a completely welded job. After welding, all joints had to be cleaned and painted.

To assemble all of this work, we had a yard on the west side of the river, and to the north of the dam. At that time of year, the Mica Dam area got a lot of rain, so a job of this nature could be a problem to fabricate out in the open. The project superintendent was a man by the name of Mr. Erickson. I called him on the radio to come and see me about this project. I explained to him the work ahead and pointed out the fact that unless we had some cover for the job, we would lose a lot of precious time. He agreed with me but didn't have the answer to the problem. He asked me if I had any ideas. I said yes, and that I was sure I could handle it with a little cooperation. He said I could have all the help possible.

He asked me what my idea was. I explained to him that we needed something fairly large to cover the job. I asked if I could have a big truck load of the big concrete forms that were being removed from the head works up at the west end of the dam. "Yes" he replied, "but I don't see your plan yet". Then I explained that I would do it with the forms. I would stand the forms on end to form walls on each side of the fabricating area. Then I would use some spare channel iron that was available around the site. I could soon build a roof, which would be movable for the crane to handle the work, and the welding and painting could be done in the dry. He agreed with me and I went ahead with the work. Very soon I had a fabricating and paint shop 40 feet x 50 feet with a removable roof that could be lifted off and replaced with the crane.

After I had the fabricating shop, or fab shop, built, and the work was progressing, everyone thought it to be a good idea. The men enjoyed working under cover out of the rain, and good progress was made with the work.

As mentioned before, these trash racks were all made from 24" I-beams. When we assembled several of these together, we had a large load to handle. These frames were all made to fit the existing steel that was embedded in the concrete at the north end of the tunnel where we installed them when they were ready.

By setting up the fab shop we were able to set up several trash rack frames at the same time. That way, two or three welders could work simultaneously and this sped up the entire job. At this time though, the weather was cooling down besides being wet.

All welded connections had to be cleaned and painted, so again our fab shop was paying off. We had a real production line going. Once the frames were painted and cured, we set them outside until we were ready to transport them to the tunnel. Placing the frames at the tunnel portal was another real project. On this part of the work they needed divers because most of the frames would be under water. Structural steel can be welded under water but it is much slower than otherwise.

Also at the portal to the tunnel, we need a large float or raft. We needed to build one. Because I had worked with divers before, I knew what we would need. North of the dam, and on the west side of the river, I found some nice and fairly big cedar trees – there was my raft. I rustled up some tools and took some men to do a little logging. These trees were close to the road, so with a small mobile crane and a low bed for hauling, we soon had all the timber needed for a raft. On the roadway above the tunnel was where we placed the crane. At this place we unloaded our logs and then built our raft. We tied the logs together with cables and then placed deck planks on the logs. Then, I had the carpenters build a small shack on the float for the divers for dressing and changing. The welding machines and compressor could be placed later.

The crane we had for this project was a real good one – a 120-ton mobile job. At the road level we also had a shack for the crew. The only access to the float was by means of a man basket handled by the crane. This could hold several men at the same time. The crew of divers arrived from Vancouver, so then we could start the installation of the trash racks. The divers were from the North Vancouver Can Dive Company. The brought their own equipment with them. This is a safety method that divers have. Since they know how the equipment has been maintained, there is no chance of any foul ups.

With the crane we placed their equipment on the raft. Then we started placing the trash rack sections under water. The foreman of the divers was a man by the name of Norm MacDonald. He had three more divers with him, and all good men. A diver has to be able to perform a lot of various jobs while working under water. Sometimes the working conditions are real tough. We got a big taste of this on this job.

It was not long until the cold weather set in and we had ice to contend with. The divers were working in pairs. This worked out very well because they could only stay under water for short periods of time. So, they worked one team and then the other, so the work was always moving ahead. They were going down under the ice and work was slowing down. Norm MacDonald said we would have to work overtime in order to finish before Christmas.

This was during December 1972. We were working late at night and also weekends. But, we managed to finish the project before Christmas.

Then we hoisted all of the diver's equipment back up to the road level for shipping. The only job remaining was lifting the tunnel gate. The big crane was capable of that lift. It was late in the afternoon on the 23rd of December. When I finally was able to get away, one of the crew that had been with me was Roy Cleminshaw. He was living near Peachland in the Okanagan. We were already too late for the ferry to Galena Bay, which was on my way home. So, I told Roy I would drive by way of Vernon and Kelowna so he would be able to get the night bus at Vernon, which would take him home. I then had to go home by way of Rock Creek, Grand Forks, and Castlegar. I arrived home at 6 am on the 24th of December.

CHAPTER 58

Kootenay Canal BC Hydro Power Project, 1973-76

ARRIVING HOME ON THE MORNING of Christmas Eve I was real tired from my long drive, so sleep was what I needed. I went to bed and did not get up until noon. Then I went downtown for some last minute Christmas shopping. Then home again to relax some more. Then I spent a nice quiet Christmas at home. My wife Sylvia gave me a nice new guitar which I really appreciated as I had not had a good guitar for a long time. I liked playing and singing. I didn't call the Union Hall to let them know that I was out of work. I was enjoying some time to myself.

The Kootenay Canal project was starting but I thought it would be some time before they would need any ironworkers. However, it was in February that I received a call to report to work at the Canal project. This was only 10 miles from my home. Doing ironwork, you can't get much closer than that. At first they only hired a few ironworkers for the unloading of material, but very soon things changed. Machines and equipment were coming in very large amounts and more men were required.

B.C. Hydro built a large camp on the site, and also a large warehouse at the railway siding, which was located about 3 miles from the jobsite.

Before the job would be finished there would be thousands of tons of material to handle for the project.

The unloading and hauling of machinery and equipment for this project was going to be a big part of the work on this job. The warehouse at the siding was able to store a lot of items, but most of the machinery had to be stored outside. Some of it had to be assembled before being used.

At this time, my ears were starting to give me some trouble. The doctor told me to stay away from noise as much as possible. He suggested I buy a farm or ranch where things were quiet. I told him that I had already done that, so now I had to work to pay for it. He laughed and told me to try and work where it was quiet. At the job, if I could have looked after the unloading and handling, I could have worked where there was the least amount of noise. Near the powerhouse the noise was terrible – big noisy engines, rock drills, screaming compressors, loaders, etc. – almost deafening. Where we unloaded most of the time, there was only the noise of the crane engine and a truck. So, this was easier on the ears. Somebody had to look after this work so that was the job that I decided would be best for me, and that was the way it worked out most of the time. Of course, at times, there wasn't any unloading to be done, and other work to take care of, which I did a lot of the time.

There was the concrete batch plant to erect and various other parts of the project, but whenever there was equipment and other material to unload and reload, that was my part of the work. Then there were the big whirly cranes to erect – one at the headworks at the top of the intake to the penstocks, and later one at the powerhouse site. These cranes were built on top of travelling towers and each one was capable of handling a four cubic yard bucket of concrete on a 120-foot boom, when the boom was in the lowest position. These cranes travelled on rail tracks more than 20 feet apart, and for a distance of 400 feet. The concrete came from the batch plant in four cubic yard buckets on big special trucks hauling four buckets each trip. There were several of these trucks in service. The concrete moved with real efficiency. The crane was equipped with an air-powered hitch that hooked up and unhooked without any manpower. These big hitches carried a bottle of compressed air and the hooks were open and closed by an air cylinder contained with the hitch. It was a very efficient piece of equipment.

The contracting company that handled the construction of the power house and head works was the Atkinson Engineering & Construction

Company of San Francisco, California. Their Canadian partner was the Commonwealth Construction Company of Vancouver, BC. Ray Moffat had been with Commonwealth for a lot of projects, so he was sent to the canal project to be the ironworkers general foreman. I had known Ray for a long time and I was glad to see him take the job. We had always had good job relations. Ray was also glad that I was on the job, especially to handle the unloading of the heavy lifts.

On this project we were not as well equipped for cranes as on some of the other dam jobs. Most of the time we were using the 70-ton mobile. We also had a 25-ton mobile for the smaller jobs. Between these two cranes we could handle most of the work. The problem was that when we used the 70-ton at the rail siding, if there were several rail cars to unload, we had to unload all of them before sending any truckloads to the job site. However, we made it all work out to suit the equipment we had.

Up at the head works, at the penstock intake, the whirly crane could handle all of the erection of the penstocks and the head gates. The only erection job at that location that was done with the 70-ton mobile was the outside crane above the head gates, but this was during the latter part of the project. Also at the powerhouse there was a similar crane over the tail race gates. The structural steel for the powerhouse could all be done with the big whirly. At the warehouse, a lot of equipment was stored by using a forklift directly on the warehouse floor. Some of the heavy lifts at the rail siding included the turbine parts – the big turbine to generator shafts, 60-ton each. This was using the crane to full capacity.

On almost all jobs there are times when work is not done in a safe and sane manner. This makes a job very hard to accomplish. This is what happened one afternoon on this project. We had for our headquarters a small shop known as the fab shop or erection shop. Ray Moffat had a small office there from where he managed the work. One afternoon I came in there to see Ray, as we were almost finished for the day. He said that we all have to go down to the powerhouse right away. I asked why. He told me that we had to reeve the load blocks of the powerhouse crane. I said, "my god Ray, it's almost quitting time and that job will be more than four or five hours work. Can't it be done tomorrow?" He said that they wanted it done that day. I said "they must be nuts."

Well, we all went down to the powerhouse to start the job. As usual when some college-educated asshole is in charge of the organizing of a job, no preparations had been made. This job should have started at 8 o'clock in the morning. By the time we got everything ready to reeve the drums and blocks on the crane, it was dark. This job required men up on the structure of the crane and men down below to handle the spool of cable. To reeve a crane properly, it should first be reeved with a rope and then the rope joined to the cable so that when the rope is pulled through the blocks, the cable automatically follows the rope. When no preparations have been made, and you think you can do the job with only a hand line, you have nothing but trouble. Previous to this I had worked on the reeving of a lot of overhead cranes, and never had such a bad time as on this one. I had a big discussion with Ray over this. I think that was the only time we ever disagreed.

The travelling crane for the head gates and the crane over the tail race gates could, in both cases, be erected with the 70-ton mobile. The crane sections hauled on a low bed truck. At the powerhouse there was plenty of room to maneuver the equipment and crane. At the head works however, it was a different picture. The mobile crane did not have much room to pick up a load and swing it into position. The low bed truck had very little room to navigate. Because the road to the head works was a narrow built road on the side of the canal, and about a ½ mile from our working yard, the low bed had to go this distance head on. The crane went first. After setting up, it had to work over the truck cab when lifting the crane sections from the low bed, and then, work over its own truck cab in order to erect the crane sections.

The crane sections were assembled at our working yard. By doing this we could erect two vertical legs and a top girder in one lift. These sections required guy lines until the cross girders could be placed. We assembled all of these sections at the yard before loading any of them. When all was ready we loaded the low bed and then stopped all other traffic from entering the road to the head works. Then we moved and everything worked the way that it was planned. After the low bed was empty it had to back slowly down the long hill, but it all went O.K.

The work sure goes differently with a little planning. Then we had the job of placing the big transformers. The power house transformers weighed up to 110 tons each so these had to be unloaded using hydraulic jacks to move them from the rail cars to the special low bed truck that B.C. Hydro had for this special work. 110 tons is an awesome piece of equipment. We had four of these to handle in this manner. At the powerhouse these were moved to their final place in the same manner.

These transformers were about the last work on this project.

After placing the transformers there was some equipment to be loaded for shipment. This wound up the work on this project, and also wound up my history of construction work.

An odd thing about this was that it was only two miles from where I had started as a green 17-year old kid in 1928. The changes in everything over the years were almost unbelievable, not only in the workplace, but in everyday living. For transportation we had paved highways, we could go to an airport and fly across the country or across the ocean. We had electricity even in all of the country places. We had more schools and colleges for the young people. And we had first class living conditions in the camps.

The wages for working men had also changed by at least 10 fold. Men now made as much in one day as they made before in a two-week pay period. There were also pensions for men that were retiring. And, this is what I did, on my little ranch in Crescent Valley, to which I have given the name of Rainbow Pines.

Epilogue

WHEN THE BIG KOOTENAY CANAL Project was finished, and because I had all of my pensions due, I thought that I could retire and take life easy. But, that is not the way things go when you have a farm or ranch to attend to. A short time previous to this, I had purchased a number of yearling beef calves at the cattle auction sales in Cranbrook. It's hard to realize how busy a bunch of animals can keep a man. If they are out in range country where they have grass and water, the workload is light. But, where you have them on a small acreage, without hired help, it is a continual chore to look after them. They require a lot of attention. There are water lines to maintain, fences to build and repair, buildings to maintain, farm machinery to maintain and repair, hay to be cut and stored, and a hundred and one things that you never gave much more than a passing thought to before.

I had always liked having horses, and I had always been able to handle them. I had bought a saddle horse a few years back – mostly for the kids – and I acquired a farm tractor, but I had the idea that I should work with horses. So, I purchased some work horses. These were two-year-old colts of the Percheron breed. I had experience with breaking horses for work from years back, so I didn't have any trouble with these colts.

One of the things I did was rebuild an old bob sleigh so we could give sleigh rides in the winter. The sleigh that I built was a four-seater, so it could handle a good number of people. It required a good heavy team of horses to pull the load because when fully loaded, it would be a ton of weight. The most important ride of each winter was the day that we had the ride for the handicapped. It is hard to believe that something so simple could bring so much joy to people, especially when I would let the team run and the bells would ring. Then when we reached the old ranch house again, my wife Sylvia would have hot chocolate and hot dogs ready for all the riders. This is the kind of thing that makes one feel good to know that you have brightened the lives of people who are not so fortunate.

When I was young I always enjoyed the books about the west in the early days, especially the ones written by Zane Grey. So, I always wanted to see the country that he wrote about. So, Sylvia and I were able to take several bus tours. We went to Colorado, Arizona, South Dakota, Oregon, and Mexico. We also went to Nashville Tennessee where we went to see and hear the Grand Old Opera entertainers. We have also been to Texas and New Mexico and to the Great Carlsbad Caverns. Also, one time, in the early spring, we went on a western Canada farm tour to Europe where we went to Holland. We saw them make wooden shoes, carve diamonds, make cheese and other products. In Germany and Switzerland we saw bridges that had been built by the Romans and were still being used. We also had a tour of several famous old cathedrals, such as the Cologne Cathedral, Notre Dame Cathedral in Paris, also a tour of the famous Palace of Versailles on the outskirts of Paris. Then in England we saw the Canterbury Cathedral and Saint Paul's Cathedral. We had tours of farms in all of the western European countries including England. The different methods are surprising.

When I was in my first year of high school in the town of Trial, my folks decided to sell the place in Trail and move out in the country again. This time it was to Tarrys, which was only two miles from where I was born. This was a nice place to live, but the only High Schools in the whole area were in Nelson and Trail. In those days, there was no such thing as school buses, so I had to forget about school and try and find work of some kind. This has been explained previously in the early part of this book. I had always wanted to finish High School. One day I received a card in the mail about a correspondence course. I answered the card and then decided to take the course. The course took two years to complete. My average mark for the course was 85%, and on three different exams I got 100%. Education is a wonderful thing at any age, but I guess there are not many people receiving their High School diploma at my age. A lot of people were talking about it. The local newspaper heard about it and came out to interview me, then the T.V. News, and then the Vancouver papers. Then I received cards, phone calls, letters, and no end of congratulations.

Now I have two wonderful honours bestowed upon me. The first one was when the local High School (Mount Sentinel Secondary in South Slocan, British Columbia) invited me to be the guest of honour with the graduating class of 2005. Then, I was invited to be the guest of honour at the Building and Construction Trades Convention in Victoria, where I received an honourary life membership in recognition of my solidarity with the Ironworkers union over all these years of construction throughout B.C. I received a beautiful wall plaque to commemorate the event. I also received a beautiful framed picture of the Ironworkers Memorial Bridge. This is now the official name of the Second Narrows crossing of Burrard Inlet in Vancouver. This is the bridge that collapsed during construction and took the lives of 21 men when it went down.

When Sylvia and I first moved to Crescent Valley we purchased a mobile home to live in because the old log house on the place was not livable and needed an awful lot of work to make it livable. It had been built in a very primitive manner, so it required a lot of work including plumbing, wiring, inside finishing, etc. etc. This all took a lot of time, but my work has been enjoyed by a lot of people. If you have two good hands and some ambition, you can accomplish a good many things. Now in our senior years we relax and enjoy. Like the old song says, let the rest of the world go by.

**BRITISH COLUMBIA & YUKON TERRITORY
BUILDING & CONSTRUCTION
TRADES COUNCIL**

Honourary Life Membership

Presented To

JOE "RED" IRVING

*IN RECOGNITION OF A LIFETIME
OF UNION SOLIDARITY AND YOUR
LASTING CONTRIBUTION TO THE
BUILDING OF THE PROVINCE OF
BRITISH COLUMBIA.*

*37th Annual Convention
November 2005*

*Award presented to Joe Irving in November 2005
for his lifetime contribution to the building of British Columbia*

ISBN 141208185-8